SHEFFIELD HALLAM UNIVERSITY
LEARNING & IT SERVICES
ͻSETTS CENTRE CITY CAMPUS
SHEFFIELD S1 1WB

D0321075

CASEBOOK SERIES

ONE WEEK LOAN

SHEFFIELD HALLAM UNIVERSITY
LEARNING CENTRE
WITHDRAWN FROM STOCK

Milton

Paradise Lost

A CASEBOOK

EDITED BY

A. E. DYSON

and

JULIAN LOVELOCK

Sheffield Hallam University
Learning and Information Service
WITHDRAWN FROM STOCK

Selection and editorial matter, Introduction, and 'Event Perverse: The Epic of Exile' © A. E. Dyson and Julian Lovelock 1973

All rights reserved. No reproduction, copy or transmission of this publication may be made without written permission.

No paragraph of this publication may be reproduced, copied or transmitted save with written permission or in accordance with the provisions of the Copyright, Designs and Patents Act 1988, or under the terms of any licence permitting limited copying issued by the Copyright Licensing Agency, 90 Tottenham Court Road, London W1T 4LP.

Any person who does any unauthorised act in relation to this publication may be liable to criminal prosecution and civil claims for damages.

The authors have asserted their rights to be identified as the authors of this work in accordance with the Copyright, Designs and Patents Act 1988.

Published by
PALGRAVE
Houndmills, Basingstoke, Hampshire RG21 6XS and
175 Fifth Avenue, New York, N.Y. 10010
Companies and representatives throughout the world

PALGRAVE is the new global academic imprint of
St. Martin's Press LLC Scholarly and Reference Division and
Palgrave Publishers Ltd (formerly Macmillan Press Ltd).

ISBN 0–333–13842–2

This book is printed on paper suitable for recycling and made from fully managed and sustained forest sources.

A catalogue record for this book is available from the British Library.

Transferred to digital print 2002

Printed and bound in Great Britain by
Antony Rowe Ltd, Chippenham and Eastbourne

CONTENTS

ACKNOWLEDGEMENTS

T. S. Eliot, 'Milton I' and 'Milton II' from *On Poetry and Poets* reprinted by permission of Faber & Faber Ltd and Farrar, Straus & Giroux; Frank Kermode, 'Adam Unparadised' from *The Living Milton* reprinted by permission of Routledge & Kegan Paul Ltd and Barnes & Noble; C. S. Lewis, extracts from *A Preface to 'Paradise Lost'* published by Oxford University Press; B. Rajan, *'Paradise Lost' and the Seventeenth Century Reader* reprinted by permission of Chatto & Windus Ltd; Christopher Ricks, 'Tincture or Reflection' from *Milton's Grand Style* reprinted by permission of the Clarendon Press, Oxford; E. M. W. Tillyard, *Studies in Milton* reprinted by permission of Miss Angela Tillyard and Chatto & Windus Ltd; R. J. Zwi Werblowsky, 'Antagonist of Heaven's Almighty King' from *Lucifer and Prometheus* reprinted by permission of Routledge & Kegan Paul Ltd; Basil Willey, *The Seventeenth Century Background* reprinted by permission of Chatto & Windus Ltd. Stanley Fish's article was published in an expanded form in *Surprised by Sin*, and is reprinted here, in the shorter version originally used in *Critical Quarterly*, by permission of Macmillan.

Quotations have been standardised to agree with *The Poems of John Milton* edited by John Carey and Alastair Fowler (Longman 1968) except where there is some particular reason in context for leaving another version.

GENERAL EDITOR'S PREFACE

Each of this series of Casebooks concerns either one well-known and influential work of literature or two or three closely linked works. The main section consists of critical readings, mostly modern, brought together from journals and books. A selection of reviews and comments by the author's contemporaries is also included, and sometimes comments from the author himself. The Editor's Introduction charts the reputation of the work from its first appearance until the present time.

The critical forum is a place of vigorous conflict and disagreement, but there is nothing in this to cause dismay. What is attested is the complexity of human experience and the richness of literature, not any chaos or relativity of taste. A critic is better seen, no doubt, as an explorer than as an 'authority', but explorers ought to be, and usually are, well equipped. The effect of good criticism is to convince us of what C. S. Lewis called 'the enormous extension of our being which we owe to authors'. A Casebook will be justified only if it helps to promote the same end.

A single volume can represent no more than a small selection of critical opinions. Some critics have been excluded for reasons of space, and it is hoped that readers will follow up the further suggestions in the Select Bibliography. Other contributions have been severed from their original context, to which some readers may wish to return. Indeed, if they take a hint from the critics represented here, they certainly will.

A. E. DYSON

INTRODUCTION

It is not that he and I see different things when we look at *Paradise Lost*. He sees and hates the very same that I see and love. Hence the disagreement between us tends to escape from the realm of literary criticism. We differ not about the nature of Milton's poetry, but about the nature of man, or even the nature of joy itself. For this, in the long run, is the real question at issue; whether man should or should not continue to be 'a noble animal, splendid in ashes and pompous in the grave'.

These words of C. S. Lewis[1] about his disagreement with F. R. Leavis possibly oversimplify; it is unlikely that the two men did 'see' the same when they looked at Milton's poetry, and it is certain that they differed about its 'nature'. But the passage forms a useful starting place for a survey of criticism of *Paradise Lost*. The poem was written to 'justify the ways of God to men'; and, while this striking aim has in itself the obvious seeds of complexity, it is at one level simple and clear. Milton's concern is to enlighten his readers, to lift their hearts and minds to divine realities, to call or recall them to a noble view of themselves. He was the last poet who would have thought of himself as a mere rhetorician, a mere linguist, a mere artist even; he was always, before these things, prophet and bard. Criticism of *Paradise Lost* cannot evade the challenge of poetry as a sublime activity, transcending, though of course encompassing, language and words. One cannot write on Milton without committing oneself to a view of man, and without knowing that great and passionate truths are at stake. C. S. Lewis was surely right to assert also that if one dislikes the heroic view of man, then one will probably dislike epic poems, epic heroes, and ritual in art.

Milton deserves critics for whom the truth or falsity of his vision is central to his greatness, and, by and large, he has attracted the critics he deserves. For editors of a Casebook this is daunting, since the problem of dispensing with the indispensable looms unusually large. No Helen Gardner or Northrop Frye; no Empson, Broadbent, Burden, Stein, or Summers : clearly claims for completeness cannot be made. The 'Select Bibliography' makes what amends it can, and lists works to which all serious students will turn. In making our selection we have compromised by centring attention on the two major controversies surrounding *Paradise Lost*, and by choosing examples of most kinds of critical approach. Our own concluding piece, published here for the first time, is from a work in progress and absolves us, we hope, from the task of actually engaging in the critical debates in this Introduction.

We are left, however, with an Introduction to attempt, in this unusually complex field. Our solution is again the one forced on us as the only reasonable possibility, to be as simple as we can. What follows is a bare description of the two major controversies surrounding *Paradise Lost,* the one on its style, the other on its portrayals of God, Satan, Adam, and Eve. Naturally the two debates overlap and run concurrently, so we have not tried to divide the articles into two specific groups; and naturally on such a small-scale map of the area the mountains look like molehills and the by-ways are invisible – the charm of the country must be taken on trust. Our aim is to point at the territory for readers new to *Paradise Lost,* and to remind them that Milton now has not only critics, but critics on critics : for instance, there is Robert Martin Adam's *Milton and the Modern Critics* and Patrick Murray's *Milton: the Modern Phase.*

THE DEBATE ON STYLE

As one can see from his own comments, Milton hoped that *Paradise Lost* would dignify the language and bring it to age. English had proved its power as a medium for a serious long poem in *The Faerie Queene* and as a medium for tragedy in Shakespeare, but it still had no epic poem to compare with Homer and Virgil in the ancient world. It had yet to prove itself suited to celebrating man at his greatest, in the *genre* attuned to the highest sublimity of thought and style.

Milton's mission was to discover new linguistic potentials in English, which would enable it at last to stand proudly alongside Latin and Greek. Given the youthfulness of the language and its notoriously mongrel ancestry, he would naturally find some genetic traits more suited than others to epic themes. The Anglo-Saxon components had proved their vitality in Chaucer and Shakespeare, but Latin components seemed more appropriate for the grandest effects. In the following pages Basil Willey and C. S. Lewis both accept the latinate vocabulary and syntax as appropriate, and defend Milton's poetry in the manner he might have chosen himself. Basil Willey places it in its classical and Renaissance background; C. S. Lewis rejoices in it as ritual, with power to involve its readers as participants.

One must always remember that Milton was writing an epic, which is a form in which style and content are most closely akin. As E. M. W. Tillyard points out in *The English Epic and its Background*, epic poetry celebrates the greatness of man and the destiny of nations, taking men and events characterised by 'magnitude' for its theme. In this aspect Milton saw it as his supreme good fortune to have a theme that was 'true', not only in its general account of man and its heroic insights, but at a level transcending any other he could have found. Homer and Virgil had made sublime art out of pagan hints and guesses, but Milton's theme came with the authority of God. Potentially his poem would be the greatest ever written; hence his long and serious devotion to the craft of poetry, and to the word of God.

From the first, there were readers who did not altogether approve of the Grand Style, and early responses to *Paradise Lost* varied widely, as our extracts show. But in general consensus Milton soon emerged as a poet who could be mentioned with Shakespeare, Homer, and Virgil, and who certainly belonged among the supreme. As an influence on other poets, he was overshadowed at first by Dryden and Pope, but after 1726, when Thomson's *Winter* was published, the ascendancy of his style became clear. He was the main and central inspiration of Thomson, Young, Akenside, Wharton, and a host of others, including Cowper, during the next fifty years. Thomson and Young achieved immense fame throughout Europe for over a century, and were commonly mentioned, along with Milton, among poets destined to be 'for all time'. In retrospect the oddity is that these poets used Milton's style not for epics, but for philosophic reflections with epic overtones; they offer high views of man, but very few myths. The result is often 'common sense' (in its Augustan meaning) dressed imposingly, but surely outlandishly, in borrowed and indisputably faded bardic robes

In the nineteenth century Milton's influence was less direct in its manifestations, but it can still be traced easily. Keats was the first major poet to sense a threat to his own poetic development in Milton's ascendancy, but he did not question Milton's own power and greatness (and would one really wish the first *Hyperion* away?). Spenser,[2] Shakespeare, the Elizabethan love poets, the ballad writers, Pope, were all now influential alongside Milton, and the major nineteenth-century poets were too great and too individual to 'derive' from any one source in a disabling way. Wordsworth, Coleridge, Shelley, Keats, Tennyson, Browning, and Arnold all developed kinds of blank verse peculiar to their own themes and purposes. Milton profoundly affected all of them (except Browning, who returned, with questionable success, to the dramatic and Jacobean tradition), but always, in the main, as a force for good. Wordsworth in particular seems to have found precisely the Miltonic qualities suited to his own epic hero ('the egotistical sublime'), and to have transmuted these, along with other influences, into something wholly distinctive and almost equally great.

It was left to our own century to mount an odd attack on Milton, which achieved notoriety partly because T. S. Eliot was its important exponent, and partly because *Scrutiny* took it up. The young Eliot found Milton a bad influence, as the young Keats had done; but from this he chose to generalise a theory of art. Milton's poetry, he said in 1936, was not *just* a bad influence, but it had to be so : 'it could *only* be an influence for the worse'. He argued that Milton's visual imagination was defective, and asserted that *Paradise Lost* has to be read twice, once for the sound, and once for the sense. In addition Milton was cast in a villainous role in the alleged seventeenth-century 'dissociation of sensibility', with its disintegration of 'the living English which was Shakespeare's' into two parts.

In all these matters Eliot was at odds with the findings of most other critics, and today his arguments look singularly unsupported and brash. In 1947 he made partial amends in an address from which we also print an extract; he retracted a number of the earlier strictures, taking himself and Middleton Murry equally to task. Murry had also attacked Milton, in *Heaven and Earth* and elsewhere, mainly in the course of defending Keats. But, as Eliot now realised, Milton ought not to be blamed for his effect on Keats, or indeed on anyone, since a great poet will inevitably do harm as well as good. He overshadows lesser poets coming after by his mere pervasiveness; and, as Eliot added, Shakespeare could as justly be accused of killing English poetic drama for hundreds of years. However, Eliot still maintained that Milton's imagination was defective (a matter on which the majority of other critics, but not all, disagree with him), and now defended Milton not as a classical poet but as a great eccentric, using language in a highly personal and idiosyncratic way. On this showing Milton's genius lay more in the direction of the individual talent than of tradition; but uniqueness is, after all, a characteristic of great art.

All of this would have been of interest chiefly to students of Eliot rather than of Milton, if F. R. Leavis had not produced a bizarre article in *Scrutiny* (1933), which announced that 'Milton's dislodgement, in the past decade, after his two centuries of predominance, was effected with remarkably little fuss'. This article was confessedly inspired by 'Mr Eliot's creative achievement', which 'gave his few critical asides – potent, it is true, by context – their finality, and made it unnecessary to elaborate a case'. Leavis's article was later incorporated in *Revaluation* (1936), where a case was still not elaborated, but where Eliot's hints about the poetic tradition blossomed into a full theory based on 'the Shakespearian use of English; one might say . . . the English use, in the essential spirit of the language, of its characteristic resources'. This organic concept of language accompanies the idea that some poets (Donne is picked out for mention) are central to its genius, while others (notably Milton) are violators.

The issues raised here are large and interesting, but any theory which makes the success of one linguistic usage a criterion for denying the success of another seems inherently perverse. To credit one's own seducer with the virtual ruin of everyone is seldom plausible (indeed the occasion central to *Paradise Lost* is the only convincing instance of which we can think); and Leavis did not even claim to be a ruined poet himself. He substitutes the English language itself as Milton's victim, making Milton a serpent in the Eden of its verse. What one must say in reply is that the notion of an *English* use of English must surely be an absurdity, if it does not include all the fine uses of English that there are. Milton believed that he was extending the potentials of English, not limiting them; and in this he was surely right. *Paradise Lost* is a poem written in English and intelligible to English speakers; it is a poem which many prize among the highest attainments of man. It is, therefore, an English poem, with every reason to be proud of itself, and a source of strength to any other English speakers who use it with tact. The corresponding truth is that while all new poets feed on the works of the past which nourish them, all great poets produce, in the end, a use of language peculiarly their own. The test is that somehow magic fusion of form and content in major art, which can be recognised when it exists, but never foreseen or prescribed.

But the other side of Leavis's article is an account of Milton's style, which is at once so dogmatic, so unargued, and so at odds with the reading experience of most other serious critics, that it suggests a real failure to read the poem at all. The grand style, says Leavis, 'calls pervasively for a kind of attention, compels an attitude towards itself, that is incompatible with a sharp, concrete realisation; just as it would seem to be, in the mind of the poet, incompatible with an interest in sensuous particularity'. He discusses the poem's rhythms in terms of 'the routine gesture, the heavy fall', 'the foreseen thud', 'the inescapable monotony', 'the routine thump'. One wonders what poem Leavis was reading; and how; did he feel the rhythms on his pulses, or read them aloud? If he couldn't *hear* the lines, no doubt he missed Milton's 'sensuous particularity'; but should music criticism be written by the tone deaf? In fact there is no routine thud or thump from beginning to end of Milton's poem (except where it is for a deliberate purpose), only an extraordinary range of specific effects. From the opening, the interplay between speaking voice and iambic norm is as startling as anything in Shakespeare or Donne : one thinks of 'Sing, heavenly Muse' in line 6, with the delighted 'Sing' surging like a great wave; or still more astonishing, that buoyant 'Rose out of chaos' in line 10. Even in Books I, II, and VI, where the 'grand style' is most evident, the mingling of magnificence and tragedy, the complex play of ironies, images, and ideas, presents an interplay of sound and meaning as little to be predicted, as gentle and as awesome, as the sea. For Eden and its human heroes there is a different music and resonance; and as he needs, Milton evolves astonishingly beautiful local moods. Consider the wonderful mixture of luminous, dreamlike, and gorgeous effects in Book VII, the great account of Creation. In this book it is as if Milton had anticipated the magnificence which Mahler was later to celebrate in his own eighth symphony : 'Imagine that the universe bursts into song. We hear no longer human voices, but those of planets and suns circling in their orbit.' (Letter to Willem Mengelberg, August 1906). God's power to light up every particle of creation is instinct in the poetry : it is a great sounding out of God's warmth and presence, of that miracle, so central to *Paradise Lost,* when emptiness, nothingness, evil even, are taken by the Creator and turned into Good. The stylistic contrast could scarcely be more marked between the whole of Book VII – perhaps the most sustained passage of sublimity in literature – and, for example, that account of 'the dismal world' in Book II (570–628), where one has an overwhelming sense of reversed creation, incipient nightmare, the abyss of un-being. Again, the contrast with Book VI, the account of the war in heaven, is especially striking, coming as these two books do at the poem's centre.

Indeed it would be hard to discover anywhere in *Paradise Lost* a passage which does not have distinctive rhythms and felicities; and fortunately, modern criticism really does 'elaborate' *this* case. The insights of critics like Basil Willey and C. S. Lewis, who are concerned with the broad sweep of the structure of *Paradise Lost,* have now been supplemented by those of critics sensitive to local effects. Christopher Ricks's *Milton's Grand Style* should be read as a whole, but the extract which we print exemplifies the author's close and useful attention to the text. Frank Kermode writes with subtle delicacy of the poem's resonances, which bear for him the main weight of its manifest power. In fact so many passages of *Paradise Lost* have now been analysed in depth, that one could piece together – from Ricks, Empson, Broadbent, Burden, Stein, Fish, and Summers especially – detailed appreciations of most of the poem's parts. We have consequently arrived at a time when Fowler, in the Introduction to his edition, can confidently dismiss the attacks of Eliot and Leavis as 'dogma, built on unexamined premises and unsupported by demonstration'.

THE SPLIT IN THE POEM

'Milton', wrote Blake, 'was a true poet, and of the Devil's party without knowing it.' Here, in a sentence, is the 'split', or alleged split, which has been debated with skill and deviousness ever since. Milton intended to expose the ways of Satan and to justify the ways of God : did he in fact do the reverse?

In making our selection we have tried to show the seeds of this debate in early criticism, and something, at least, of its current harvest. Much has necessarily been omitted; and it is important to remember that many of the books on Milton recently published have felt obliged to have a chapter about, or an extended sequence of references to, the previous debates. We have also had to juggle with possibilities at every point. By choosing to have Lewis on Milton's style, we have had to exclude his famous chapters on God and Satan; by choosing Rajan on Satan, we have had to exclude other parts of his excellent book, which sets about reconstructing the reading response of an 'ideal' seventeenth-century reader. From the 'devil's party', we could have readily chosen extracts from Empson (satanist in chief?), Waldock (an earlier, but intellectually blunter exponent), or Peter; but we decided in the end on Werblowsky, who is not a polemical satanist, but a Jungian psychologist, with a specifically modern sense of ambivalences in Milton's archetypes. This is an interesting approach, very unlike most of the others, and a useful contrast to

Rajan's; it is also, we think, sounder as criticism than the competing pieces. The 'satanist' critics tend to share the intelligence of their hero, but also his blindnesses; as Fowler's edition demonstrates, their work already wears an eccentric look. From the more modern critics we have chosen Kermode, who goes to the heart of the poem by a route not often taken, and Fish, whose account of the poem's rhetorical structure is a nemesis for Satan, at which the archfiend himself might ruefully nod. But in choosing Fish we have had to exclude Burden, Stein, and Summers, each of whom writes outstandingly illuminatingly and well. We have been forced, again, to exclude Broadbent, whose book is a mine of insights – some illuminating, some ingenious, all learned and thought-provoking – but whose structure does not lend itself to representation by extract. (Fortunately Fowler's edition refers in its notes to Burden and Broadbent.) More sadly still, we have found no room for Helen Gardner and Northrop Frye, whose short books are among the classics of Milton criticism. We make amends by recording that these two books, together with C. S. Lewis's, would be our ultimate choice for highest acclaim.

The simplest assertion of a 'split' in the poem comes from those who feel that though Milton thought of himself as a Christian, he was mistaken; his inner sympathies with rebellion, anger, revolution colour the poem, do what he will. The apparent contradictions in his own life are often pointed to. In politics he was a revolutionary and a regicide, devoted to extreme democratic and egalitarian ideals. He denounced most forms of authority – kings, bishops and magistrates in particular; he attacked censorship, and campaigned for legal divorce. How, then, could such a man become a great singer of cosmic harmony, and stigmatise 'disobedience' as the first and greatest sin? How, more importantly, could he be 'against' a Satan who denounces the person of God and the laws of heaven in impassioned diatribes which bear such a striking resemblance to the tone and mood of his own early prose?

To this simple puzzlement is added the Romantic antinomianism documented by Mario Praz in his classic work *The Romantic Agony,* and clearly evident in extracts from Blake, Shelley and others printed here. The 'metamorphosis of Satan', as Praz calls it, is the process whereby Satan became cast in the role of archetypal defender of personal autonomy and freedom, fighting arbitrary law and tyranny embodied, in *Paradise Lost*, in the person and nature of God.

To such doubts and difficulties there is no simple answer; but it should be remembered that Milton was a scriptural fundamentalist, whose textbook of revolution was in the first place the Old Testament, and not any secular source. In the Old Testament God is continually saying that false kings and prophets have usurped His authority, and that if divine authority is to be restored, these must first be swept away. Thus Milton saw a dichotomy rather than a continuity between heavenly and earthly hierarchies, and found divine sanctions for believing that the highest form of religious obedience might be political revolution. In this matter he depended not only on a high view of human nature (which arguably *does* foreshadow romantic primitivism in certain exalted moments), but, more importantly, on absolute confidence in the prophetic and active role of God. Milton believed in the 1640s that God was about to produce a purgation of England by revolution, which would be followed by a rule of the saints. He did not, therefore, take the Hobbesian view that revolution would lead to anarchy and to the loss of freedom; he believed that a monstrous tyranny, imposed by God's enemies in God's name, would be replaced by the glorious liberty of the children of God. Always he would have taken for granted that disobedience to earthly leaders might be true obedience, but that the same attitude, when turned against God Himself, was the essence of sin and death. Admittedly, we might doubt his self-knowledge and disagree with his analysis; and it is here that the 'satanist' critics usually start. But it would be naive to impose upon Milton the modern notion that the mainsprings of action can be considered apart from 'belief'.

The simple 'satanist' case is, then, that Milton allowed the revolutionary in himself to take root in Satan, and made God, unwittingly, in the image of a Stuart king. In other words the theology of the epic might 'come out right' in the poem's formal structure (as Lewis demonstrates) but the emotional energy undercuts this with a different tale. For good measure it is some-

times added that God, as depicted in *Paradise Lost*, exemplifies
law and justice but not love, forgiveness, or mercy; and that
Christ, far from being the suffering servant crucified, is depicted
as a warrior hero of stoic cast.

Waldock argued the case that a split of this kind runs through
the whole poem, and appealed to our reading experience to
bear him out. Peter followed him in general, with special attention
to the depiction of God. Werblowsky throws his stress on the
fluidity of the archetypes themselves, pointing out that the
classical story of Zeus and Prometheus has an archetypal
similarity to the opposition of God and Satan, but that the
classical tale is more easily recast in a romantic mould. Zeus is not
a god of love, and is no friend to man; Prometheus, in giving
forbidden knowledge, is not man's enemy – in intention at least –
but his friend. A human reader is likely to empathise with
Prometheus and fear Zeus, even turning Prometheus, as Shelley
does, into martyr and hero. The possibility is therefore open that
Milton accidentally transposed his archetypes; and that his own
psychology predisposed this response, unknown to himself.

In such ways it is possible for critics to decide that Milton
achieved not what he set out to do but something almost the
opposite and yet to feel that the blame lies with Milton's art, not
with Christian truth. But, if Werblowsky approaches the latter
view, Empson goes further; he sees Milton as grappling with
Christianity, bringing out imaginatively its internal difficulties and
contradictions, and, in doing so, exposing the 'real' nature of the
Christian God. Empson believes that *Paradise Lost* is a great
poem partly because it shows that God is, after all, a tyrant and
torturer. His book *Milton's God* manages therefore to combine a
tribute to Milton's poetic power – and many fine insights into the
local effects of the poem – with a polemical purpose much at odds
with Milton's own. It is a robustly atheistic attack on the Christian
religion, using Milton, one of the religion's finest creative minds,
for the attack.

Clearly matters could not rest here; there have been numerous
'answers' to Empson, one of the most interesting of which is
Stanley Fish's *Surprised by Sin*. Fish's basic point is that Empson's
reading, or Waldock's or Peter's, is perfectly valid and sensitive,

but that it is the one actually intended by Milton as part of his design. Whereas the 'satanist' critics see Milton accidentally betraying himself, or betraying his religion, Fish sees him as a master rhetorician, leading his readers a highly educative dance. As Fish says, we *are* fallen men; the poem is true in its analysis; and Milton's aim was to bring this home in our reading response. In discovering that Satan is attractive, God fearful and alien, we discover the reality of a moral twist in ourselves. To read the poem is to re-enact its inner assertions; it is to become ourselves entangled in sin and doubt. We find our intellects clouded, our anger, envy, lust played upon; we are brought to the actual place of the original fall. We discover that Satan remains as real and powerful an enemy, even in the twentieth century, with its wholly different mythologies, as he would have been to Rajan's seventeenth-century reader for whom Milton wrote. Fish suggests, in fact, that in being made to re-enact the fall – to nod our agreement with Empson – we are made to discover that we are, in truth, sons of Adam, and in exile still. In this enterprise, Milton might have pressed his own bitter political experiences into service, but he wrote in a manner wholly insulated from merely provincial affairs. *Paradise Lost* demonstrates that since love and reason can exist only in a world in tune with its Creator, the divide between right and wrong responses to creation, between heaven and hell, will always remain.

In the course of his book Fish virually attacks the notion that works of art generate their own organic unity, at least if this view is made an enemy of structure and tone. He sees the writer's games with the reader as central, if the original intention is to be transmitted from the one to the other through structure and recaptured as a living response. In effect he comes close to suggesting that we should read *Paradise Lost* as Wayne Booth has taught us to read major novels – as a highly sophisticated structure, with a devious rather than a simple organisation, and with the hand of a master rhetorician working just out of sight.

In our view Fish does better justice to the poem's structure than any other critic, and he has moved the criticism of Milton on to permanently new ground. The approach to *Paradise Lost* in our final article is perhaps more directly indebted to Lewis and Kermode – in their very different emphases – but Fish's work allows us, along with other writers on the poem, to regard certain old controversies as now at rest.

As one looks back at the 'satanist' critics, it seems likely that they have been disposed, in the main, to take the allegory too literally. Some critics even seem to base their criticism of Milton's visual imagination on this kind of misreading, as if they were looking for the type of consistency that a 'painterly' poet might show. But there is no lack of clarity, either visual or intellectual, in the poem which shows Satan chained eternally to a lake of fire at one moment, and free to come and go through the universe at the next. These images depict different aspects of hell; they are not discrepancies, but the natural means for expressing realities which transcend time. God's tone cannot be criticised therefore as though he were a schoolmaster (*pace* Pope), nor can the war in Heaven be taken as a literal event. If you *do* take it over-literally then of course there are problems; the heroic encounters between apparent equals might seem to contradict the underlying religious vision that love and hatred, creation and negation, reality and nonsense, must always exist on different planes. There is the problem that the war will look faked (in much the same way, and for similar reasons, that E. M. W. Tillyard argues here that the psychology of the fall is faked). Since God and Christ are bound to win, their victory will seem a matter of brilliant and even cynical stage management, rather than the costly experience of love which it actually is. Again there is something inherently absurd in the notion of angels engaging in a combat where they cannot be killed and where they can only be transiently injured, if a too literal reading is rigidly enforced. Milton must have realised that he ran such dangers (in Book vi notably), and the supreme comment on them – partly because it exists in a work of genius, and partly because it is good-natured fun, not solemn criticism – is, of course, Pope's jokes about the sylphs throughout *The Rape of the Lock*. But Milton both knew and forced his readers to know the nature of allegory, and he persistently dislocates any rigid attempt to pin down place or time. The images are best received, as they were intended to be, as an arena of powerful and shifting impressions, through which one is moved into ever deeper perceptions of hate and love, chaos and order, fall and redemption.

How, then, do we test the poem? We are thrown back on experience, which confronts us in different ways, but at every point. We shall perhaps be less inclined to worry, with Tillyard, about the metaphysics of original temptation, if we recognise both the power of the ideal, and the reality of exile, in ourselves. We shall be less ready to justify Satan by abstract argument if we recognise that we feel like Satan often and to feel so is hell. We shall be less ready to call hell glamorous and heaven empty, if we respond – especially in Books IV and VII – to the vision that each day can be a glad whole, with beginning, middle and end turned to worship, where people and events are gladly received, and gladly surrendered again to the love of God. We shall be less ready to find fault with God's tone and proclaim Him a tyrant if we discover in the poem the miracle of evil taken and turned into good.

A. E. DYSON
JULIAN LOVELOCK

NOTES

1. *A Preface to Paradise Lost,* ch. 19. For references to authors and works mentioned in this Introduction, see 'Select Bibliography', pp. 243–5.

2. Spenser was also, of course, an important influence in the mid-eighteenth century alongside Milton, notably in Thomson's enchanting and influential *The Castle of Indolence.* But it would be fair to assert that he was never taken as seriously as Milton.

PART ONE

Extracts from Milton's writings

The following section is taken from Milton's works.

The earliest notes for *Paradise Lost* date from about 1640, and form part of the Trinity College Cambridge MS. There are four drafts, which Alastair Fowler reprints at the beginning of the Introduction to his edition. It is clear that Milton intended to write a tragic drama, but there are many suggestions of the later epic. Draft III is headed 'Paradise Lost', draft IV 'Adam Unparadised'.

Edward Phillips, in his *Life* (1694) quotes *Paradise Lost* IV 32–41 as having been shown to him several years before the epic was begun, as the opening lines of a tragedy.

Though Milton may have composed parts of the poem over many years, the main poem was written, according to Phillips and Aubrey, between 1658 and 1663. Fowler records that Milton usually composed during the winter, mostly in the night or early morning. He dictated in the first part of the day to any amanuensis who was available, dictating up to forty lines, and then reducing to about half the number. From time to time Phillips corrected the orthography and pointing.

The poem was published in 1667, at first in ten books, and later, in 1674, in twelve. (The first Book VII became Books VII and VIII; the first Book X became Books XI and XII.) Fowler gives full details of the early printing history. The first edition sold 1300 copies, for which Milton received £10.

MILTON ON HIMSELF AND HIS ART

I

Do not *you* look down on song divine, creation of the bard; for naught graces more finely than does song his heavenly source, his heavenly seed, his mind mortal in origin – for song still keeps holy traces of Prometheus' fire. The gods above love song, and song has power to rouse the quaking depths of Tartarus, to bind fast the gods of the deeps below; song restrains with triple adamant the unfeeling Manes. By song the secrets of the far-distant future are revealed by the daughters of Phœbus, and by quivering Sibyls, pale of lips . . . Persist not, I pray you, to hold cheap the holy Muses, nor think them idle, poor. . . .

SOURCE: 'To My Father' (1632?)

II

Then, admidst the hymns and hallelujahs of saints, someone may perhaps be heard offering at high strains in new and lofty measures to sing and celebrate Thy divine mercies and marvellous judgements in this land throughout the ages, whereby this great and warlike nation, instructed and inured to the fervent and continual practice of truth and righteousness, and casting far from her the rags of her whole vices, may press on hard to that high and happy emulation to be found the soberest, wisest, and most Christian people at that day, when Thou, the eternal and shortly expected king, shall open the clouds to judge the several kingdoms of the world, and . . . shalt put an end to all earthly tyrannies, proclaiming Thy universal and mild monarchy through heaven and earth.

SOURCE: *Of Reformation* (1641)

III

... In the private academies of Italy ... I began ... to assent ... to an inward prompting which now grew daily upon me, that by labour and intent study (which I take to be my portion in this life) joined with the strong propensity of nature, I might perhaps leave something so written to aftertimes, as they should not willingly let it die. These thoughts at once possessed me, and these other: that if I were certain to write as men buy leases, for three lives and downward, there ought no regard be sooner had than to God's glory by the honour and instruction of my country. For which cause, and not only for that I knew it would be hard to arrive at the second rank among the Latins, I applied myself to that resolution which Ariosto followed against the persuasions of Bembo, to fix all the industry and art I could unite to the adorning of my native tongue; not to make verbal curiosities the end (that were a toilsome vanity), but to be an interpreter and relater of the best and sagest things among mine own citizens throughout this island, in the mother dialect. That what the greatest and choicest wits of Athens, Rome, or modern Italy, and those Hebrews of old, did for their country, I in my proportion with this over and above of being a Christian, might do for mine: not caring to be once named abroad, though perhaps I could attain to that, but content with these British Islands as my world, whose fortune hath hitherto been, that if the Athenians, as some say, made their small deeds great and renowned by their eloquent writers, England hath had her noble achievements made small by the unskilful handling of monks and mechanics. ...

Neither do I think it shame to covenant with any knowing reader that for some few years yet I may go on trust with him toward the payment of what I am now indebted, as being a work not to be raised from the heat of youth or the vapours of wine, like that which flows at waste from the pen of some vulgar amorist or the trencher fury of a rhyming parasite, nor to be obtained by the invocation of Dame Memory and her siren daughters, but by devout prayer to that eternal Spirit who can enrich with all utterance and knowledge, and sends out His seraphim with the hallowed fire of His altar to touch and purify the lips of whom

He pleases : to this must be added industrious and select reading, steady observation, insight into all seemly and generous arts and affairs. . . .

SOURCE : *Reason of Church Government* (1642)

IV

. . . he who would not be frustrate of his hope to write well hereafter in laudable things, ought himself to be a true poem, that is, a composition and pattern of the best and honourablest things, not presuming to sing high praises of heroic men or famous cities unless he have in himself the experience and the practice of all that which is praiseworthy.

SOURCE : *Apology for Smectymnuus* (1642)

V

And indeed from my youth upward I had been fired with a zeal which kept urging me, if not to do great deeds myself, at least to celebrate them.

SOURCE : *First Defence* . . . (1651)

EXTRACTS FROM *PARADISE LOST*

Of man's first disobedience, and the fruit
Of that forbidden tree, whose mortal taste
Brought death into the world, and all our woe,
With loss of Eden, till one greater man

Restore us, and regain the blissful seat,
Sing heavenly Muse, that on the secret top
Of Oreb, or of Sinai, didst inspire
That shepherd, who first taught the chosen seed,
In the beginning how the heavens and earth
Rose out of chaos : or if Sion hill
Delight thee more, and Siloa's brook that flowed
Fast by the oracle of God; I thence
Invoke thy aid to my adventurous song,
That with no middle flight intends to soar
Above the Aonian mount, while it pursues
Things unattempted yet in prose or rhyme.
And chiefly thou O Spirit, that dost prefer
Before all temples the upright heart and pure,
Instruct me, for thou know'st; thou from the first
Wast present, and with mighty wings outspread
Dove-like sat'st brooding on the vast abyss
And madest it pregnant : what in me is dark
Illumine, what is low raise and support;
That to the highth of this great argument
I may assert eternal providence,
And justify the ways of God to men.

SOURCE : Book 1, 1–26 (1667).

II

No more of talk where God or angel guest
With man, as with his friend, familiar used
To sit indulgent, and with him partake
Rural repast, permitting him the while
Venial discourse unblamed : I now must change
Those notes to tragic; foul distrust, and breach
Disloyal on the part of man, revolt,
And disobedience : on the part of heaven
Now alienated, distance and distaste,
Anger and just rebuke, and judgment given,
That brought into this world a world of woe,

Sin and her shadow Death, and Misery
Death's harbinger : sad task, yet argument
Not less but more heroic than the wrath
Of stern Achilles on his foe pursued
Thrice fugitive about Troy wall; or rage
Of Turnus for Lavinia disespoused,
Or Neptune's ire or Juno's, that so long
Perplexed the Greek and Cytherea's son;
If answerable style I can obtain
Of my celestial patroness, who deigns
Her nightly visitation unimplored,
And dictates to me slumbering, or inspires
Easy my unpremeditated verse :
Since first this subject for heroic song
Pleased me long choosing, and beginning late;
Not sedulous by nature to indite
Wars, hitherto the only argument
Heroic deemed, chief mastery to dissect
With long and tedious havoc fabled knights
In battles feigned; the better fortitude
Of patience and heroic martyrdom
Unsung; or to describe races and games,
Or tilting furniture, emblazoned shields,
Impreses quaint, caparisons and steeds;
Bases and tinsel trappings, gorgeous knights
At joust and tournament; then marshalled feast
Served up in hall with sewers, and seneschals;
The skill of artifice or office mean,
Not that which justly gives heroic name
To person or to poem. Me of these
Nor skilled nor studious, higher argument
Remains, sufficient of it self to raise
That name, unless an age too late, or cold
Climate, or years damp my intended wing
Depressed, and much they may, if all be mine,
Not hers who brings it nightly to my ear.

SOURCE : Book IX, 1–47 (1667).

THE VERSIFICATION OF
PARADISE LOST

(This was inserted in 1668 'for the satisfaction of many that have desired it', in copies of the first edition of *Paradise Lost* still in the hands of the printer. [Eds]).

The measure is English heroic verse without rhyme, as that of Homer in Greek and of Virgil in Latin, rhyme being no necessary adjunct or true ornament of poem or good verse, in longer works especially, but the invention of a barbarous age to set off wretched matter and lame metre, graced indeed since by the use of some famous modern poets, carried away by custom, but much to their own vexation, hindrance, and constraint to express many things otherwise, and for the most part worse, than else they would have expressed them. Not without cause therefore some both Italian and Spanish poets of prime note have rejected rhyme both in longer and shorter works, as have also long since our best English tragedies, as a thing of itself to all judicious ears, trivial and of no true musical delight – which consists only in apt numbers, fit quantity of syllables, and the sense variously drawn out from one verse into another, not in the jingling sound of like endings, a fault avoided by the learned ancients both in poetry and all good oratory. This neglect then of rhyme so little is to be taken for a defect, though it may seem so perhaps to vulgar readers, that it rather is to be esteemed an example set, the first in English, of ancient liberty recovered to heroic poem from the troublesome and modern bondage of rhyming.

SOURCE: 'Note on the Versification of *Paradise Lost*' (1668).

PART TWO

Milton's Earlier Critics

Andrew Marvell

That Majesty which through thy Work doth Reign
Draws the Devout, deterring the Profane.
And things divine thou treat'st of in such state
As them preserves, and thee, inviolate.
At once delight and horror on us seise,
Thou sing'st with so much gravity and ease;
And above humane flight dost soar aloft
With Plume so strong, so equal, and so soft,
The Bird nam'd from that Paradise you sing
So never flags, but always keeps on Wing....
Thy Verse created like thy Theme sublime,
In Number, Weight, and Meausre, needs not Rime.

SOURCE: 'On *Paradise Lost*' (1674).

John Dennis

I

I am not so miserably mistaken, as to think rhiming essential to our *English* Poetry. I am far better acquainted with *Milton*, than that comes to. Who without the assistance of Rhime, is one of the most sublime of our *English* Poets. Nay, there is something so transcendently sublime in his first, second, and sixth Books, that were the Language as pure as the Images are vast and daring, I do not believe it could be equall'd, no, not in all Antiquity.

SOURCE: 'The Preface to *The Passion of Byblis*' (1692).

II

By all which we may see, that *Milton,* to introduce his Devils
with success, saw that it was necessary to give them something that
was allied to Goodness. Upon which he very dextrously feign'd,
that the Change which was caus'd by their Fall, was not wrought
in them all at once; and that there was not an entire Alteration
work'd in them, till they had a second time provok'd their
Creatour by succeeding in their attempt upon Man.

SOURCE : 'Remarks on a Book Entitled, *Prince Arthur, an*
Heroick Poem' (1696)

John Dryden

It is true, he runs into a flat of thought, sometimes for a hundred
lines together, but it is when he is got into a track of Scripture.
His antiquated words were his choice, not his necessity; for therein he imitated Spenser, as Spenser did Chaucer. And though,
perhaps, the love of their masters may have transported both too
far, in the frequent use of them, yet, in my opinion, obsolete
words may then be laudably revived, when either they are more
sounding, or more significant, than those in practice; and when
their obscurity is taken away, by joining other words to them,
which clear the sense; according to the rule of Horace, for the
admission of new words. But in both cases a moderation is to be
observed in the use of them : for unnecessary coinage, as well as
unnecessary revival, runs into affection; a fault to be avoided on
either hand. Neither will I justify Milton for his blank verse,
though I may excuse him, by the example of Hannibal Caro,
and other Italians, who have used it; for whatever causes he
alleges for the abolishing of rhyme, (which I have not now the
leisure to examine,) his own particular reason is plainly this, that

rhyme was not his talent; he had neither the ease of doing it, nor the graces of it; which is manifest in his *Juvenilia*, or verses written in his youth, where his rhyme is always constrained and forced, and comes hardly from him, at an age when the soul is most pliant, and the passion of love makes almost every man a rhymer, though not a poet. . . .

SOURCE : 'Original and Progress of Satire' (1693).

Patrick Hume

The Forfeiture of this Innocent and Blissful Seat, by the Disobedience of our first Parents, and their deserved Expulsion out of this *Paradise*, is the sad Subject of this unparallell'd Poem . . .

It imports much to know, nor can it be determined, what kind this Interdicted Tree was of, the Prohibition having no regard to, or influence on, its Fruit, more than it was made the Trial of Man's entire Obedience to his Maker.

SOURCE : 'Annotations on Milton's *Paradise Lost*' (1695).

Joseph Addison

There is another objection against Milton's fable . . . namely, That the hero in the *Paradise Lost* is unsuccessful, and by no means a match for his enemies. This gave occasion to Mr. Dryden's reflection, that the devil was in reality Milton's hero . . . The *Paradise Lost* is an epic, or a narrative poem, and he that looks for an hero in it, searches for that which Milton never intended; but if he

will needs fix the name of an hero upon any person in it, it is
certainly the Messiah who is the hero, both in the principal
action, and in the chief episodes. Paganism could not furnish out
a real action for a fable greater than that of the *Iliad* or *Aeneid*,
and therefore an heathen could not form a higher notion of a
poem than one of that kind which they call an heroic. Whether
Milton's is not of a sublimer nature I will not presume to determine : it is sufficient, that I show there is in the *Paradise Lost* all
the greatness of plan, regularity and design, and masterly beauties
which we discover in Homer and Virgil.

SOURCE : *Spectator*, number 297 (9 February 1712).

Voltaire

What *Milton* so boldly undertook, he perform'd with a superior
Strength of Judgment, and with an Imagination productive of
Beauties not dream'd of before him. The Meaness (if there is any)
of some Parts of the Subject is lost in the Immensity of the
Poetical Invention. There is something above the reach of human
Forces to have attempted the Creation *without* Bombast, to have
describ'd the Gluttony and Curiosity of a Woman without Flat-
ness, to have brought Probability and Reason amidst the Hurry
of imaginary Things belonging to another World, and as far
remote from the Limits of our Notions as they are from our
Earth; in short to force the Reader to say, 'If God, if the Angels,
if Satan would speak, I believe they would speak as they do in
Milton.'

I have often admir'd how barren the Subject appears, and
fruitful it grows under his Hands.

SOURCE : *An Essay upon the Civil Wars of France . . . and also
upon the Epick Poetry of the European Nations from Homer to
Milton* (1727).

Alexander Pope

The imitators of Milton, like most other imitators, are not copies but caricatures of their original; they are a hundred times more obsolete and cramp than he, and equally so in all places : whereas it should have been observed of Milton, that he is not lavish of his exotic words and phrases every where alike, but employs them much more when the subject is marvellous, vast, and strange, as in the scenes of Heaven, Hell, Chaos, &c., than where it is turned to the natural or agreeable, as in the pictures of paradise, the loves of our first parents, the entertainments of angels, and the like. In general, this unusual style better serves to awaken our ideas in the descriptions and in the imaging and picturesque parts, than it agrees with the lower sort of narrations, the character of which is simplicity and purity. Milton has several of the latter, where we find not an antiquated, affected, or uncouth word, for some hundred lines together; as in his fifth book, the latter part of the eighth, the former of the tenth and eleventh books, and in the narration of Michael in the twelfth. I wonder indeed that he, who ventured (contrary to the practice of all other Epic Poets) to imitate Homer's lownesses in the narrative, should not also have copied his plainness and perspicuity in the dramatic parts : since in his speeches (where clearness above all is necessary) there is frequently such transposition and forced construction, that the very sense is not to be discovered without a second or third reading : and in this certainly he ought to be no example.

SOURCE : 'Postscript to the *Odyssey*' (1723).

Milton's strong pinion now not Heav'n can bound,
Now serpent-like, in prose he sweeps the ground,
In Quibbles, Angel and Archangel join,
And God the Father turns a School-Divine.

SOURCE : *Imitations of Horace*, Ep. II, i, 99–102.

Jonathan Richardson

Milton's language is English, but 'tis Milton's English; 'tis Latin, 'tis Greek English; not only the words, the phraseology, the transpositions, but the ancient idiom is seen in all he writes, so that a learned foreigner will think Milton the easiest to be understood of all the English writers. This peculiar English is most conspicuously seen in *Paradise Lost*, for this is the work which he long before intended should enrich and adorn his native tongue. . . .

SOURCE : 'Explanatory Notes and Remarks on Milton's *Paradise Lost*' (1734).

Samuel Johnson

Great events can be hastened or retarded only by persons of elevated dignity. Before the greatness displayed in Milton's poem, all other greatness shrinks away. The weakest of his agents are the highest and noblest of human beings, the original parents of mankind; with whose actions the elements consented; on whose rectitude, or deviation of will, depended the state of terrestrial nature, and the condition of all the future inhabitants of the globe.

Of the other agents in the poem, the chief are such as it is irreverence to name on slight occasions. . . .

Of the evil angels the characters are more diversified. To Satan, as Addison observes, such sentiments are given as suit *the most exalted and most depraved being*. Milton has been censured, by Clarke, for the impiety which sometimes breaks from Satan's mouth. For there are thoughts, as he justly remarks, which no observation of character can justify, because no good man would willingly permit them to pass, however transiently, through his own mind. To make Satan speak as a rebel, without any such expressions as might taint the reader's imagination, was indeed one of the great difficulties in Milton's undertaking, and I cannot but think that he has extricated himself with great happiness. There is in Satan's speeches little that can give pain to a pious ear. The language of rebellion cannot be the same with that of obedience. The malignity of Satan foams in haughtiness and obstinacy; but his expressions are commonly general, and no otherwise offensive than as they are wicked.

The other chiefs of the celestial rebellion are very judiciously discriminated in the first and second books; and the ferocious character of Moloch appears, both in the battle and the council, with exact consistency.

To Adam and Eve are given, during their innocence, such sentiments as innocence can generate and utter. Their love is pure benevolence and mutual veneration; their repasts are without luxury, and their diligence without toil. Their addresses to their Maker have little more than the voice of admiration and gratitude. Fruition left them nothing to ask, and Innocence left them nothing to fear.

But with guilt enter distrust and discord, mutual accusation, and stubborn self-defence; they regard each other with alienated minds, and dread their Creator as the avenger of their transgression. At last they seek shelter in his mercy, soften to repentance, and melt in supplication. Both before and after the Fall, the superiority of Adam is diligently sustained.

Of the *probable* and the *marvellous,* two parts of a vulgar epick poem, which immerge the critick in deep consideration, the *Paradise Lost* requires little to be said. It contains the history of a miracle, of Creation and Redemption; it displays the power and the mercy of the Supreme Being; the probable therefore is marvellous, and the marvellous is probable. The substance of the narrative is truth; and as truth allows no choice, it is, like necessity, superior to rule. To the accidental or adventitious parts, as to every thing human, some slight exceptions may be made. But the main fabrick is immovably supported.

It is justly remarked by Addison, that this poem has, by the nature of its subject, the advantage above all others, that it is universally and perpetually interesting. All mankind will, through all ages, bear the same relation to Adam and to Eve, and must partake of that good and evil which extend to themselves. . . .

The plan of *Paradise Lost* has this inconvenience, that it comprises neither human actions nor human manners. The man and woman who act and suffer, are in a state which no other man or woman can ever know. The reader finds no transaction in which he can be engaged; beholds no condition in which he can by any effort of imagination place himself; he has, therefore, little natural curiosity or sympathy.

We all, indeed, feel the effects of Adam's disobedience; we all sin like Adam, and like him must all bewail our offences; we have restless and insidious enemies in the fallen angels, and in the blessed spirits we have guardians and friends; in the Redemption of mankind we hope to be included; in the description of heaven and hell we are surely interested, as we are all to reside hereafter either in the regions of horrour or of bliss.

But these truths are too important to be new; they have been taught to our infancy; they have mingled with our solitary thoughts and familiar conversation, and are habitually interwoven with the whole texture of life. Being therefore not new, they raise no unaccustomed emotion in the mind; what we knew before, we cannot learn; what is not unexpected, cannot surprise. . . .

Milton's allegory of Sin and Death is undoubtedly faulty. Sin is indeed the mother of Death, and may be allowed to be the portress of hell; but when they stop the journey of Satan, a journey described as real, and when Death offers him battle, the allegory is broken. That Sin and Death should have shewn the way to hell, might have been allowed; but they cannot facilitate the passage by building a bridge, because the difficulty of Satan's passage is described as real and sensible, and the bridge ought to be only figurative. The hell assigned to the rebellious spirits is described as not less local than the residence of man. It is placed in some distant part of space, separated from the regions of harmony and order by a chaotick waste and an unoccupied vacuity; but *Sin* and *Death* worked up a *mole of aggravated soil*, cemented with *asphaltus*; a work too bulky for ideal architects.

This unskilful allegory appears to me one of the greatest faults of the poem. ...

Poetry may subsist without rhyme, but English poetry will not often please; nor can rhyme ever be safely spared but where the subject is able to support itself. Blank verse makes some approach to that which is called the *lapidary style*; has neither the easiness of prose, nor the melody of numbers, and therefore tires by long continuance. Of the Italian writers without rhyme, whom Milton alleges as precedents, not one is popular; what reason could urge in its defence, has been confuted by the ear.

But, whatever be the advantage of rhyme, I cannot prevail on myself to wish that Milton had been a rhymer; for I cannot wish his work to be other than it is; yet, like other heroes, he is to be admired rather than imitated. He that thinks himself capable of astonishing, may write blank verse; but those that hope only to please, must condescend to rhyme.

The highest praise of genius is original invention. Milton cannot be said to have contrived the structure of an epick poem, and therefore owes reverence to that vigour and amplitude of mind to which all generations must be indebted for the art of poetical narration, for the texture of the fable, the variation of incidents, the interposition of dialogue, and all the stratagems that surprise and enchain attention. But, of all the borrowers from Homer, Milton is perhaps the least indebted. He was naturally a thinker for himself, confident of his own abilities, and disdainful of help or hindrance: he did not refuse admission to the thought or images of his predecessors, but he did not seek them. From his contemporaries he neither courted nor received support; there is in his writings nothing by which the pride of other authors might be gratified, or favour gained; no exchange of praise, nor solicitation of support. His great works were performed under discountenance, and in blindness, but difficulties vanished at his touch; he was born for whatever is arduous; and his work is not the greatest of heroick poems, only because it is not the first.

SOURCE : 'Milton', *The Lives of the English Poets* (1779).

William Blake

Those who restrain desire, do so because theirs is weak enough to be restrained; and the restrainer or reason usurps its place & governs the unwilling.

And being restrain'd, it by degrees becomes passive, till it is only the shadow of desire.

The history of this is written in *Paradise Lost*, & the Governor of Reason is call'd Messiah.

And the original Archangel, or possessor of the command of the heavenly host, is call'd the Devil or Satan, and his children are call'd Sin & Death.

But in the Book of Job, Milton's Messiah is call'd Satan.

For this history has been adopted by both parties.

It indeed appear'd to Reason as if Desire was cast out; but the Devil's account is, that the Messiah fell, & formed a heaven of what he stole from the Abyss.

This is shewn in the Gospel, where he prays to the Father to send the comforter, or Desire, that Reason may have Ideas to build on; the Jehovah of the Bible being no other than he who dwells in flaming fire.

Know that after Christ's death, he became Jehovah.

But in Milton, the Father is Destiny, the Son a Ratio of the five senses, & the Holy-ghost Vacuum!

Note: The reason Milton wrote in fetters when he wrote of Angels & God, and at liberty when of Devils & Hell, is because he was a true poet and of the Devil's party without knowing it.

SOURCE: *The Marriage of Heaven and Hell* (1790).

William Wordsworth

I

MILTON! thou shouldst be living at this hour:
England hath need of thee: she is a fen

Of stagnant waters : altar, sword, and pen,
Fireside, the heroic wealth of hall and bower,
Have forfeited their ancient English dower
Of inward happiness. We are selfish men;
Oh ! raise us up, return to us again;
And give us manners, virtue, freedom, power.
Thy soul was like a Star, and dwelt apart;
Thou hadst a voice whose sound was like the sea :
Pure as the naked heavens, majestic, free,
So didst thou travel on life's common way,
In cheerful godliness; and yet thy heart
The lowliest duties on herself did lay.

(1802)

II

Milton wrote chiefly from the Imagination which you may place
where you like in head, heart, liver or veins. *Him* the Almighty
Power hurled headlong &c. [*P.L.,* 1 44–9] see one of the most
wonderful sentences ever formed by the mind of man. The instances of imaginative and impassioned inversion in Milton are
innumerable. Take for instance the first sentence of his Poem.

SOURCE : 'Annotations to Richard Payne Knight, *Analytical
Inquiry into the Principles of Taste*' (1808).

III

I have long been persuaded that Milton formed his blank verse
upon the model of the *Georgics* and the *Æneid*, and I am so
much struck with this resemblance, that I should have attempted
Virgil in blank verse, had I not been persuaded that no ancient
author can be with advantage so rendered. Their religion, their
warfare, their course of action and feeling are too remote from
modern interest to allow it.

SOURCE : Letter to Lord Lonsdale (February 1819).

IV

Look at the case of Milton, he thought it his duty to take an active part in the troubles of his country, and consequently from his early manhood to the decline of his life he abandoned Poetry. Dante wrote his Poem in a great measure, perhaps entirely, when exile had separated him from the passions and what he thought the social duties of his native City. Cervantes, Camoens and other illustrious foreigners wrote in prison and in exile, when they were cut off from all other employments. So it will be found with most others, they composed either under similar circumstances, or like Virgil and Horace, at entire leisure, in which they were placed by Patronage, and charged themselves with no other leading duty than fulfilling their mission in their several ways as Poets.

SOURCE : Letter to Isabella Fenwick (October 1844).

V

The Wordsworths and Quillinans sat two hours with us. He said he thought [Dr Arnold] was mistaken in the philosophy of his view of the danger of Milton's Satan being represented without horns and hoofs; that Milton's conception was as true as it was grand; that making sin ugly was a commonplace notion compared with making it beautiful outwardly, and inwardly a hell. It assumed every form of ambition and worldliness, the form in which sin attacks the highest natures.

SOURCE : Reminiscences of Lady Richardson (1844).

Samuel Taylor Coleridge

I

A Reader of Milton must be always on his Duty : he is surrounded with sense; it rises in every line; every word is to the purpose. There are no lazy intervals : all has been considered and demands & merits observation.

If this be called obscurity, let it be remembered tis such a one as is complaisant to the Reader : not that vicious obscurity, which proceeds from a muddled head &c.

SOURCE : *Notes* (1797).

II

I dare not pronounce such passages as these to be absolutely unnatural, not merely because I consider the author a much better judge than I can be, but because I can understand and allow for an effort of the mind, when it would describe what it cannot satisfy itself with the description of, to reconcile opposites and qualify contradictions, leaving a middle state of mind more strictly appropriate to the imagination than any other, when it is, as it were, hovering between images. As soon as it is fixed on one image, it becomes understanding : but while it is unfixed and wavering between them, attaching itself permanently to none, it is imagination. Such is the fine description of Death in Milton :

> The other shape,
> If shape it might be called, that shape had none
> Distinguishable in member, joint, or limb,
> Or substance might be called, that shadow seemed.
> For each seemed either : black it stood as night,
> Fierce as ten Furies, terrible as hell,
> And shook a dreadful dart; what seemed his head
> The likeness of a kingly crown had on. (II, 666–73)

The grandest efforts of poetry are where the imagination is called forth, not to produce a distinct form, but a strong working of the mind, still offering what is still repelled, and again creating what is again rejected : the result being what the poet wishes to impress, namely, the substitution of a sublime feeling of the unimaginable for a mere image. I have sometimes thought that the passage just read might be quoted as exhibiting the narrow limit of painting, as compared with the boundless power of poetry :

painting cannot go beyond a certain point; poetry rejects all control, all confinement. Yet we know that sundry painters have attempted pictures of the meeting between Satan and Death at the gates of Hell; and how was Death represented? Not as Milton has described him, but by the most defined thing that can be imagined—a skeleton, the dryest and hardest image that it is possible to discover; which, instead of keeping the mind in a state of activity, reduces it to the merest passivity – an image, compared with which a square, a triangle, or any other mathematical figure, is a luxuriant fancy.

SOURCE: 'Seventeen Lectures on Shakespeare and Milton for the London Philosophical Society' (1811–12), Lecture VII (1811).

III

In its state of immanence or indwelling in reason and religion, the will appears indifferently as wisdom or as love : two names of the same power, the former more intelligential, the latter more spiritual, the former more frequent in the Old, the latter in the New, Testament. But in its utmost abstraction and consequent state of reprobation, the will becomes Satanic pride and rebellious self-idolatry in the relations of the spirit to itself, and remorseless despotism relatively to others; the more hopeless as the more obdurate by its subjugation of sensual impulses, by its superiority to toil and pain and pleasure; in short, by the fearful resolve to find in itself alone the one absolute motive of action, under which all other motives from within and from without must be either subordinated or crushed. . . .

This is the character which Milton has so philosophically as well as sublimely embodied in the Satan of his *Paradise Lost*.

SOURCE: *The Statesman's Manual* (1816).

IV

Difficult as I shall find it to turn over these leaves without catching some passage, which would tempt me to stop, I propose to consider, 1st, the general plan and arrangement of the work – 2ndly, the subject with its difficulties and advantages; – 3rdly, the poet's object, the spirit in the letter, the ἐνθύμιον ἐν μύθῳ, the true school-divinity; and lastly, the characteristic excellencies of the poem, in what they consist, and by what means they were produced.

1. As to the plan and ordonnance of the Poem.

Compare it with the *Iliad,* many of the books of which might change places without any injury to the thread of the story. Indeed, I doubt the original existence of the *Iliad* as one poem; it seems more probable that it was put together about the time of the Pisistratidae. The *Iliad* – and, more or less, all epic poems, the subjects of which are taken from history – have no rounded conclusion; they remain, after all, but single chapters from the volume of history, although they are ornamental chapters. Consider the exquisite simplicity of the *Paradise Lost.* It and it alone really possesses a beginning, a middle, and an end; it has the totality of the poem as distinguished from the *ab ovo* birth and parentage, or straight line, of history.

2. As to the subject –

In Homer, the supposed importance of the subject, as the first effort of confederated Greece, is an after-thought of the critics; and the interest, such as it is, derived from the events themselves, as distinguished from the manner of representing them, is very languid to all but Greeks. It is a Greek poem. The superiority of the *Paradise Lost* is obvious in this respect, that the interest transcends the limits of a nation. But we do not generally dwell on this excellence of the *Paradise Lost,* because it seems attributable to Christianity itself – yet in fact the interest is wider than Christendom, and comprehends the Jewish and Mohammedan worlds – nay, still further, inasmuch as it represents the origin of evil, and the combat of evil and good, it contains matter of deep interest to all mankind, as forming the basis of all religion, and the true occasion of all philosophy whatsoever.

The FALL of Man is the subject; Satan is the cause; man's blissful state the immediate object of his enmity and attack; man is warned by an angel who gives him an account of all that was requisite to be known, to make the warning at once intelligible and awful; then the temptation ensues, and the Fall; then the immediate sensible consequence; then the consolation, wherein an angel presents a vision of the history of men with the ultimate triumph of the Redeemer. Nothing is touched in this vision but what is of general interest in religion : anything else would have been improper.

The inferiority of Klopstock's *Messiah* is inexpressible. I admit the prerogative of poetic feeling, and poetic faith; but I cannot suspend the judgment even for a moment. A poem may in one sense be a dream, but it must be a waking dream. In Milton you have a religious faith combined with the moral nature; it is an efflux; you go along with it. In Klopstock there is a wilfulness; he makes things so and so. The feigned speeches and events in the *Messiah* shock us like falsehoods; but nothing of that sort is felt in the *Paradise Lost*, in which no particulars, at least very few indeed, are touched which can come into collision or juxtaposition with recorded matter.

But notwithstanding the advantages in Milton's subject, there were concomitant insuperable difficulties, and Milton has exhibited marvellous skill in keeping most of them out of sight. High poetry is the translation of reality into the ideal under the predicament of succession of time only. The poet is an historian, upon condition of moral power being the only force in the universe. The very grandeur of his subject ministered a difficulty to Milton. The statement of a being of high intellect, warring against the supreme Being, seems to contradict the idea of a supreme Being. Milton precludes our feeling this, as much as possible, by keeping the peculiar attributes of divinity less in sight, making them to a certain extent allegorical only. Again, poetry implies the language of excitement; yet how to reconcile such language with God? Hence Milton confines the poetic passion in God's speeches to the language of scripture; and once only allows the *passio vera*, or *quasihumana*, to appear, in the passage, where the Father contemplates his own likeness in the Son before the battle –

> Go then thou mightiest in thy Father's might,
> Ascend my chariot, guide the rapid wheels
> That shake heaven's basis, bring forth all my war,
> My bow and thunder, my almighty arms

> Gird on, and sword upon thy puissant thigh;
> Pursue these sons of darkness, drive them out
> From all heaven's bounds into the utter deep :
> There let them learn, as likes them, to despise
> God and Messiah his anointed king. (IV 710–18)

3. As to Milton's object –

It was to justify the ways of God to man! The controversial spirit observable in many parts of the poem, especially in God's speeches, is immediately attributable to the great controversy of that age, the origination of evil. The Arminians considered it a mere calamity. The Calvinists took away all human will. Milton asserted the will, but declared for the enslavement of the will out of an act of the will itself. There are three powers in us, which distinguish us from the beasts that perish – 1, reason; 2, the power of viewing universal truth; and 3, the power of contracting universal truth into particulars. Religion is the will in the reason, and love in the will.

The character of Satan is pride and sensual indulgence, finding in self the sole motive of action. It is the character so often seen *in little* on the political stage. It exhibits all the restlessness, temerity, and cunning which have marked the mighty hunters of mankind from Nimrod to Napoleon. The common fascination of men is, that these great men, as they are called, must act from some great motive. Milton has carefully marked in his Satan the intense selfishness, the alcohol of egotism, which would rather reign in hell than serve in heaven. To place this lust of self in opposition to denial of self or duty, and to show what exertions it would make, and what pains endure to accomplish its end, is Milton's particular object in the character of Satan. But around this character he has thrown a singularity of daring, a grandeur of sufferance, and a ruined splendour, which constitute the very height of poetic sublimity.

Lastly, as to the execution –

The language and versification of the *Paradise Lost* are peculiar in being so much more necessarily correspondent to each other than those in any other poem or poet. The connexion of the sentences and the position of the words are exquisitely artificial;

but the position is rather according to the logic of passion or universal logic, than to the logic of grammar. Milton attempted to make the English language obey the logic of passion as perfectly as the Greek and Latin. Hence the occasional harshness in the construction.

Sublimity is the pre-eminent characteristic of the *Paradise Lost*. It is not an arithmetical sublime like Klopstock's, whose rule always is to treat what we might think large as contemptibly small. Klopstock mistakes bigness for greatness. There is a greatness arising from images of effort and daring, and also from those of moral endurance; in Milton both are united. The fallen angels are human passions, invested with a dramatic reality.

The apostrophe to light at the commencement of the third book is particularly beautiful as an intermediate link between Hell and Heaven; observe, how the second and third books support the subjective character of the poem. In all modern poetry in Christendom there is an under consciousness of a sinful nature, a fleeting away of external things, the mind or subject greater than the object, the reflective character predominant. In the *Paradise Lost* the sublimest parts are the revelations of Milton's own mind, producing itself and evolving its own greatness; and this is so truly so, that when that which is merely entertaining for its objective beauty is introduced, it at first seems a discord.

In the description of Paradise itself you have Milton's sunny side as a man; here his descriptive powers are exercised to the utmost, and he draws deep upon his Italian resources. In the description of Eve, and throughout this part of the poem, the poet is predominant over the theologian. Dress is the symbol of the Fall, but the mark of intellect; and the metaphysics of dress are, the hiding what is not symbolic and displaying by discrimination what is. The love of Adam and Eve in Paradise is of the highest merit – not phantomatic, and yet removed from every thing degrading. It is the sentiment of one rational being towards another made tender by a specific difference in that which is essentially the same in both; it is a union of opposites, a giving and receiving mutually of the permanent in either, a completion of each in the other.

Milton is not a picturesque, but a musical, poet; although he has this merit that the object chosen by him for any particular foreground always remains prominent to the end, enriched, but not incumbered, by the opulence of descriptive details furnished by an exhaustless imagination. I wish the *Paradise Lost* were more carefully read and studied than I can see any ground for believing it is, especially those parts which, from the habit of always looking for a story in poetry, are scarcely read at all—as, for example, Adam's vision of future events in the 11th and 12th books. No one can rise from the perusal of this immortal poem without a deep sense of the grandeur and the purity of Milton's soul, or without feeling how susceptible of domestic enjoyments he really was, notwithstanding the discomforts which actually resulted from an apparently unhappy choice in marriage. He was, as every truly great poet has ever been, a good man; but finding it impossible to realize his own aspirations, either in religion, or politics, or society, he gave up his heart to the living spirit and light within him, and avenged himself on the world by enriching it with this record of his own transcendent ideal.

SOURCE: 'Fourteen Lectures for the London Philosophical Society', Lecture x (1818).

v

The general characteristic of the style of our literature down to the period which I have just mentioned, was gravity, and in Milton and some other writers of his day there are perceptible traces of the sternness of republicanism. Soon after the Restoration a material change took place, and the cause of royalism was graced, sometimes disgraced, by every shade of lightness of manner.

SOURCE: Lecture xiv (1818).

vi

In the *Paradise Lost* – indeed in every one of his poems – it is Milton himself whom you see; his Satan, his Adam, his Raphael, almost his Eve – are all John Milton; and it is a sense of this intense egotism that gives me the greatest pleasure in reading Milton's works. The egotism of such a man is a revelation of spirit.

SOURCE: *Table Talk* (18 August 1833).

VII

In my judgment, an epic poem must either be national or mundane. As to Arthur, you could not by any means make a poem on him national to Englishmen. What have *we* to do with him? Milton saw this, and with a judgment at least equal to his genius, took a mundane theme – one common to all mankind. His Adam and Eve are all men and women inclusively. Pope satirizes Milton for making God the Father talk like a school divine. Pope was hardly the man to criticize Milton. The truth is, the judgment of Milton in the conduct of the celestial part of his story is very exquisite. Wherever God is represented as directly acting as Creator, without any exhibition of his own essence, Milton adopts the simplest and sternest language of the Scriptures. He ventures upon no poetic diction, no amplification, no pathos, no affection. It is truly the Voice or the Word of the Lord coming to, and acting on, the subject Chaos. But, as some personal interest was demanded for the purposes of poetry, Milton takes advantage of the dramatic representation of God's address to the Son, the Filial Alterity, and in *those addresses* slips in, as it were by stealth, language of affection, or thought, or sentiment. Indeed, although Milton was undoubtedly a high Arian in his mature life, he does in the necessity of poetry give a greater objectivity to the Father and the Son, than he would have justified in argument. He was very wise in adopting the strong anthropomorphism of the Hebrew Scriptures at once. Compare the *Paradise Lost* with Klopstock's Messiah, and you will learn to appreciate Milton's judgment and skill quite as much as his genius.

SOURCE: *Table Talk* (4 September 1833).

Charles Lamb

Nothing can be more unlike to my fancy than Homer and Milton. Homer is perfect prattle, tho' exquisite prattle, compared to the deep oracular voice of Milton. In Milton you love to stop, and saturate your mind with every great image or sentiment; in Homer you want to go on, to have more of his agreeable narrative.

SOURCE: Letter to Charles Lloyd (31 July 1809).

William Hazlitt

I

Milton has borrowed more than any other writer; yet he is perfectly distinct from every other writer. The power of his mind is stamped on every line. He is a writer of centos, and yet in originality only inferior to Homer. The quantity of art shews the strength of his genius; so much art would have overloaded any other writer. Milton's learning has all the effect of intuition. He describes objects of which he had only read in books, with the vividness of actual observation. His imagination has the force of nature. He makes words tell as pictures . . . There is also a decided tone in his descriptions, an eloquent dogmatism, as if the poet spoke from thorough conviction, which Milton probably derived from his spirit of partisanship, or else his spirit of partisanship from the natural firmness and vehemence of his mind. In this Milton resembles Dante (the only one of the moderns with whom he has anything in common), and it is remarkable that Dante, as well as Milton, was a political partisan. That approximation to the severity of impassioned prose which has been made an objection to Milton's poetry, is one of its chief excellencies. It has been suggested, that the vividness with which he describes visible objects, might be owing to their having acquired a greater strength in his mind after the privation of sight; but we find the same palpableness and solidity in the descriptions which occur in his early poems. There is, indeed, the same depth of impression in his descriptions of the objects of the other senses. Milton had as much of what is meant by *gusto* as any poet. He forms the most intense conceptions of things, and then embodies them by a single stroke of his pen. Force of style is perhaps his first excellence. Hence he stimulates us most in the reading, and less afterwards.

SOURCE: *Round Table* (1817).

II

The difference between the character of *Eve* in Milton and Shakspeare's female characters is very striking, and it appears to us to be this: Milton describes *Eve* not only as full of love and tenderness for *Adam*, but as the constant object of admiration in herself. She is the idol of the poet's imagination, and he paints her whole person with a studied profusion of charms. She is the wife, but she is still as much as ever the mistress, of *Adam*. She is represented, indeed, as devoted to her husband, as twining round him for support 'as the vine curls her tendrils' (IV, 307) but her own grace and beauty are never lost sight of in the picture of conjugal felicity. *Adam's* attention and regard are as much turned to her as hers to him : for 'in that first garden of their innocence', he had no other objects or pursuits to distract his attention; she was both his business and his pleasure. Shakespeare's females, on the contrary, seem to exist only in their attachment to others. They are pure abstractions of the affections. Their features are not painted, nor the colour of their hair. Their hearts only are laid open. We are acquainted with *Imogen, Miranda, Ophelia,* or *Desdemona*, by what they thought and felt, but we cannot tell whether they were black, brown, or fair. But Milton's *Eve* is all of ivory and gold. Shakspeare seldom tantalises the reader with a luxurious display of the personal charms of his heroines, with a curious inventory of particular beauties, except indirectly, and for some other purpose, as where *Jachimo* describes *Imogen* asleep, or the old men in the *Winter's Tale* vie with each other

in invidious praise of *Perdita*. Even in *Juliet*, the most voluptuous
and glowing of the class of characters here spoken of, we are
reminded chiefly of circumstances connected with the physiog-
nomy of passion, as in her leaning with her cheek upon her arm,
or which only convey the general impression of enthusiasm made
on her lover's brain. One thing may be said, that Shakespeare
had not the same opportunities as Milton : for his women were
clothed, and it cannot be denied that Milton took *Eve* at a con-
siderable disadvantage in this respect. He had accordingly
described her in all the loveliness of nature, tempting to sight as the
fruit of the Hesperides guarded by that Dragon old, herself the
fairest among the flowers of Paradise ! . . .

That which distinguishes Milton from the other poets, who
have pampered the eye and fed the imagination with exuberant
descriptions of female beauty, is the moral severity with which he
has tempered them. There is not a line in his works which tends to
licentiousness, or the impression of which, if it has such a tendency,
is not effectually checked by thought and sentiment.

SOURCE : *Round Table* (1817).

III

To proceed to a consideration of the merits of *Paradise Lost*, in
the most essential point of view, I mean as to the poetry of character and passion. I shall say nothing of the fable, or of other technical objections or excellences; but I shall try to explain at once
the foundation of the interest belonging to the poem. I am ready
to give up the dialogues in Heaven, where, as Pope justly observes,
'God the Father turns a school-divine'; nor do I consider the
battle of the angels as the climax of sublimity, or the most successful effort of Milton's pen. In a word, the interest of the poem
arises from the daring ambition and fierce passions of Satan, and
from the account of the paradisaical happiness, and the loss of it
by our first parents. Three-fourths of the work are taken up with
these characters, and nearly all that relates to them is unmixed
sublimity and beauty. The two first books alone are like two massy
pillars of solid gold.

Satan is the most heroic subject that ever was chosen for a poem; and the execution is as perfect as the design is lofty. He was the first of created beings, who, for endeavouring to be equal with the highest, and to divide the empire of heaven with the Almighty, was hurled down to hell. His aim was no less than the throne of the universe; his means, myriads of angelic armies bright, the third part of the heavens, whom he lured after him with his countenance, and who durst defy the Omnipotent in arms. His ambition was the greatest, and his punishment was the greatest; but not so his despair, for his fortitude was as great as his sufferings. His strength of mind was matchless as his strength of body; the vastness of his designs did not surpass the firm, inflexible determination with which he submitted to his irreversible doom, and final loss of all good. His power of action and of suffering was equal. He was the greatest power that was ever overthrown, with the strongest will left to resist or to endure. He was baffled, not confounded. He stood like a tower; or

> — As when heaven's fire
> Hath scathed the forest oaks or mountain pines.

He was still surrounded with hosts of rebel angels, armed warriors, who own him as their sovereign leader, and with whose fate he sympathises as he views them round, far as the eye can reach; though he keeps aloof from them in his own mind, and holds supreme counsel only with his own breast. An outcast from Heaven, Hell trembles beneath his feet, Sin and Death are at his heels, and mankind are his easy prey.

> All is not lost; the unconquerable will,
> And study of revenge, immortal hate,
> And courage never to submit or yield,
> And what is else not to be overcome,

are still his. The sense of his punishment seems lost in the magnitude of it; the fierceness of tormenting flames is qualified and made innoxious by the greater fierceness of his pride; the loss of infinite happiness to himself is compensated in thought, by the power of inflicting infinite misery on others. Yet Satan is not the principle of malignity, or of the abstract love of evil — but of the abstract love of power, of pride, of self-will personified, to which last principle all other good and evil, and even his own, are subordinate. From this principle he never once flinches. His love of power and contempt for suffering are never once relaxed from the highest pitch of intensity. His thoughts burn like hell within him; but the power of thought holds dominion in his mind over every other consideration. The consciousness of a determined purpose, of 'that intellectual being, those thoughts that wander through eternity', though accompanied with endless pain, he prefers to nonentity, to 'being swallowed up and lost in the wide womb of uncreated night'. He expresses the sum and substance of all ambition in one line. 'Fallen cherub, to be weak is miserable, doing or suffering!' After such a conflict as his, and such a defeat, to retreat in order, to rally, to make terms, to exist at all, is something; but he does more than this – he founds a new empire in hell, and from it conquers this new world, whither he bends his undaunted flight, forcing his way through nether and surrounding fires. The poet has not in all this given us a mere shadowy outline; the strength is equal to the magnitude of the conception. The Achilles of Homer is not more distinct; the Titans were not more vast; Prometheus chained to his rock was not a more terrific example of suffering and of crime. Wherever the figure of Satan is introduced, whether he walks or flies, 'rising aloft incumbent on the dusky air', it is illustrated with the most striking and appropriate images : so that we see it always before us, gigantic, irregular, portentous, uneasy, and disturbed – but dazzling in its faded splendour, the clouded ruins of a god. The deformity of Satan is only in the depravity of his will; he has no bodily deformity to excite our loathing or disgust. The horns and tail are not there, poor emblems of the unbending, unconquered spirit, of the writhing agonies within. Milton was too magnanimous and open an antagonist to support his argument by the bye-tricks of a hump and cloven foot; to bring into the fair field of controversy the good old catholic prejudices of which Tasso and Dante have availed themselves, and which the mystic German critics would restore. He relied on the justice of his cause, and did not scruple to give the devil his due. Some persons may think that he has carried his liberality too far, and injured the cause he professed to espouse by making him the chief person in his poem. Considering the nature of his subject, he would be equally in danger of running into this fault, from his faith in religion, and his love of rebellion; and perhaps each of these motives had its full share in determining the choice of his subject.

Not only the figure of Satan, but his speeches in council, his soliloquies, his address to Eve, his share in the war in heaven, or in the fall of man, shew the same decided superiority of character. To give only one instance, almost the first speech he makes:

> Is this the region, this the soil, the clime,
> Said then the lost archangel, this the seat
> That we must change for heaven, this mournful gloom
> For that celestial light? Be it so, since he
> Who now is sovereign can dispose and bid
> What shall be right: furthest from him is best
> Whom reason hath equalled, force hath made supreme
> Above his equals. Farewell happy fields
> Where joy for ever dwells: hail horrors, hail
> Infernal world, and thou profoundest hell
> Receive thy new possessor: one who brings
> A mind not to be changed by place or time.
> The mind is its own place, and in itself
> Can make a heaven of hell, a hell of heaven.
> What matter where, if I be still the same,
> And what I should be, all but less than he
> Whom thunder hath made greater? Here at least
> We shall be free; the almighty hath not built
> Here for his envy, will not drive us hence:
> Here we may reign secure, and in my choice
> To reign is worth ambition though in hell:
> Better to reign in hell, than serve in heaven.

The whole of the speeches and debates in Pandemonium are well worthy of the place and the occasion – with Gods for speakers, and angels and archangels for hearers. There is a decided manly tone in the arguments and sentiments, an eloquent dogmatism, as if each person spoke from thorough conviction; an excellence which Milton probably borrowed from his spirit of partisanship, or else his spirit of partisanship from the natural firmness and vigour of his mind. In this respect Milton resembles

Dante (the only modern writer with whom he has any thing in common) and it is remarkable that Dante, as well as Milton, was a political partisan. That approximation to the severity of impassioned prose which has been made an objection to Milton's poetry, and which is chiefly to be met with in these bitter invectives, is one of its great excellences. The author might here turn his philippics against Salmasius to good account. The rout in Heaven is like the fall of some mighty structure, nodding to its base, 'with hideous ruin and combustion down'. But, perhaps, of all the passages in *Paradise Lost*, the description of the employments of the angels during the absence of Satan, some of whom 'retreated in a silent valley, sing with notes angelical to many a harp their own heroic deeds and hapless fall by doom of battle', is the most perfect example of mingled pathos and sublimity. – What proves the truth of this noble picture in every part, and that the frequent complaint of want of interest in it is the fault of the reader, not of the poet, is that when any interest of a practical kind takes a shape that can be at all turned into this (and there is little doubt that Milton had some such in his eye in writing it) each party converts it to its own purposes, feels the absolute identity of these abstracted and high speculations; and that, in fact, a noted political writer of the present day has exhausted nearly the whole account of Satan in the *Paradise Lost*, by applying it to a character whom he considered as after the devil (though I do not know whether he would make even that exception) the greatest enemy of the human race. This may serve to shew that Milton's Satan is not a very insipid personage.

Of Adam and Eve it has been said, that the ordinary reader can feel little interest in them, because they have none of the passions, pursuits, or even relations of human life, except that of man and wife, the least interesting of all others, if not to the parties concerned, at least to the by-standers. The preference has on this account been given to Homer, who, it is said, has left very vivid and infinitely diversified pictures of all the passions and affections, public and private, incident to human nature – the relations of son, of brother, parent, friend, citizen, and many others. Longinus preferred the *Iliad* to the *Odyssey*, on account of the greater number of battles it contains; but I can neither agree to his criticism, nor assent to the present objection. It is true, there is little action in this part of Milton's poem; but there is much repose, and more enjoyment. There are none of the every-day occurrences, contentions, disputes, wars, fightings, feuds, jealousies, trades, professions, liveries, and common handicrafts of life; 'no kind of traffic; letters are not known; no use of service, of riches, poverty, contract, succession, bourne, bound of land, tilth, vineyard none; no occupation, no treason, felony, sword, pike, knife, gun, nor need of any engine'. So much the better; thank Heaven, all these were yet to come. But still the die was cast, and in them our doom was sealed. In them

> The generations were prepared; the pangs,
> The internal pangs, were ready, the dread strife
> Of poor humanity's afflicted will,
> Struggling in vain with ruthless destiny.

In their first false step we trace all our future woe, with loss of Eden. But there was a short and precious interval between, like the first blush of morning before the day is overcast with tempest, the dawn of the world, the birth of nature from 'the unapparent deep', with its first dews and freshness on its cheek, breathing odours. Theirs was the first delicious taste of life, and on them depended all that was to come of it. In them hung trembling all our hopes and fears. They were as yet alone in the world, in the eye of nature, wondering at their new being, full of enjoyment and enraptured with one another, with the voice of their Maker walking in the garden, and ministering angels attendant on their steps, winged messengers from heaven like rosy clouds descending in their sight. Nature played around them her virgin fancies wild; and spread for them a repast where no crude surfeit reigned. Was there nothing in this scene, which God and nature alone witnessed, to interest a modern critic? What need was there of action, where the heart was full of bliss and innocence without it! They had nothing to do but feel their own happiness, and 'know to know no more'. 'They toiled not, neither did they spin; yet Solomon in all his glory was not arrayed like one of these.' All things seem to acquire fresh sweetness, and to be clothed with fresh beauty in their sight. They tasted as it were for themselves

and us, of all that there ever was pure in human bliss. 'In them
the burden of the mystery, the heavy and the weary weight of all
this unintelligible world, is lightened.' They stood awhile perfect,
but they afterwards fell, and were driven out of Paradise, tasting
the first fruits of bitterness as they had done of bliss. But their
pangs were such as a pure spirit might feel at the sight – their
tears 'such as angels weep'. The pathos is of that mild contem-
plative kind which arises from regret for the loss of unspeakable
happiness, and resignation to inevitable fate. There is none of the
fierceness of intemperate passion, none of the agony of mind and
turbulence of action, which is the result of the habitual struggles
of the will with circumstances, irritated by repeated disappointment, and constantly setting its desires most eagerly on that which
there is an impossibility of attaining. This would have destroyed
the beauty of the whole picture. They had received their un-
looked-for happiness as a free gift from their Creator's hands, and
they submitted to its loss, not without sorrow, but without impious
and stubborn repining.

> In either hand the hastening angel caught
> Our lingering parents, and to the eastern gate
> Led them direct, and down the cliff as fast
> To the subjected plain; then disappeared.
> They looking back, all the eastern side beheld
> Of Paradise, so late their happy seat,
> Waved over by that flaming brand, the gate
> With dreadful faces thronged and fiery arms :
> Some natural tears they dropped, but wiped them soon;
> The world was all before them, where to choose
> Their place of rest, and providence their guide. . . .

SOURCE : Lecture III – 'On Shakespeare and Milton' (1818).

Thomas De Quincey

A purpose of the same nature is answered by the higher literature,
viz. the literature of power. What do you learn from *Paradise*

Lost? Nothing at all. What do you learn from a cookery-book? Something new, something that you did not know before, in every paragraph. But would you therefore put the wretched cookery-book on a higher level of estimation than the divine poem? What you owe to Milton is not any knowledge, of which a million separate items are still but a million of advancing steps on the same earthly level; what you owe is *power* – that is, exercise and expansion to your own latent capacity of sympathy with the infinite, where every pulse and each separate influx is a step upwards, a step ascending as upon a Jacob's ladder from earth to mysterious altitudes above the earth. *All* the steps of knowledge, from first to last, carry you further on the same plane, but could never raise you one foot above your ancient level of earth : whereas the very *first* step in power is a flight – is an ascending movement into another element where earth is forgotten. . . .

Poetry, or any one of the fine arts (all of which alike speak through the genial nature of man and his excited sensibilities), can teach only as nature teaches, as forests teach, as the sea teaches, as infancy teaches – viz. by deep impulse, by hieroglyphic suggestion. Their teaching is not indirect or explicit, but lurking, implicit, masked in deep incarnations. To teach formally and professedly is to abandon the very differential character and principle of poetry. If poetry could condescend to teach anything, it would be truths moral or religious. But even these it can utter only through symbols and actions. The great moral, for instance, the last result, of the *Paradise Lost* is once formally announced – viz. *to justify the ways of God to man* (I 26); but it teaches itself only by diffusing its lesson through the entire poem in the total succession of events and purposes : and even this succession teaches it only when the whole is gathered into unity by a reflex act of meditation, just as the pulsation of the physical heart can exist only when all the parts in an animal system are locked into one organisation.

SOURCE : 'The Poetry of Pope' (August 1848).

Percy Bysshe Shelley

Milton's Devil as a moral being is as far superior to his God, as one who perseveres in some person which he had conceived to be excellent, in spite of adversity and torture, is to one who in the cold security of undoubted triumph inflicts the most horrible revenge upon his enemy – not from any mistaken notion of bringing him to repent of a perseverance in enmity, but with the open and alleged design of exasperating him to deserve new torments. . . .

There is also another view of the subject, suggested by mythological writers, which strongly recommends the Devil to our sympathy and compassion, though [it] is less consistent with the theory of God's omnipotence than that already stated. The Devil, it is said, before his fall, as an Angel of the highest rank and the most splendid accomplishments placed his peculiar delight in doing good. But the inflexible grandeur of his spirit, mailed and nourished by the consciousness [of] the purest and loftiest designs, was so secure from the assault of any gross or common torments, that God was considerably puzzled to invent what he considered an adequate punishment for his rebellion; he exhausted all the varieties of smothering and burning and freezing and cruelly-lacerating his external frame, and the Devil laughed at the impotent revenge of his conqueror. At last the benevolent and amiable disposition which distinguished his adversary, furnished God with the true method of executing an enduring and a terrible vengeance. He turned his good into evil, and, by virtue of his omnipotence, inspired him with such impulses, as, in spite of his better nature, irresistibly determined him to act what he most abhorred, and to be a minister of those designs and schemes of which he was the chief and the original victim. He is for ever tortured with compassion and affection for those whom he betrays and ruins; he is racked by a vain abhorrence for the desolation of which he is the instrument; he is like a man compelled by a tyrant to set fire to his own possessions, and to appear as witness against, and the accuser of his dearest friends and most intimate connexions; and then to be their executioner, and to inflict the most subtle and protracted torments upon them. As a man, were he deprived of all other refuge, he might hold his breath and die – but God is represented as omnipotent and the Devil as eternal. Milton has expressed this view of the subject with the sublimest pathos.

SOURCE: *On the Devil, and Devils* (1819).

John Keats

I

There is a greatness which the *Paradise Lost* possesses over every other Poem – *the Magnitude of Contrast* and that is softened by the contrast being ungrotesque to a degree. Heaven moves on like music throughout – Hell is also peopled with angels it also moves[s] on like music not grating and ha[r]sh but like a grand accompaniment in the Base to Heaven –

SOURCE: Annotations to *Paradise Lost* (1818).

II

I am convinced more and more day by day that fine writing is next to fine doing the top thing in the world; the *Paradise Lost* becomes a greater wonder.

SOURCE: Letter to J. H. Reynolds (24 August 1819).

III

I have given up Hyperion – there were too many Miltonic inversions in it – Miltonic verse cannot be written but in an artful or rather artist's humour. I wish to give myself up to other sensations. English ought to be kept up. It may be interesting to you to pick out some lines from Hyperion and put a mark ✕ to the false beauty proceeding from art, and one ‖ to the true voice of feeling. Upon my soul 'twas imagination I cannot make the distinction – Every now & then there is a Miltonic intonation – But I cannot make the division properly. . . .

SOURCE : Letter to J. H. Reynolds (21 September 1819).

IV

I shall never become attach'd to a foreign idiom so as to put it into my writings. The *Paradise Lost* though so fine in itself is a corruption of our Language – it should be kept as it is unique – a curiosity, a beautiful and grand Curiosity. The most remarkable Production of the world – A northen dialect accommodating itself to Greek and Latin inversions and intonations. The purest English I think – or what ought to be the purest – is Chatterton's – The Language had existed long enough to be entirely uncorrupted of Chaucer's gallicisms and still the old words are used – Chatterton's language is entirely northern – I prefer the native music of it to Milton's cut by feet. I have but lately stood my guard against Milton. Life to him would be death to me. Miltonic verse cannot be written but i[n] the vein of art – I wish to devote myself to another sensation –

SOURCE : Letter to the George Keatses (24 September 1819).

Matthew Arnold

If to our English race an inadequate sense for perfection of work is a real danger, if the discipline of respect for a high and flawless excellence is peculiarly needed by us, Milton is of all our gifted men the best lesson, the most salutary influence. In the sure and flawless perfection of his rhythm and diction he is as admirable as Virgil or Dante, and in this respect he is unique amongst us. No one else in English literature and art possesses the like distinction. . . .

To what does he owe this supreme distinction? To nature first and foremost, to that bent of nature for inequality which to the worshippers of the average man is so unacceptable; to a gift, a divine favour. 'The older one grows,' says Goethe, 'the more one prizes natural gifts, because by no possibility can they be procured and stuck on.' Nature formed Milton to be a great poet. But what other poet has shown so sincere a sense of the grandeur of his vocation, and a moral effort so constant and sublime to make and keep himself worthy of it? The Milton of religious and political controversy, and perhaps of domestic life also, is not seldom disfigured by want of amenity, by acerbity. The Milton of poetry, on the other hand, is one of those great men 'who are modest' – to quote a fine remark of Leopardi, that gifted and stricken young Italian, who in his sense for poetic style is worthy to be named with Dante and Milton – 'who are modest, because they continually compare themselves, not with other men, but with that idea of the perfect which they have before their mind'. The Milton of poetry is the man, in his own magnificent phrase, of 'devout prayer to that Eternal Spirit that can enrich with all utterance and knowledge, and sends out his Seraphim with the hallowed fire of his altar, to touch and purify the lips of whom he pleases'. And finally, the Milton of poetry is, in his own words again, the man of 'industrious and select reading'. Continually he lived in companionship with high and rare excellence, with the great Hebrew poets and prophets, with the great poets of Greece and Rome. The Hebrew compositions were not in verse, and can be not inadequately represented by the grand, measured prose of our English Bible. The verse of the poets of Greece and Rome no translation can adequately reproduce. Prose cannot have the power of verse; verse-translation may give whatever of charm is in the soul and talent of the translator himself, but never the specific charm of the verse and poet translated. In our race are thousands of readers, presently there will be millions, who know not a word of Greek and Latin, and will never learn those languages. If this host of readers are ever to gain any sense of the power and charm of the great poets of antiquity, their way to gain it is not through translations of the ancients, but through the original poetry of Milton, who has the like power and charm, because he has the like great style.

Through Milton they may gain it, for, in conclusion, Milton is English; this master in the great style of the ancients is English. Virgil, whom Milton loved and honoured, has at the end of the *Aeneid* a noble passage, where Juno, seeing the defeat of Turnus and the Italians imminent, the victory of the Trojan invaders assured, entreats Jupiter that Italy may nevertheless survive and be herself still, may retain her own mind, manners, and language, and not adopt those of the conqueror.

> Sit Latium, sint Albani per secula reges !

Jupiter grants the prayer; he promises perpetuity and the future to Italy – Italy reinforced by whatever virtue the Trojan race has, but Italy, not Troy. This we may take as a sort of parable suiting ourselves. All the Anglo-Saxon contagion, all the flood of Anglo-Saxon commonness, beats vainly against the great style but cannot shake it, and has to accept its triumph. But it triumphs in Milton, in one of our own race, tongue, faith, and morals. Milton has made the great style no longer an exotic here; he has made it an inmate amongst us, a leaven, and a power. Nevertheless he, and his hearers on both sides of the Atlantic, are English, and will remain English –

> Sermonem Ausonii patrium moresque tenebunt.

The English race overspreads the world, and at the same time the ideal of an excellence the most high and the most rare abides a possession with it for ever.

SOURCE : 'Milton' (1888).

PART THREE
Modern Criticism

Basil Willey

THE HEROIC POEM (1934)

In the seventeenth century there was one poetic genre which enjoyed such peculiar and special prestige that it was proof against the cold climate of 'an age too late' – the Heroic Poem. Only the Bible could claim a greater share of reverence than Homer and Virgil. This was a legacy of the Renaissance, when as is well known, the desire to emulate the noblest achievements of the ancients had become fused with the patriotic nationalism of the time, and poets in each country had aspired to 'illustrate' their vernaculars by composing in them works worthy to be set beside the *Iliad* and the *Aeneid*. The continued vitality of this tradition is well illustrated in Dryden's describing the Heroic Poem, at the very end of the century and of his own life (1697), as 'undoubtedly the greatest work which the soul of man is capable to perform'.[1] It is outside my purpose to account for this veneration for epic poetry, but a few of its credentials may well be mentioned. The ancients had produced their crowning master-pieces in this kind; Aristotle had canonised it; and Dante, Ariosto, and Tasso had in their several ways raised Italian nearly to a level with the classical languages. Not until a work of equal scope, ordonnance and elevation had been produced in French, for instance, or in English, could those modern dialects claim to have emerged from mediaeval barbarism. Moreover, the subject-matter of epic was normally some great act in the drama of national history, and through it, therefore, could be expressed the new-found pride of nationhood, and the passion for great doing, which distinguished the Renaissance. Above all, the comparative invulnerability of heroic poetry, even in an age of scientific enlightenment, was due to this, that though it might make use of fiction, though its history might be 'fained', its object was something as important as Truth itself, namely moral edification.

On this point the critics from the Renaissance onwards were unanimous, and Dryden's remark, which recalls Spenser's, may be taken as typical :

> The design of it is to form the mind to heroic virtue by example;
> 'tis conveyed in verse, that it may delight, while it instructs.[2]

In order to acquit himself worthily in heroic poetry, then, a poet must possess the loftiest genius as an artist and the highest qualities as a man. The very difficulty of the task invested the whole topic with a glamour which can now be more easily understood than felt; and this to some extent explains the extraordinary fact, noted by W. P. Ker,[3] that

> The 'Heroic Poem' is not commonly mentioned in histories of Europe as a matter of serious interest : yet from the days of Petrarch and Boccaccio to those of Dr Johnson, and more especially from the sixteenth century onward, it was a subject that engaged some of the strongest intellects in the world (among them Hobbes, Gibbon and Hume); it was studied and discussed as fully and with as much thought as any of the problems by which the face of the world was changed in those countries. There might be difference of opinion about the essence of the Heroic Poem or the Tragedy, but there was no doubt about their value. Truth about them was ascertainable, and truth about them was necessary to the intellect of man, for they were the noblest things belonging to him.

English poetry had had its Spenser, who had hoped to overgo Ariosto. But he was not felt to have succeeded; for, as Dryden remarked, in reviewing the achievement in this field,[4] there was no uniformity in his design; he had a new hero for each adventure, and as each one represented a particular moral virtue, they are 'all equal, without subordination or preference'. And apart from these and other faults (the 'ill choice of his stanza', for instance), the work was incomplete. The absolute epic in English was still unwritten. Part at least of Milton's purpose was to write it, and so to realise at last, for England, this cherished ambition of the Renaissance. In a famous passage of the *Reason of Church Government*, Milton relates how the great idea came to him that by labour and intense study . . . joined with the strong propensity of nature, I might perhaps leave something so written to aftertimes, as they should not willingly let it die.

And it became clear to him, also, that like a true poet of the Renaissance, his aim must be the adorning of his native tongue, and the honour and instruction of his country :

That what the greatest and choicest wits of Athens, Rome, or modern Italy, and those Hebrews of old did for their country, I, in my proportion, with this over and above, of being a Christian, might do for mine; not caring to be once named abroad, though perhaps I could attain to that, but content with these British islands as my world. . . .[5]

Dryden will not grant that even Milton had realised the idea of the heroic poem. . . . But he would have agreed that Milton was pre-eminently fitted, both in genius and in character, to succeed where others had failed. Loftily as they conceived of the heroic poem, no poet or critic of the Renaissance could approach Milton in grandeur of purpose and intensity of self-devotion. It is not for me here to do more than remind readers how, 'long choosing and beginning late', Milton dedicated himself to the intellectual and moral discipline which he considered necessary for his purpose; of his realisation that

he who would not be frustrate of his hope to write well hereafter in laudable things, ought himself to be a true poem; that is, a composition and pattern of the best and honourablest things;[6]

and of his magnificent request, twenty years before the completion of *Paradise Lost*, for yet more time, since his was

a work not to be raised from the heat of youth, or the vapours of wine; like that which flows at waste from the pen of some vulgar amourist, or the trencher fury of a rhyming parasite; nor to be obtained by the invocation of dame memory and her siren daughters, but by devout prayer to that eternal Spirit, who can enrich with all utterance and knowledge, and sends out his seraphim, with the hallowed fire of his altar, to touch and purify the lips of whom he pleases.[7]

Nor was Milton actuated, it need hardly be said, merely by the literary and patriotic ambition to rival the ancients in English; with him the moral purpose, always a part of the Renaissance theory of epic, was of supreme importance. His work was to be 'doctrinal and exemplary to a nation', for it was the true office of poetic genius, he held,

to imbreed and cherish in a great people the seeds of virtue and public civility, to allay the perturbations of the mind, and set the affections in right tune; to celebrate in glorious and lofty hymns the throne and equipage of God's almightiness, and what he works, and what he suffers to be wrought with high providence in his church; to sing victorious agonies of martyrs and saints, the deeds and triumphs of just and pious nations, doing valiantly through faith against the enemies of Christ. . . . Teaching over the whole book of sanctity and virtue, through all the instances of example. . . .[8]

The appearance of *Paradise Lost* in the midst of the seventeenth century, then, may be attributed in the first place to the fact that in Milton the Renaissance idea of the heroic poem, alive as ever though hitherto 'laid up in some heaven to which the true scholar might rise',[9] at last found its destined English exponent.

SOURCE : *Seventeenth Century Background* (1934).

NOTES

1. *Dedication of the Aeneis.*
2. Ibid.
3. *Essays of Dryden*, vol. I, introduction, p. XVI.
4. *Discourse Concerning the Original and Progress of Satire.*
5. *Milton's Prose Works* (Bohn), vol. II, p. 478.
6. *Apology for Smectymnuus* (Bohn), vol. III, p. 118.
7. *Reason of Church Government* (Bohn), vol. II, p. 481.
8. Ibid., p. 479.
9. Ker, op. cit., introduction, p. XV.

T. S. Eliot

MILTON: STYLE AND TRADITION
(1936 and 1947)

A disadvantage of the rhetorical style appears to be, that a dis-location takes place, through the hypertrophy of the auditory imagination at the expense of the visual and tactile, so that the inner meaning is separated from the surface, and tends to become something occult, or at least without effect upon the reader until fully understood. To extract everything possible from *Paradise Lost*, it would seem necessary to read it in two different ways, first solely for the sound, and second for the sense. The full beauty of his long periods can hardly be enjoyed while we are wrestling with the meaning as well; and for the pleasure of the ear the meaning is hardly necessary, except in so far as certain key-words indicate the emotional tone of the passage. Now Shakespeare, or Dante, will bear innumerable readings, but at each reading all the ele-ments of appreciation can be present. There is no interruption between the surface that these poets present to you and the core. While, therefore, I cannot pretend to have penetrated to any 'secret' of these poets, I feel that such appreciation of their work as I am capable of points in the right direction; whereas I cannot feel that my appreciation of Milton leads anywhere outside of the mazes of sound. That, I feel, would be the matter for a separate study, like that of Blake's prophetic books; it might be well worth the trouble, but would have little to do with my interest in the poetry. So far as I perceive anything, it is a glimpse of a theology that I find in large part repellent, expressed through a mythology which would have better been left in the Book of *Genesis,* upon which Milton has not improved. There seems to me to be a divi-sion, in Milton, between the philosopher or theologian and the poet; and, for the latter, I suspect also that this concentration

upon the auditory imagination leads to at least an occasional
levity. I can enjoy the roll of

> ... Cambula, seat of Cathaian Can
> And Samarchand by Oxus, Temir's throne,
> To Paquin of Sinaean kings, and thence
> To Agra and Lahor of great Mogul
> Down to the golden Chersonese, or where
> The Persian in Ecbatan sate, or since
> In Hispahan, or where the Russian Ksar
> On Mosco, of the Sultan in Bizance,
> Turchestan-born . . . ,[1]

and the rest of it, but I feel that this is not serious poetry, not
poetry fully occupied about its business, but rather a solemn game.
More often, admittedly, Milton uses proper names in moderation,
to obtain the same effect of magnificence with them as does
Marlowe – nowhere perhaps better than in the passage from
Lycidas :

> Whether beyond the stormy Hebrides,
> Where thou perhaps under the whelming tide
> Visit'st the bottom of the monstrous world ;
> Or whether thou to our moist vows deny'd
> Sleep'st by the fable of Bellerus old,
> Where the great vision of the guarded Mount
> Looks toward Namancos and Bayona's hold ...

than which for the single effect of grandeur of sound, there is
nothing finer in poetry.

SOURCE : *On Poetry and Poets* (1957). First published 1936.

II

'Milton's style was not modified by his subject; what is shown
with greater extent in *Paradise Lost* may be found in *Comus*. One
source of his peculiarity was his familiarity with the Tuscan poets;
the disposition of his words is, I think, frequently Italian; perhaps
sometimes combined with other tongues. Of him, at last, may be

said what Jonson said of Spenser, that he *wrote no language*, but had formed what Butler called a *Babylonish dialect*, in itself harsh and barbarous, but made by exalted genius and extensive learning the vehicle of so much instruction and so much pleasure, that, like other lovers, we find grace in its deformity.' [Johnson]

This criticism seems to me substantially true : indeed unless we accept it, I do not think we are in the way to appreciate the peculiar greatness of Milton. His style is not a *classic* style, in that it is not the elevation of a *common* style, by the final touch of genius, to greatness. It is, from the foundation, and in every particular, a personal style, not based upon common speech, or common prose, or direct communication of meaning. Of some great poetry one has difficulty in pronouncing just what it is, what infinitesimal touch, that has made all the difference from a plain statement which anyone could make; the slight transformation which, while it leaves a plain statement a plain statement, has always the maximal, never the minimal, alteration of ordinary language. Every distortion of construction, the foreign idiom, the use of a word in a foreign way or with the meaning of the foreign word from which it is derived rather than the accepted meaning in English, every idiosyncrasy is a particular act of violence which Milton has been the first to commit. There is no cliché, no poetic diction in the derogatory sense, but a perpetual sequence of original acts of lawlessness. Of all modern writers of verse, the nearest analogy seems to me to be Mallarmé, a much smaller poet, though still a great one. The personalities, the poetic theories of the two men could not have been more different; but in respect of the violence which they could do to language, and justify, there is a remote similarity. Milton's poetry is poetry as the farthest possible remove from prose; his prose seems to me too near to half-formed poetry to be a good prose.

To say that the work of a poet is at the farthest possible remove from prose would once have struck me as condemnatory : it now seems to me simply, when we have to do with a Milton, the precision of its peculiar greatness. As a poet, Milton seems to me probably the greatest of all eccentrics. His work illustrates no general principles of good writing; the only principles of writing that it illustrates are such as are valid only for Milton himself to observe. There are two kinds of poet who can ordinarily be of use to other poets. There are those who suggest, to one or another of their successors, something which they have not done themselves, or who provoke a different way of doing the same thing : these are likely to be not the greatest, but smaller, imperfect poets with whom later poets discover an affinity. And there are the great poets from whom we can learn negative rules : no poet can teach another to write well, but some great poets can teach others some of the things to avoid. They teach us what to avoid, by showing us what great poetry can do without – how *bare* it can be. Of these are Dante and Racine. But if we are ever to make use of Milton we must do so in quite a different way. Even a small poet can learn something from the study of Dante, or from the study of Chaucer : we must perhaps wait for a great poet before we find one who can profit from the study of Milton.

I repeat that the remoteness of Milton's verse from ordinary speech, his invention of his own poetic language, seems to me one of the marks of his greatness. Other marks are his sense of structure, both in the general design of *Paradise Lost* and *Samson*, and in his syntax; and finally, and not least, his inerrancy, conscious or unconscious, in writing so as to make the best display of his talents, and the best concealment of his weaknesses.

The appropriateness of the subject of *Samson* is too obvious to expatiate upon : it was probably the one dramatic story out of which Milton could have made a masterpiece. But the complete suitability of *Paradise Lost* has not, I think, been so often remarked. It was surely an intuitive perception of what he could not do, that arrested Milton's project of an epic on King Arthur. For one thing, he had little interest in, or understanding of, individual human beings. In *Paradise Lost* he was not called upon for any of that understanding which comes from an affectionate observation of men and women. But such an interest in human beings was not required – indeed its *absence* was a necessary condition – for the creation of his figures of Adam and Eve. These are not a man and woman such as any we know : if they were, they would not be Adam and Eve. They are the original *Man* and *Woman*, not types, but prototypes. They have the general characteristics of men and women, such that we can recognize, in the temptation and the fall, the first motions of the faults and virtues, the abjection and the nobility, of all their descendants. They have ordinary humanity to the right degree, and yet are not, and should not be, ordinary mortals. Were they more particularized they would be false, and if Milton had been more interested in humanity, he could not have created them. Other critics have remarked upon the exactness, without defect of exaggeration, with which Moloch, Belial, and Mammon, in the second book, speak according to the particular sin which each represents. It would not be suitable that the infernal powers should have, in the human sense, characters, for a character is always mixed; but in the hands of an inferior manipulator, they might easily have been reduced to *humours*.

The appropriateness of the material of *Paradise Lost* to the genius and the limitations of Milton, is still more evident when we consider the visual imagery. I have already remarked, in a paper written some years ago, on Milton's weakness of visual observation, a weakness which I think was always present – the effect of his blindness may have been rather to strengthen the compensatory qualities than to increase a fault which was already present. Mr Wilson Knight, who has devoted close study to recurrent imagery in poetry, has called attention to Milton's propensity towards images of engineering and mechanics; to me it seems that Milton is at his best in imagery suggestive of vast size, limitless space, abysmal depth, and light and darkness. No theme and no setting, other than that which he chose in *Paradise Lost*, could have given him such scope for the kind of imagery in which he excelled, or made less demand upon those powers of visual imagination which were in him defective.

Most of the absurdities and inconsistencies to which Johnson calls attention, and which, so far as they can justly be isolated in this way, he properly condemns, will I think appear in a more correct proportion if we consider them in relation to this general judgment. I do not think that we should attempt to *see* very clearly any scene that Milton depicts : it should be accepted as a shifting phantasmagory. To complain, because we first find the arch-fiend 'Chained on the burning lake', and in a minute or two see him making his way to the shore, is to expect a kind of consistency which the world to which Milton has introduced us does not require.

This limitation of visual power, like Milton's limited interest in human beings, turns out to be not merely a negligible defect, but a positive virtue, when we visit Adam and Eve in Eden. Just as a higher degree of characterization of Adam and Eve would have been unsuitable, so a more vivid picture of the earthly Paradise would have been less paradisiacal. For a greater definiteness, a more detailed account of flora and fauna, could only have assimilated Eden to the landscapes of earth with which we are familiar. As it is, the impression of Eden which we retain, is the most suitable, and is that which Milton was most qualified to give : the impression of *light* – a daylight and a starlight, a light of dawn and of dusk, the light which, remembered by a man in his blindness, has a supernatural glory unexperienced by men of normal vision.

We must, then, in reading *Paradise Lost*, not expect to see clearly; our sense of sight must be blurred, so that our *hearing* may become more acute. *Paradise Lost*, like *Finnegans Wake* (for I can think of no work which provides a more interesting parallel : two books by great blind musicians, each writing a language of his own based upon English) makes this peculiar demand for a readjustment of the reader's mode of apprehension. The emphasis is on the sound, not the vision, upon the word, not the idea; and in the end it is the unique versification that is the most certain sign of Milton's intellectual mastership.

On the subject of Milton's versification, so far as I am aware, little enough has been written. We have Johnson's essay in the *Rambler*, which deserves more study than it has received, and we have a short treatise by Robert Bridges on *Milton's Prosody*. I speak of Bridges with respect, for no poet of our time has given such close attention to prosody as he. Bridges catalogues the systematic irregularities which give perpetual variety to Milton's verse, and I can find no fault with his analysis. But however interesting these analyses are, I do not think that it is by such means that we gain an appreciation of the peculiar rhythm of a poet. It seems to me also that Milton's verse is especially refractory to yielding up its secrets to examination of the single line. For his verse is not formed in this way. It is the period, the sentence and still more the paragraph, that is the unit of Milton's verse; and emphasis on the line structure is the minimum necessary to provide a counter-pattern to the period structure. It is only in the period that the wave-length of Milton's verse is to be found: it is his ability to give a perfect and unique pattern to every paragraph, such that the full beauty of the line is found in its context, and his ability to work in larger musical units than any other poet – that is to me the most conclusive evidence of Milton's supreme mastery. The peculiar feeling, almost a physical sensation of a breathless leap, communicated by Milton's long periods, and by his alone, is impossible to procure from rhymed verse. Indeed, this mastery is more conclusive evidence of his intellectual power, than is his grasp of any *ideas* that he borrowed or invented. To be able to control so many words at once is the token of a mind of most exceptional energy.

It is interesting at this point to recall the general observations upon blank verse, which a consideration of *Paradise Lost* prompted Johnson to make towards the end of his essay.

'The music of the English heroic lines strikes the ear so faintly, that it is easily lost, unless all the syllables of every line co-operate together; this co-operation can only be obtained by the preservation of every verse unmingled with another as a distinct system of sounds; and this distinctness is obtained and preserved by the artifice of rhyme. The variety of pauses, so much boasted by the lovers of blank verse, changes the measures of an English poet to the periods of a declaimer; and there are only a few skilful and happy readers of Milton, who enable their audience to perceive where the lines end or begin. *Blank verse*, said an ingenious critic, *seems to be verse only to the eye.*'

Some of my audience may recall that this last remark, in almost the same words, was often made, a literary generation ago, about the 'free verse' of the period: and even without this encouragement from Johnson it would have occurred to my mind to declare Milton to be the greatest master of free verse in our language. What is interesting about Johnson's paragraph, however, is that it represents the judgment of a man who had by no means a deaf ear, but simply a *specialized* ear, for verbal music. Within the limits of the poetry of his own period, Johnson is a very good judge of the relative merits of several poets as writers of blank verse. But on the whole, the blank verse of his age might more properly be called unrhymed verse; and nowhere is this difference more evident than in the verse of his own tragedy *Irene*: the phrasing is admirable, the style elevated and correct, but each line cries out for a companion to rhyme with it. Indeed, it is only with labour, or by occasional inspiration, or by submission to the influence of the older dramatists, that the blank verse of the nineteenth century succeeds in making the absence of rhyme inevitable and right, with the rightness of Milton. Even Johnson admitted that he could not wish that Milton had been a rhymer. Nor did the nineteenth century succeed in giving to blank verse the flexibility which it needs if the tone of common speech, talking of the topics of common intercourse, is to be employed; so that when our more modern practitioners of blank verse do not touch the sublime, they frequently sink to the ridiculous. Milton perfected non-dramatic blank verse and at the same time imposed limitations, very hard to break, upon the use to which it may be put if its greatest musical possibilities are to be exploited.

SOURCE : *On Poetry and Poets* (1957). First published 1947.

NOTE

1. [The quotations are left in the version used by Eliot. Eds.].

C. S. Lewis

THE STYLE OF SECONDARY EPIC (1942)

> Forms and figures of speech originally the offspring of passion, but now the adopted children of power.
>
> COLERIDGE

I

The style of Virgil and Milton arises as the solution of a very definite problem. The Secondary epic aims at an even higher solemnity than the Primary; but it has lost all those external aids to solemnity which the Primary enjoyed. There is no robed and garlanded *aoidos*, no altar, not even a feast in a hall – only a private person reading a book in an armchair. Yet somehow or other, that private person must be made to feel that he is assisting at an august ritual, for if he does not, he will not be receptive of the true epic exhilaration. The sheer writing of the poem, therefore, must now do, of itself, what the whole occasion helped to do for Homer. The Virgilian and Miltonic style is there to compensate for – to counteract – the privacy and informality of silent reading in a man's own study. Every judgment on it which does not realize this will be inept. To blame it for being ritualistic or incantatory, for lacking intimacy or the speaking voice, is to blame it for being just what it intends to be and ought to be. It is like damning an opera or an oratorio because the personages sing instead of speaking.

In a general and obvious sense this effect is achieved by what is called the 'grandeur' or 'elevation' of the style. As far as Milton is concerned (for I am not scholar enough to analyse Virgil) this grandeur is produced mainly by three things. (1) The use of slightly unfamiliar words and constructions, including archaisms. (2) The use of proper names, not solely nor chiefly for their sound, but because they are the names of splendid, remote, terrible, voluptuous, or celebrated things. They are there to encourage a sweep of the reader's eye over the richness and variety of the world – to supply that *largior aether* which we breathe as long as the poem lasts. (3) Continued allusion to all the sources of heightened interest in our sense experience (light, darkness, storm, flowers, jewels, sexual love, and the like), but all over-topped and 'managed' with an air of magnanimous austerity. Hence comes the feeling of sensual excitement *without* surrender or relaxation, the extremely tonic, yet also extremely rich, quality of our experience while we read. But all this you might have in great poems which were not epic. What I chiefly want to point out is something else – the poet's unremitting *manipulation* of his readers – how he sweeps us along as though we were attending an actual recitation and nowhere allows us to settle down and luxuriate on any one line or paragraph. It is common to speak of Milton's style as organ music. It might be more helpful to regard the reader as the organ and Milton as the organist. It is on us he plays, if we will let him.

Consider the opening paragraph. The ostensible philosophical purpose of the poem (to justify the ways of God to Man) is here of quite secondary importance. The real function of these twenty-six lines is to give us the sensation *that some great thing is now about to begin.* If the poet succeeds in doing that sufficiently, we shall be clay in his hands for the rest of Book I and perhaps longer; for be it noted that in this kind of poetry most of the poet's battles are won in advance. And as far as I am concerned, he succeeds completely, and I think I see something of how he does it. Firstly, there is the quality of weight, produced by the fact that nearly all the lines end in long, heavy monosyllables. Secondly, there is the direct suggestion of deep spiritual preparation at two points – *O spirit who dost prefer* and *What in me is dark.* But notice how cunningly this direct suggestion of great beginnings is reinforced by allusion to the creation of the world itself (*Dove-like sat'st brooding*), and then by images of rising and lifting (*With no middle flight intends to soar . . . raise and support – Highth of this great argument*) and then again how reaction and rising come potently together when we are reminded that Heaven and Earth *rose out of Chaos,* and how in addition to this we have that brisk, morning promise of good things to come, borrowed from Ariosto (*things unattempted yet*), and how *till one greater Man* makes us feel we are about to read an epic that spans over the whole of history with its arch. All images that can suggest a great thing beginning have been brought together and our very muscles respond as we read. But look again and you will see that the ostensible and logical connection between these images is not exactly the same as the emotional connection which I have been tracing. The point is important. In one respect, Milton's technique is very like that of some moderns. He throws ideas together because of those emotional relations which they have in the very recesses of our consciousness. But unlike the moderns he always provides a façade of logical connections as well. The virtue of this is that it lulls our logical faculty to sleep and enables us to accept what we are given without question.

This distinction between the logical connections which the poet puts on the surface and the emotional connections whereby he really manipulates our imagination is the key to many of his similes. The Miltonic simile does not always serve to illustrate what it pretends to be illustrating. The likeness between the two things compared is often trivial, and is, indeed, required only to save the face of the logical censor. At the end of Book 1 the fiends are compared to elves. Smallness is the only point of resemblance. The first use of the simile is to provide contrast and relief, to refresh us by a transition from Hell to a moonlit English lane. Its second use becomes apparent when we suddenly return to where

> far within
> And in their own dimensions like themselves
> The great seraphic lords and cherubim
> In close recess and secret conclave sat
> A thousand demi-gods on golden seats ... (1 792–6)

It is by contrast with the fairies that these councillors have grown so huge, and by contrast with the fanciful simile that the hush

before their debate becomes so intense, and it is by that intensity
that we are so well prepared for the opening of Book II. It
would be possible to go further and to say that this simile is simply
the point at which the whole purpose of transforming the fiends to
dwarfish stature is achieved, and that this transformation itself
has a retrospective effect on the hugeness of Pandemonium. For
the logician it may appear as something 'dragged in by the heels',
but in poetry it turns out to be so bound up with the whole close
of the first Book and the opening of the second that if it were
omitted the wound would spread over about a hundred lines.
Nearly every sentence in Milton has that power which physicists
sometimes think we shall have to attribute to matter – the power
of action at a distance.

Examples of this subterranean virtue (so to call it) in the
Miltonic simile will easily occur to every one's memory. Paradise
is compared to the field of Enna – one beautiful landscape to
another (IV 268). But, of course, the deeper value of the simile
lies in the resemblance which is not explicitly noted as a resemblance at all, the fact that in both these places the young and the
beautiful while gathering flowers was ravished by a dark power
risen up from the underworld. A moment later Eden is compared
to the *Nyseian isle* and to *Mount Amara*. Unlearned readers
may reassure themselves. In order to get the good out of this
simile it is not at all necessary to look up these places in the notes,
nor has pedantry any share in the poet's motives for selecting
them. All that we need to know the poet tells us. The one was a
river island and the other a high mountain, and both were
hiding places. If only we will read on, asking no questions, the
sense of Eden's secrecy, of things infinitely precious, guarded,
locked up, and put away, will come out of that simile and enrich
what Milton is all the time trying to evoke in each reader – the
consciousness of Paradise. Sometimes, I admit, the poet goes too
far and the feint of logical connection is too outrageous to be
accepted. In IV 160–71 Milton wants to make us feel the full
obscenity of Satan's presence in Eden by bringing a sudden stink
of fish across the sweet smell of the flowers, and alluding to one of
the most unpleasant Hebrew stories. But the pretence of logical
connection (that Satan liked the flowers of Paradise *better* than

Asmodeus liked the smell of burning fish) is too strained. We feel its absurdity.

This power of manipulation is not, of course, confined to the similes. Towards the end of Book III Milton takes Satan to visit the sun. To keep on harping on heat and brightness would be no use; it would end only in that bog of superlatives which is the destination of many bad poets. But Milton makes the next hundred lines as Solar as they could possibly be. We have first (583) the picture of the sun *gently warming* the universe, and a hint of the enormous distances to which this *virtue* penetrates. Then at line 588, by means of what is not much more than a pun on the word *spot* we have Galileo's recent discovery of the sun-spots. After that we plunge into alchemy because the almost limitless powers attributed to gold in that science and the connection of gold with the solar influence make a kind of mirror in which we can view the regal, the vivifying, the *arch-chemic* properties of the sun. Then, still working indirectly, Milton makes us realize the marvel of a shadowless world (614–20). After that we meet Uriel (*Fire of God*), and because the sun (as every child knew from Spenser and Ovid, if not from Pliny and Bernardus) is the *world's eye*, we are told that Uriel is one of those spirits who are God's eyes (650) and is even, in a special sense, God's singular *eye* in this material world (660) and 'the sharpest sighted spirit of all in heaven' (691). This is not, of course, the sun of modern science; but almost everything which the sun had meant to man up till Milton's day has been gathered together and the whole passage in his own phrase, 'runs potable gold'.

A great deal of what is mistaken for pedantry in Milton (we hear too often of his 'immense learning') is in reality evocation. If Heaven and Earth are ransacked for simile and allusion, this is not done for display, but in order to guide our imaginations with unobtrusive pressure into the channels where the poet wishes them to flow; and as we have already seen, the learning which a reader requires in responding to a given allusion does not equal the learning Milton needed to find it. When we have understood this it will perhaps be possible to approach that feature of Milton's style which has been most severely criticized – the Latinism of his contructions.

Continuity is an essential of the epic style. If the mere printed page is to affect us like the voice of a bard chanting in a hall, then the chant must *go on* – smoothly, irresistibly, 'upborne with indefatigable wings'. We must not be allowed to settle down at the end of each sentence. Even the fuller pause at the end of a paragraph must be felt as we feel the pause in a piece of music, where the silence is part of the music, and not as we feel the pause between one item of a concert and the next. Even between one Book and the next we must not wholly wake from the enchantment nor quite put off our festal clothes. A boat will not answer to the rudder unless it is in motion; the poet can work upon us only as long as we are kept on the move.

Roughly speaking, Milton avoids discontinuity by an avoidance of what grammarians call the simple sentence. Now, if the sort of things he was saying were at all like the things that Donne or Shakespeare say, this would be intolerably tiring. He therefore compensates for the complexity of his syntax by the simplicity of the broad imaginative effects beneath it and the perfect rightness of their sequence. For us readers, this means in fact that our receptivity can be mainly laid open to the underlying simplicity, while we have only to *play* at the complex syntax. It is not in the least necessary to go to the very bottom of these verse sentences as you go to the bottom of Hooker's sentences in prose. The general feeling (which will usually be found to be correct if you insist on analysing it) that something highly concatenated is before you, that the flow of speech does not fall apart into separate lumps, that you are following a great unflagging voice – this is enough to keep the 'weigh' on you by means of which the poet steers. Let us take an example :

> If thou beest he ; but O how fallen ! how changed
> From him, who in the happy realms of light
> Clothed with transcendent brightness didst outshine
> Myriads though bright : if he whom mutual league,
> United thoughts and counsels, equal hope
> And hazard in the glorious enterprise,
> Joined with me once, now misery hath joined
> In equal ruin : into what pit thou seest
> From what highth fallen ... (I 84–92)

This is a pretty complicated sentence. On the other hand, if you read it (and let the ghost of a chanting, not a talking, voice be in your ear) without bothering about the syntax, you receive in their most natural order all the required impressions – the lost glories of heaven, the first plotting and planning, the hopes and hazards of the actual war, and then the misery, the ruin, and the pit. But the complex syntax has not been useless. It has preserved the *cantabile,* it has enabled you to feel, even within these few lines, the enormous onward pressure of the great stream on which you are embarked. And almost any sentence in the poem will illustrate the same point.

The extremely Latin connections between the sentences serve the same purposes, and involve, like the similes, a fair amount of illusion. A good example is *nor sometimes forget,* in III 32. In this passage Milton is directly calling up what he indirectly suggests throughout, the figure of the great blind bard. It will, of course, be greatly enriched if the mythical blind bards of antiquity are brought to bear on us. A poet like Spenser would simply begin a new stanza with *Likewise dan Homer* or something of the sort. But that will not quite serve Milton's purpose : it is a little too like rambling, it might suggest the garrulity of an old gentleman in his chair. *Nor sometimes forget* gets him across from *Sion and the flowery brooks* to *Blind Thamyris* with an appearance of continuity, like the stylized movement by which a dancer passes from one position to another. *Yet not the more* in line 26 is another example. So are *sad task, yet argument* (IX 13) and *Since first this subject* (IX 25). These expressions do not represent real connections of thought, any more than the prolonged syllables in Handel represent real pronunciation.

It must also be noticed that while Milton's Latin constructions in one way tighten up our language, in another way they make it more fluid. A fixed order of words is the price – an all but ruinous price – which English pays for being uninflected. The Miltonic constructions enable the poet to depart, in some degree, from this fixed order and thus to drop the ideas into his sentence in any order he chooses. Thus, for example,

> soft oppression seized
> My drowsed sense, untroubled, though I thought
> I then was passing to my former state
> Insensible, and forthwith to dissolve. . . . (VIII 288–91)

The syntax is so artificial that it is ambiguous. I do not know whether *untroubled* qualifies *me* understood, or *sense*, and similar doubts arise about *insensible* and the construction of *to dissolve*. But then I don't need to know. The sequence *drowsed – untroubled – my former state – insensible – dissolve* is exactly right; the very crumbling of consciousness is before us and the fringe of syntactical mystery helps rather than hinders the effect. Thus, in another passage, I read

> heaven opened wide
> Her ever during gates, harmonious sound
> On golden hinges moving (VII 205–7)

Moving might be a transitive participle agreeing with *gates* and governing *sound*; or again the whole phrase form *harmonious* to *moving* might be an ablative absolute. The effect of the passage, however, is the same whichever we choose. An extreme modern might have attempted to reach it with

> Gates open wide. Glide
> On golden hinges . . .
> Moving . . .
> Harmonious sound.

This melting down of the ordinary units of speech, this plunge back into something more like the indivisible, flowing quality of immediate experience, Milton also achieves. But by his appearance of an extremely carpentered structure he avoids the suggestion of fever, preserves the sense of dignity, and does not irritate the mind to ask questions.

Finally, it remains to judge this style not merely as an epic style, but as a style for that particular story which Milton has chosen. I must ask the reader to bear with me while I examine it at its actual work of narration. Milton's theme leads him to deal with certain very basic images in the human mind – with the archetypal patterns, as Miss Bodkin would call them, of Heaven, Hell, Paradise, God, Devil, the Winged Warrior, the Naked Bride, the Outer Void. Whether these images come to us from real spiritual perception or from pre-natal and infantile experience confusedly remembered, is not here in question; how the poet arouses them, perfects them, and then makes them re-act on one another in our minds is the critic's concern. I use the word 'arouses' advisedly. The naif reader thinks Milton is going to *describe* Paradise as Milton imagines it; in reality the poet knows (or behaves as if he knew) that this is useless. His own private image of the happy garden, like yours and mine, is full of irrelevant particularities – notably, of memories from the first garden he ever played in as a child. And the more thoroughly he describes those particularities the further we are getting away from the Paradisal idea as it exists in our minds, or even in his own. For it is something coming *through* the particularities, some light which transfigures them, that really counts, and if you concentrate on them you will find them turning dead and cold under your hands. The more elaborately, in *that* way, we build the temple, the more certainly we shall find, on completing it, that the god has flown. Yet Milton must *seem* to describe – you cannot just say nothing about Paradise in *Paradise Lost*. While seeming to describe his own imagination he must actually arouse ours, and arouse it not to make definite pictures, but to find again in our own depth the Paradisal light of which all explicit images are only the momentary reflection. We are his organ : when he appears to be describing Paradise he is in fact drawing out the Paradisal Stop in us. The place where he chiefly does so (IV 131–286) is worth examination in detail.

It begins (131) *so on he fares. On* is the operative word. He is going on and on. Paradise is a long way off. At present we are approaching only its *border*. Distance means gradualness of approach. It is *now nearer* (133). Then come the obstacles; a *steep wilderness* with *hairy sides* (135). Do not overlook *hairy*. The Freudian idea that the happy garden is an image of the human body would not have frightened Milton in the least, though, of course, the main point is that the ascent was *grotesque*

and wild (136) and *access denied* (137). But we want something more than obstacle. Remember that in this kind of poetry
the poet's battles are mainly won in advance. If he can gives us
the idea of increasing expectancy, the idea of the Paradisal light
coming but not yet come, then, when at last he has to make a
show of describing the garden itself, we shall be already conquered. He is doing his work *now* so that when the climax comes
we shall actually do the work for ourselves. Therefore, at line
137, he begins playing on the note of progression – upward progression, a vertical serialism. *Overhead is insuperable height* of
trees (138). But that is not enough. The trees are ladder-like or
serial trees (cedar, pine, and fir) with one traditionally eastern
and triumphal tree (the palm) thrown in (139). They stand up
like a stage set (140) where Milton is thinking of *silvis scaena
coruscis*. They go up in tiers like a theatre (140–2). Already,
while I read, I feel as if my neck ached with looking higher and
higher. Then quite unexpectedly, as in dream landscapes, we find
that what seemed the top is not the top. Above all these trees, *yet
higher* (142) springs up the green, living wall of Paradise. And
now a moment's rest from our looking upward; at a wave of the
wand we are seeing the whole thing reversed – we are Adam,
King of Earth, looking *down* from that green rampart into this
lower world (144–5) – and, of course, when we return it seems
loftier still. For even that wall was not the real top. Above the wall
– yes, at last, almost beyond belief, we see for once with mortal
eyes the trees of Paradise itself. In lines 147–9 we get the first bit
of direct description. *Of course*, the trees have golden fruit. We
always knew they would. Every myth has told us so; to ask for
'originality' at this point is stark insensibility. But we are not
allowed to go on looking at them. The simile of the rainbow
(150–2) is introduced, and at once our glimpse of Paradise
recedes to the rainbow's end. Then the theme of serialism is picked
up again – the air is growing purer every minute (153); and this
idea (*Quan la douss aura venta*) at once passes into a nineteen-
line exploitation of the most evocative of the senses, suddenly
countered by the stench of Satan (167). Then a pause, as if after
a crashing piece of orchestration, and we go back to the images
of gradual approach, Satan still journeying *on* (172). Now the

obstacles grow more formidable and it presently turns out (as the Trojans had found on sighting Italy) that the real entrance is *on the other side* (179). What follows is concerned with the main theme of the story and may be omitted here. We return to Paradise at 205. We are in at last, and now the poet has to do something in the way of description: well for him that the Paradise-complex in us is now thoroughly awake and that almost any particular image he gives us will be caught up and assimilated. But he does not begin with a particular image, rather with an idea –*in narrow room nature's whole wealth.* The 'narrow room', the sense of a small guarded place, of sweetness rolled into a ball, is essential. God had *planted* it all (210). Not created it, but planted it – an anthropomorphic God out of Ezekiel 31, the God of our childhood and man's, making a toy garden as *we* made them when we were children. The earliest and lowest levels are being uncovered. And all this realm was studded once with rich and ancient cities; a *pleasant soil* (214), but the mountain of Paradise, like a jewel set in gold, *far more pleasant* (215) so that an emotion stolen from the splendour of the cities now flows into our feeling of Paradise. Then come the trees, the mythical and numinous trees, and *vegetable gold* from the garden of Hesperus (217–22). Then the rivers, which like Alph plunge into darkness and rise from it through *pores* at the bidding of *kindly thirst* (228), and Paradise again reminds us of a human body; and in contrast with this organic dark we have *crisped brooks* above (237) and the hard, bright suggestions of *pearl* and *gold* (238). Finally, from line 246 to 265, we get actual description. It is all, most rightly, generalized, and it is short. A reader who dislikes this kind of poetry would possibly express his objection to Milton's Paradise by saying it contained 'all the right things' – odorous gums, golden fruit, thornless roses, murmuring falls – and would prefer something he had not expected. But the unexpected has here no place. These references to the obvious and the immemorial are there not to give us new ideas about the lost garden but to make us know that the garden is found, that we have come home at last and reached the centre of the maze – our centre, humanity's centre, not some private centre of the poet's. And they last only long enough to do so. The representa-

tion begins swelling and trembling at 264 with the nervous re-
iteration of *airs* in order that it may *burst* in the following lines –
may flow over into a riot of mythology where we are, so to speak,
drenched. That is the real climax; and then, having been
emparadised, we are ready at line 288 to meet at last the white,
erect, severe, voluptuous forms of our first parents.

II

One hand a Mathematique Christall swayes,
Which, gathering in one line a thousand rayes
From her[1] bright eyes, *Confusion* burnes to death,
And all estates of men distinguisheth.
By it *Morallitie* and *Comelinesse*
Themselves in all their sightly figures dresse.
Her other hand a lawrell rod applies,
To beate back *Barbarisme* and *Avarice*,
That follow'd, eating earth and excrement
And human limbs; and would make proud ascent
To seates of gods, were *Ceremonie* slaine.

> CHAPMAN : *Hero and Leander*, III

I believe I am right in saying that the reaction of many readers
to the foregoing reflections might be expressed in the following words. 'You have described exactly what we do *not* call
poetry. This manipulation of the audience which you attribute to
Milton is just what distinguishes the vile art of the rhetorician
and the propagandist from the disinterested activity of the poet.
This evocation of stock responses to conventional situations, which
you choose to call Archetypal Patterns, is the very mark of the
cheap writer. This calculated pomp and grandiosity is the sheer
antithesis of true poetic sincerity – a miserable attempt to appear
high by mounting on stilts. In brief, we always suspected that
Milton was bogus, and you have confirmed our suspicion.
Habemus confitentem reum.' I hardly expect to convert many of
those who take such a view; but it would be a mistake not to
make clear that the difference between us is essential. If these are
my errors they are not errors into which I have fallen inadver-

tently, but the very lie in the soul. If these are my truths, then they are basic truths the loss of which means imaginative death.

First, as to Manipulation. I do not think (and no great civilization has ever thought) that the art of the rhetorician is necessarily vile. It is in itself noble, though of course, like most arts, it can be wickedly used. I do not think that Rhetoric and Poetry are distinguished by manipulation of an audience in the one hand and, in the other, a pure self expression, regarded as its own end, and indifferent to any audience. Both these arts, in my opinion, definitely aim at doing something to an audience. And both do it by using language to control what already exists in our minds. The differentia of Rhetoric is that it wishes to produce in our minds some practical resolve (to condemn Warren Hastings or to declare war on Philip) and it does this by calling the passions to the aid of reason. It is honestly practised when the orator honestly believes that the thing which he calls the passions to support *is* reason, and usefully practised when this belief of his is in fact correct. It is mischievously practised when that which he summons the passions to aid is, in fact, unreason, and dishonestly practised when he himself knows that it is unreason. The proper use is lawful and necessary because, as Aristotle points out, intellect of itself 'moves nothing' : the transition from thinking to doing, in nearly all men at nearly all moments, needs to be assisted by appropriate states of feeling. Because the end of rhetoric is in the world of action, the objects it deals with appear foreshortened and much of their reality is omitted. Thus the ambitions of Philip are shown only in so far as they are wicked and dangerous, because indignation and moderate fear are emotional channels through which men pass from thinking to doing. Now good poetry, if it dealt with the ambitions of Philip, would give you something much more like their total reality – what it felt like to be Philip and Philip's place in the whole system of things. Its Philip would, in fact, be more *concrete* than the Philip of the orator. That is because poetry aims at producing something more like vision than it is like action. But vision, in this sense, includes passions. Certain things, if not seen as lovely or detestable, are not being correctly seen at all. When we try to rouse someone's hate of toothache in order to persuade him to

ring up the dentist, this is rhetoric; but even if there were no
practical issue involved, even if we only wanted to convey the
reality of toothache for some speculative purpose or for its own
sake, we should still have failed if the idea produced in our
friend's mind did not include the hatefulness of toothache.
Toothache, with that left out, is an abstraction. Hence the
awakening and moulding of the reader's or hearer's emotions is a
necessary element in that vision of concrete reality which poetry
hopes to produce. Very roughly, we might almost say that in
Rhetoric imagination is present for the sake of passion (and,
therefore, in the long run, for the sake of action), while in poetry
passion is present for the sake of imagination, and therefore, in
the long run, for the sake of wisdom or spiritual health – the rightness and richness of a man's total response to the world. Such
rightness, of course, has a tendency to contribute indirectly to
right action, besides being in itself exhilarating and tranquilliz-
ing; that is why the old critics were right enough when they
said that Poetry taught by delighting, or delighted by teaching.
The rival theories of Dr Richards and Professor D. G. James are
therefore perhaps not so different that we cannot recognize a
point of contact. Poetry, for Dr Richards, produces a wholesome
equilibrium of our psychological attitudes. For Professor James,
it presents an object of 'secondary imagination', gives us a view
of the world. But a concrete (as opposed to a purely conceptual)
view of reality would in fact involve right attitudes; and the
totality of right attitudes, if man is a creature at all adapted to the
world he inhabits, would presumably be in wholesome equilibrium. But however this may be, Poetry certainly aims at making
the reader's mind what it was not before. The idea of a poetry
which exists only for the poet – a poetry which the public rather
overhears than hears – is a foolish novelty in criticism. There is
nothing specially admirable in talking to oneself. Indeed, it is
arguable that Himself is the very audience before whom a man
postures most and on whom he practises the most elaborate
deceptions.

Next comes the question of Stock Responses. By a Stock
Response Dr I. A. Richards means a deliberately organized attitude which is substituted for 'the direct free play of experience'.

In my opinion such deliberate organization is one of the first necessities of human life, and one of the main functions of art is to assist it. All that we describe as constancy in love or friendship, as loyalty in political life, or, in general, as perseverance – all solid virtue and stable pleasure – depends on organizing chosen attitudes and maintaining them against the eternal flux (or 'direct free play') of mere immediate experience. This Dr Richards would not perhaps deny. But his school puts the emphasis the other way. They talk as if improvement of our responses were always required in the direction of finer discrimination and greater particularity; never as if men needed responses more normal and more traditional than they now have. To me, on the other hand, it seems that most people's responses are not 'stock' enough, and that the play of experience is too free and too direct in most of us for safety or happiness or human dignity. A number of causes may be assigned for the opposite belief. (1) The decay of Logic, resulting in an untroubled assumption that the particular is real and the universal is not. (2) A Romantic Primitivism (not shared by Dr Richards himself) which prefers the merely natural to the elaborated, the un-willed to the willed. Hence a loss of the old conviction (once shared by Hindoo, Platonist, Stoic, Christian, and 'humanist' alike) that simple 'experience', so far from being something venerable, is in itself mere raw material, to be mastered, shaped, and worked up by the will. (3) A confusion (arising from the fact that both are voluntary) between the organization of a response and the pretence of a response. Von Hügel says somewhere, 'I kiss my son not only because I love him, but in order that I may love him.' That is organization, and good. But you may also kiss children in order to make it *appear* that you love them. That is pretence, and bad. The distinction must not be overlooked. Sensitive critics are so tired of seeing good Stock responses aped by bad writers that when at last they meet the reality they mistake it for one more instance of posturing. They are rather like a man I knew who had seen so many bad pictures of moonlight on water that he criticized a real weir under a real moon as 'conventional'. (4) A belief (not unconnected with the doctrine of the Unchanging Human Heart . . .) that a certain elementary rectitude of human response is 'given' by nature herself, and may be taken for granted, so that poets, secure of this basis, are free to devote themselves to the more advanced work of teaching us ever finer and finer discrimination. I believe this to be a dangerous delusion. Children like dabbling in dirt; they have to be *taught* the stock response to it. Normal sexuality, far from being a *datum*, is achieved by a long and delicate process of suggestion and adjustment which proves too difficult for some individuals and, at times, for whole societies. The Stock response to Pride, which Milton reckoned on when he delineated his Satan, has been decaying ever since the Romantic Movement began – that is one of the reasons why I am composing these lectures. The Stock response to treachery has become uncertain; only the other day I heard a respectable working man defend Lord Haw-Haw by remarking coolly (and with no hint of anger or of irony), 'You've got to remember that's how he earns his pay.' The Stock response to death has become uncertain. I have heard a man say that the only 'amusing' thing that happened while he was in hospital was the death of a patient in the same ward. The Stock response to pain has become uncertain. I have heard Mr Eliot's comparison of evening to a patient on an operating table praised, nay gloated over, not as a striking picture of sensibility in decay, but because it was so 'pleasantly unpleasant'. Even the Stock response to pleasure cannot be depended on; I have heard a man (and a young man, too) condemn Donne's more erotic poetry because 'sex', as he called it, always 'made him think of lysol and rubber goods'. That elementary rectitude of human response, at which we are so ready to fling the unkind epithets of 'stock', 'crude', 'bourgeois', and 'conventional', so far from being 'given' is a delicate balance of trained habits, laboriously acquired and easily lost, on the maintenance of which depend both our virtues and our pleasures and even, perhaps, the survival of our species. For though the human heart is not unchanging (nay, changes almost out of recognition in the twinkling of an eye) the laws of causation are. When poisons become fashionable they do not cease to kill.

The examples I have cited warn us that those Stock responses which we need in order to be even human are already in danger. In the light of that alarming discovery there is no need to apologize for Milton or for any other pre-Romantic poet. The older poetry, by continually insisting on certain Stock themes – as that love is sweet, death bitter, virtue lovely, and children or gardens delightful – was performing a service not only of moral and civil, but even of biological, importance. Once again, the old critics were quite right when they said that poetry 'instructed by delighting', for poetry was formerly one of the chief means whereby each new generation learned, not to copy, but by copying to make,[2] the good Stock responses. Since poetry has abandoned that office the world has not bettered. While the moderns have been pressing forward to conquer new territories of consciousness, the old territory, in which alone man can live, has been left unguarded, and we are in danger of finding the enemy in our rear. We need most urgently to recover the lost poetic art of enriching a response without making it eccentric, and of being normal without being vulgar. Meanwhile – until that recovery is made – such poetry as Milton's is more than ever necessary to us.

There is, furthermore, a special reason why mythical poetry ought not to attempt novelty in respect of its ingredients. What it does with the ingredients may be as novel as you please. But giants, dragons, paradises, gods, and the like are themselves the expression of certain basic elements in man's spiritual experience. In that sense they are more like words – the words of a language which speaks the else unspeakable – than they are like the people and places in a novel. To give them radically new characters is not so much original as ungrammatical. That strange blend of genius and vulgarity, the film of *Snow-White*, will illustrate the point. There was good unoriginality in the drawing of the queen. She was the very archetype of all beautiful, cruel queens: the thing one expected to see, save that it was truer to type than one had dared to hope for. There was bad originality in the bloated, drunken, low comedy faces of the dwarfs. Neither the wisdom, the avarice, nor the earthiness of true dwarfs were there, but an imbecility of arbitrary invention. But in the scene where Snow-White wakes in the woods both the right originality and the right unoriginality were used together. The good unoriginality lay in the use of small, delicate animals as comforters, in the true *märchen* style. The good originality lay in letting us at first mis-

take their eyes for the eyes of monsters. The whole art consists not
in evoking the unexpected, but in evoking with a perfection and
accuracy beyond expectation the very image that has haunted us
all our lives. The marvel about Milton's Paradise or Milton's Hell
is simply that they are there – that the thing has at last been done
– that our dream stands before us and does not melt. Not many
poets can thus draw out leviathan with a hook. Compared with
this the short-lived pleasure of any novelty the poet might have
inserted would be a mere kickshaw.

The charge of calculated grandiosity, of 'stilts', remains. The
difficulty here is that the modern critic tends to think Milton is
somehow trying to deceive. We feel the pressure of the poet on
every word – the *builded* quality of the verse – and since this is the
last effect most poets wish to produce to-day, we are in danger of
supposing that Milton also would have concealed it if he could,
that it is a tell-tale indication of his failure to achieve spontaneity.
But does Milton want to sound spontaneous? He tells us that his
verse was unpremeditated in fact and attributes this to the Muse.
Perhaps it was. Perhaps by that time his own epic style had become 'a language which thinks and poetizes of itself'. But that is
hardly the point. The real question is whether an *air* of spontaneity – an impression that this is the direct outcome of immediate personal emotion – would be in the least proper to this kind
of work. I believe it would not. We should miss the all-important
sense that *something out of the ordinary is being done*. Bad poets
in the tradition of Donne write artfully and try to make it sound
colloquial. If Milton were to practise deception, it would be the
other way round. A man performing a rite is not trying to make
you think that this is his natural way of walking, these the unpremeditated gestures of his own domestic life. If long usage has in
fact made the ritual unconscious, he must labour to make it look
deliberate, in order that we, the assistants, may feel the weight
of the solemnity pressing on his shoulders as well as on our own.
Anything casual or familiar in his manner is not 'sincerity' or
'spontaneity', but impertinence. Even if his robes were not heavy
in fact, they ought to *look* heavy. But there is no need to suppose
any deception. Habit and devout concentration of mind, or something else for which the Muse is as good a name as any other,

may well have brought it to pass that the verse of *Paradise Lost* flowed into his mind without labour; but what flowed was something stylized, remote from conversation, hierophantic. The style is not pretending to be 'natural' any more than a singer is pretending to talk.

Even the poet, when he appears in the first person within his own poem, is not to be taken as the private individual John Milton. If he were that, he would be an irrelevance. He also becomes an image – the image of the Blind Bard – and we are told about him nothing that does not help that archetypal pattern. It is his office, not his person, that is sung. It would be a gross error to regard the opening of *Samson* and the opening of Book III as giving us respectively what Milton really felt, and what he would be thought to feel, about his blindness. The real man, of course, being a man, felt many more things, and less interesting things, about it than are expressed in either. From that total experience the poet selects, for his epic and for his tragedy, what is proper to each. The impatience, the humiliation, the questionings of Providence go into *Samson* because the business of tragedy is 'by raising pity and fear, or terror, to purge the mind of those and such-like passions . . . with a kind of delight stirred up by reading or seeing those passions well imitated'. If he had not been blind himself, he would still (though with less knowledge to guide him) have put just those elements of a blind man's experience into the mouth of Samson : for the 'disposition of his fable' so as to 'stand best with verisimilitude and decorum' requires them. On the other hand, whatever is calm and great, whatever associations make blindness venerable – all this he selects for the opening of Book III. Sincerity and insincerity are words that have no application to either case. We want a great blind poet in the one, we want a suffering and questioning prisoner in the other. 'Decorum is the grand masterpiece.'

The grandeur which the poet assumes in his poetic capacity should not arouse hostile reactions. It is for our benefit. He makes his epic a rite so that we may share it; the more ritual it becomes, the more we are elevated to the rank of participants. Precisely because the poet appears not as a private person, but as a Hierophant or Choregus, we are summoned not to hear what one particular man thought and felt about the Fall, but to take part, under his leadership, in a great mimetic dance of all Christendom, ourselves soaring and ruining from Heaven, ourselves enacting Hell and Paradise, the Fall and the repentance.

Thus far of Milton's style on the assumption that it is in fact as remote and artificial as is thought. No part of my defence depends on questioning that assumption, for I think it ought to be remote and artificial. But it would not be honest to suppress my conviction that the degree to which it possesses these qualities has been exaggerated. Much that we think typically 'Poetic Diction' in *Paradise Lost* was nothing of the sort, and has since become Poetic Diction only because Milton used it. When he writes of an *optic glass* (I 288) we think this a poetical periphrasis because we are remembering Thomson or Akenside; but it seems to have been an ordinary expression in Milton's time. When we read *ruin and combustion* (I 46) we naturally exclaim *aut Miltonus aut diabolus!* Yet the identical words are said to occur in a document of the Long Parliament. *Alchemy* (II 517) sounds like the Miltonic vague : it is really almost a trade name. *Numerous* as applied to verse (V 150) sounds 'poetic', but was not. If we could read *Paradise Lost* as it really was we should see more play of muscles than we see now. But only a little more. I am defending Milton's style as a ritual style.

I think the older critics may have misled us by saying that 'admiration' or 'astonishment' is the proper response to such poetry. Certainly if 'admiration' is taken in its modern sense, the misunderstanding becomes disastrous. I should say rather that joy or exhilaration was what it produced – an overplus of robust and tranquil well-being in a total experience which contains both rapturous and painful elements. In the *Dry Salvages* Mr Eliot speaks of 'music heard so deeply that it is not heard at all'. Only as we emerge from the mode of consciousness induced by the symphony do we begin once more to attend explicitly to the sounds which induced it. In the same way, when we are caught up into the experience which a 'grand' style communicates, we are, in a sense, no longer conscious of the style. Incense is consumed by being used. The poem kindles admirations which leave us no leisure to admire the poem. When our participation in a rite becomes perfect we think no more of ritual, but are engrossed by that *about which* the rite is performed; but afterwards we recognize that ritual was the sole method by which this concentration could be achieved. Those who in reading *Paradise Lost* find themselves forced to attend throughout to the sound and the manner have simply not discovered what this sound and this manner were intended to do. A schoolboy who reads a page of Milton by chance, for the first time, and then looks up and says, 'By gum!' not in the least knowing how the thing has worked, but only that new strength and width and brightness and zest have transformed his world, is nearer to the truth than they.

SOURCE : *Preface to 'Paradise Lost'* (1942).

NOTES

1. Those of the goddess Ceremony.
2. 'We learn how to do things by doing the things we are learning how to do,' as Aristotle observes (*Ethics,* II i).

B. Rajan

THE PROBLEM OF SATAN (1947)

'Satan', wrote Sir Walter Raleigh, 'unavoidably reminds us of Prometheus, and although there are essential differences, we are not made to feel them essential. His very situation as the fearless antagonist of Omnipotence makes him either a fool or a hero, and Milton is far indeed from permitting us to think him a fool.'[1] Raleigh's conclusion reflects very fairly the trend of opinion in the preceding century, which, while not always insisting that Satan was a hero,[2] invariably endowed him with his share of heroic qualities. It is only recently that critics have become audible who prefer the less noble of the opposed alternatives. Charles Williams, the first of them, in brief but thought-provoking introduction to Milton's poetry, spoke ominously of Satan's 'solemn antics'.[3] C. S. Lewis then took the hint up and developed it more aggressively. Satan became for him 'a personified self-contradiction', a being ultimately farcical, a creature who could not be brought into contact with the real without laughter arising 'just as steam *must* when water meets fire'.[4] So challenging a formulation could naturally not pass unchallenged and Professor Stoll, backed by the resources of nineteenth-century criticism, demanded at some length that the devil be given his due.[5] Mr Rostrevor Hamilton, using Raleigh's antithesis for a title, insisted that the poet had his reasons of which the Puritan knew nothing, and that the Satan created by Milton's imagination was nobler and more admirable than the devil conceived by his intellect.[6] The controversy died away except for occasional salvoes in learned periodicals,[7] but the issues it raised are sufficiently important to be discussed again in somewhat different surroundings.

Now when a problem of this kind is presented to us the first thing we need to ask about is the adequacy of the vocabulary in which it is formulated. That 'hero or fool?' is a leading question is not in itself regrettable. What is regrettable is that it is the sort of leading question which is bound to result in a misleading answer. Given certain ethical systems Satan is ultimately heroic and given others he is ultimately farcical. But what we are concerned with is poetry rather than ethics and Satan considered as a poetic force is different from Satan as a cosmic principle. For when that principle becomes dramatically real, when it comes alive in the radius of human experience, you cannot bring to its poetic deployment the simple emotions of mirth or admiration. Your response to it must not be unconditional. You have to see it as an element in a concerted whole, a single fact in a poetic process. Therefore to understand its nature and function you need to relate it to the pattern it fulfils and the background of belief against which it is presented.

It is when we undertake this reconsideration that critical differences of shading begin to emerge. Our response to Satan is, I imagine, one of cautious interest. We think of him either as an abstract conception or else, more immediately, as someone in whom evil is mixed with good but who is doomed to destruction by the flaw of self-love. But with Milton's contemporaries the response was predominantly one of fear. If like Calvin they thought of Satan as 'an engine that is in courage most hardie, in strength most mightie, in policies most subtle, in diligence and celeritie unweariable, with all sorts of engins plenteously furnishd, in skill of warre most readie',[8] that was only so that they could stand guard more vigilantly against their relentless opponent. If like Defoe they saw him as 'a mighty, a terrible, an immortal Being; infinitely superior to man, as well in the dignity of his nature, as in the dreadful powers he retains still about him',[9] the vision served to remind them inescapably that it was only by God's grace that they could hope to overcome the enormous forces against which they were contending. When Milton's great figure is silhouetted against this background the effect must be as Addison points out 'to raise and terrify our imaginations'.[10] So the heroic qualities which Satan brings to his mission, the fortitude, the steadfast hate, the implacable resolution which is founded on despair are qualities not to be imitated or admired. They are defiled by the evil to which they are consecrated. If

Milton dwells upon them it is because he knows that you will put them in their context, that you will see Satan's virtues as perverted by their end and darkening therefore to their inevitable eclipse, corroded and eaten out by the nemesis beyond them. The moral condemnation is never explicitly, or even poetically, denied. Touched on repeatedly in parenthesis, it is also always there as an undertone to the imagery. Words like Memphis and Alcairo may be nothing more than brilliant names to us. To Milton's contemporaries they were darkened with contempt. When Satan was described to them as a 'great Sultan' the phrase would have reminded them of tyranny rather than splendour. When the fallen angels were likened to the cavalry of Egypt, a plague of locusts and a barbarian invasion, they would have given full weight to the mounting disapproval which lies behind the simile. As for the great Satanic defiances, they would have admired them for their strength and deplored them for their perversity. To quote Addison once more, Satan's sentiments 'are every way answerable to his character, and suitable to a created Being of the most exalted and most depraved nature. . . . Amidst the impieties which this enraged Spirit utters . . . the author has taken care to introduce none that is not big with absurdity and incapable of shocking a religious reader'.[11] The sympathy for Satan which the poetry imposes, the admiration it compels for his Promethean qualities, are meant to be controlled by this sort of moral reaction. And the same sense of proportion should cover his intellectual argument. When Satan appeals to 'just right and the fixed laws of Heav'n', when he grounds his mandate on the ultimate nature of things, and when, in betraying overtones, he couples God's 'tyranny' with 'the excess of joy', you are not supposed to take these statements at their face value. Other politicians have made claims somewhat similar, and Satan's assertions as the champion of liberty would amuse, rather than perplex, those who were brought up to think of him as the first liar.

But to set aside the problem at this point is to leave its most interesting elements unstated. It is right to insist that Milton's Satan is not presented in a moral vacuum, that there is a background of unremitting hostility against which his poetic presence must be built up. But though the system within which he exists is never questioned, though it is seldom ignored and frequently remembered, its immediate implications are progressively subdued. We know, and even Satan knows, that the God against whom he is contending is omnipotent. But against the settled strength of his heroism, against the desperate and deliberate valour of Hell, that fact dies down to an abstract and distant necessity. When the weight of the poetry is thus thrown in on Satan's side, the effect must be to equalize in our imaginations the relative magnitude of the contending forces. We see Satan so clearly that we can hardly see anything else, and though conscious, we are not always or inescapably conscious, of the strength and authority of the forces which control him. The conflict, then, is neither Promethean nor farcical. It is dramatically real in proportion as you assent to the illusion of equality which the poem communicates.

That illusion, however, is not intended to last. In our first glimpse of the solemnities of heaven, in the deliberations of the celestial council, in the love and mercy which are poured into the Son's sacrifice, the stature of the whole infernal enterprise is meant to be implicitly reduced. But Milton's verse is not equal to the occasion. His reliance on biblical phrasing undoubtedly meant far more to his contemporaries than it can ever mean to us, but even when every allowance has been made for this difference in impact, the drab legalities of Milton's celestial style are too curt and chill to be poetically successful. It is only in the speech on Mount Niphates, when the external magnificence surrounding Satan is stripped away, that we find his stature visibly reduced and his heroic grandeur battered and corroded by the endless siege of contraries within him.

> ... horror and doubt distract
> His troubled thoughts, and from the bottom stir
> The hell within him, for within him hell
> He brings, and round about him, nor from hell
> One step no more than from himself can fly
> By change of place (iv 18–23)

Pinned on this torment he is driven from concession to concession. He admits that God is omnipotent and his own revolt unjustified. He wishes that he were ordained an 'inferior Angel', only to realize that if he were less exalted he would not be less evil. He curses God's love but ends by cursing himself. He thinks of submission but his pride rejects it; then, as desperation forces him to consider the idea, he finds that the breach between him and God is so great that no atonement could possibly heal it and that, in the last analysis, he has not even the power to atone. When we are brought up in this manner against Satan's inner helplessness, his sheer inability to be other than he is, the splendour of his presence starts to crumble. It is one of the functions of the Niphates speech to effect this reduction in scale for by doing so it helps to link two conceptions of Satan which might otherwise be harassingly opposed. On the one hand we have the 'apostate Angel', the leader of all but unconquerable armies, the antagonist to God in the theatre of world history. On the other hand we need to have someone whose characteristic qualities are cunning and subtlety rather than heroic valour, someone sufficiently small to be met and conquered by Adam and Eve in the arena of their original righteousness. One hastens to add that the two conceptions are not contradictory and are in fact meant to be imaginatively reconciled in a true understanding of the nature of evil. Jeremy Taylor achieves the synthesis memorably in prose :

His [God's] mercies make contemptible means instrumental to great purposes, and a small herb the remedy of the greatest diseases; he impedes the Devil's rage and infatuates his counsels, he diverts his malice, and defeats his purposes, he bindes him in the chaine of darknesse and gives him no power over the children of light; he suffers him to walk in solitary places and yet fetters him that he cannot disturb the sleep of a childe; he hath given him mighty power and yet a young maiden that resists him shall make him flee away; he hath given him a vast knowledge and yet an ignorant man can confute him with the twelve articles of his creed, he gave him power over the winds and made him Prince of the air and yet the breath of a holy prayer can drive him as far as the utmost sea ;[12]

The same contrast is realized poetically by Milton. Satan's omnipotence against the background of evil blends into his impotence in the presence of good. The transition from one state to the other probably begins with his deception of Uriel but it is felt most inescapably in that devouring inner chaos which is revealed to us in the Niphates soliloquy. When we see Satan transfixed upon the rocks of his hatred, confirmed in evil as the servant of his selfhood, able only to do as his inner logic demands, we see him, in his limitations, more clearly as our antagonist and know ourselves sufficient to stand against him. The imagery accordingly becomes more and more homilectical; it is addressed to Everyman in the familiar traditions of the pulpit, in figures whose content is plain and unmistakable and whose moral meaning is insistently asserted. Thus Satan appearing before Uriel as a stripling Cherub, may remind us of Burton's claim that the Devil sometimes 'transforms himself into an angel of light, and is so cunning that he is able, if it were possible, to deceive the very elect'.[13] But Milton makes sure that we will draw the necessary inference by using the occasion for a sermon on hypocrisy. Again when Satan descends from Mount Niphates, smoothing his perturbations 'with outward calm' the preacher's voice informs us that he was the first 'that practised falsehood under saintly show'. When the fiend leaps into Paradise Milton begins by appealing to his audience in the country :

> As when a prowling wolf,
> Whom hunger drives to seek new haunt for prey,
> Watching where shepherds pen their flocks at eve
> In hurdled cotes amid the field secure,
> Leaps o'er the fence with ease into the fold : (IV 183–7)

But to make condemnation doubly sure this is followed by a simile for Everyman in Bread Street :

> Or as a thief bent to unhoard the cash
> Of some rich burgher, whose substantial doors,
> Cross-barred and bolted fast, fear no assault,
> In at the window climbs, or o'er the tiles;
> So clomb this first grand thief into God's fold ...
>
> (IV 188–92)

And the pamphleteer in Milton cannot resist the afterthought :

> So since into his church lewd hirelings climb.

After about two hundred lines of the fourth book this homely
didacticism begins to have its way. Satan's dimensions are reduced so effectively that we hardly notice how, in the process, his
titles lose their lustre, how the 'Archfiend' of the first book becomes 'the Fiend' or the 'arch-fellon' and how for the first time
he begins to be 'the Devil'. It is fitting that this new being should
sit like a cormorant on the tree of life, and even his malicious
leering at the happiness of Eve and Adam is well in keeping with
the Satan of popular sentiment. Protestants had long opposed the
exaltation of the single above the married state, thinking of it, in
Ames's words as 'a diabolical presumption'.[14] It is only a step from
this, and not a large one poetically, to make the Devil jealous of
wedded love. But even before this Satan has begun to posture
and protest, according to the conventions of his villainy. His pity
for Adam and Eve is eventually only an elaborate form of self-
pity.

> Ah gentle pair, ye little think how nigh
> Your change approaches, when all these delights
> Will vanish and deliver ye to woe,
> More woe, the more your taste is now of joy;
> Happy, but for so happy ill secured
> Long to continue, and this high seat your heaven
> Ill fenced for heaven to keep out such a foe
> As now is entered; yet no purposed foe
> To you whom I could pity thus forlorn
> Though I unpitied : league with you I seek,
> And mutual amity so strait, so close,
> That I with you must dwell, or you with me
> Henceforth; my dwelling haply may not please
> Like this fair Paradise, your sense, yet such
> Accept your maker's work; he gave it me,
> Which I as freely give; hell shall unfold
> To entertain you two, her widest gates
> And send forth all her kings; there will be room,
> Not like these narrow limits, to receive

> Your numerous offspring; if no better place,
> Thank him who puts me loth to this revenge
> On you who wrong me not for him who wronged.
>
> (IV 367–87)

No more impressive evidence of Satan's degeneration could be cited. The lamentations mingled with the macabre gloating, the horrific irony seasoned with complaint are all confessions of his inner emptiness. And this vacancy is reflected in the texture of the verse. Lines like 'That I with you must dwell, or you with me' are symptomatically lacking in any sense of direction. Their tiredness stands in unmistakable contrast to the rock-like assurance of the Archangel's words in Hell :

> Fallen cherub, to be weak is miserable
> Doing or suffering : but of this be sure,
> To do aught good never will be our task,
> But ever to do ill our sole delight,
> As being the contrary to his high will
> Whom we resist. If then his providence
> Out of our evil seek to bring forth good,
> Our labour must be to pervert that end,
> And out of good still to find means of evil; (I 157–65)

Even the invocation here is meaningful and moving. It has about it the strength of native courtesy, the condescension of intrinsic merit, the responsibility mingled with protective guidance which, in a great leader, is noblest in defeat. How different it all is from the crocodile condolences of the Devil inspecting Paradise. And how different are the threatenings of the passage in Book IV, the palpable attempt to make your flesh creep, from the strange force of poetic concentration which settles implacably on that one word *pervert*. The words in the first book are steadfast and impregnable with the long stressed monosyllables aiding and buttressing their massive resolution. They preach perversion without apology or comment, and for the moment you feel that perversion absolute, unalterable as a fact in nature, an element in the geography of Hell. By contrast, the passage from the fourth book is forced and undecided. The level monosyllables are listless rather than militant. The being who speaks these words, torn and transfixed by self-interrogation, is one who invites this scornful comment of Zephon :

> Think not, revolted spirit, thy shape the same,
> Or undiminished brightness, to be known
> As when thou stood'st in heaven upright and pure;
> That glory then, when thou no more wast good,
> Departed from thee, and thou resemblest now
> Thy sin and place of doom obscure and foul. (IV 835–40)

And Satan himself is forced to accept this verdict

> . . . abashed the devil stood
> And felt how awful goodness is, and saw
> Virtue in her shape how lovely, saw, and pined
> His loss; but chiefly to find here observed
> His lustre visibly impaired; yet seemed
> Undaunted. (IV 846–51)

The form of the ruined Archangel is inexorably losing its brightness. Once indeed, under the lash of Gabriel's comments it flares into a reminiscence of its former splendour. But the 'alarmed' Satan dilated 'like *Teneriff* or *Atlas*' is never quite as impressive as the 'Unterrified' Satan who challenges Death at the outset of his journey through Chaos. He is too concerned with winning verbal victories, with shifty deceits and elaborate evasions. He accepts (as one cannot imagine the earlier Satan accepting) the symbolic verdict of the scales suspended in Heaven. The implication plainly is that the heroic in Satan is yielding to the perverted, and that the passions which led him to war with his creator are beginning to recoil on the intelligence which released them.

In the fifth book we revert to a Satan who, chronologically, ought to be at his noblest. Instead, we find only a professional politician, a propagandist who, like all propagandists, is an ardent champion of the Rights of Man and is therefore able to be generously indignant about the despotic tendencies of government in Heaven. It is a Satan notably different from the Archangel of the first books, and those who feel this discrepancy are compelled either to assume that Milton changed his mind about Satan as he drew him, or else find ways of making the difference acceptable. One way of dealing with the evidence is to assume that Satan is chiefly what the occasion makes him. What he is, depends on what he does. The intruder in Eden is not quite the explorer of Chaos and both of them differ from the 'false Archangel' whom Abdiel conquers in 'debate of truth'. The battle in Heaven is, we should remember, part of a Sermon preached to Adam; it is intended to warn him against an opponent who may conquer him by force of persuasion but cannot conquer him by force of arms. So the qualities stressed are Satan's specious plausibility in argument and, side by side with this, his very real ineptness when he is faced with the weapons of reason and the right. Milton's contemporaries could hardly have taken Satan's complaints seriously. But even if they were inclined to do so, they would have been set right by the evidence of the Niphates soliloquy, with its betraying confession that God's service was never onerous, and that ambition, not altruism, drove Satan to revolt. The other half of Milton's poetic intention is to suggest Satan's tawdriness and triviality when he is measured against the values of Heaven. It is a tawdriness first felt in the Devil's encounter with Gabriel but confirmed now by a style which can be fantastically complicated, by speeches which bristle with the equipment of the orator, with jaunty sarcasm and irrelevant puns.

> That we were formd then say'st thou? And the work
> Of secondary hands, by task transferred
> From Father to his Son? Strange point and new!
> Doctrine which we would know whence learned : who saw
> When this creation was? Remember'st thou
> Thy making, while the maker gave thee being?
> We know no time when we were not as now;
> Know none before us, self-begot, self-raised
> By our own quickening power, when fatal course
> Had circled his full orb, the birth mature
> Of this our native heaven, ethereal sons.
> Our puissance is our own, our own right hand
> Shall teach us highest deeds, by proof to try
> Who is our equal : then thou shalt behold

> Whether by supplication we intend
> Address, and to begirt the almighty throne,
> Beseeching or besieging. (v 853–69)

The spectacle of the arch-heretic accusing the saints of heresy (Milton frequently calls the loyal angels saints)[15] is one which would certainly have encouraged the violent dislike which every saint felt for Satan. And their feelings would not have been moderated by Satan's extraordinary arguments, his perverse insolence in calling Abdiel seditious, and his uncouth explanations of how he was 'self-begot'. Such behaviour for them would have justified Abdiel's verdict: 'Thyself not free but to thyself enthrall'd.' In Satan's utter incomprehension of the joyous obedience which binds man to right reason, in his persistent confusion of servitude with service, they would have seen the flaws in the rhetoric Abdiel mastered, and the diabolic persuasions which they too must subdue, within themselves, on the field of Christian warfare.

When we next see Satan his fortunes have sunk much lower. He has had to journey in darkness seven times round the earth to avoid the vigilance of the angels guarding Paradise. Now, having entered the garden by an underground river at midnight, he pours his 'bursting passion' into 'plaints' that invite comparison with his earlier soliloquy. This time he addresses the earth instead of the sun and, just as the sun once reminded him of the glory he had lost, the earth now suggests to him the glory he is to recover. It is a glory which at most can be only a shadow of his former brightness, but Satan is now so much the victim of his eloquence that he convinces himself that Earth is superior to Heaven.[16] The creature who finds ease 'only in destroying' is the embodiment of the evil he accepted as his good. Unable to alleviate his misery he finds solace only in making others as miserable as he is. His mind is diseased with the obsession of revenge. He talks of man as the 'Favourite of Heaven' and of the creation as an act of spite. He envies, only less than God, the 'gentle pair' whom he once said he could pity. If he is good it is because he is 'stupidly good' in a momentary, bewildered abstraction from himself. Yet even in this depth of degradation he can still rise to what the occasion makes him. The classics come, as so often, to his rescue, the proper names glitter to suit his serpentine stratagems and, mounting on the pedestal of an occasional simile, he becomes as lovely as temptation is to the tempted. Admittedly when the deed has been done, he slinks away to escape the judgment of God but, despite the implications of this incident, he is allowed to masquerade as an 'angel bright' and to strut through Chaos with his diabolic progeny. Meeting the infernal council in surroundings suitably Turkish, he can still outshine the stars in 'permissive glory'. He addresses them on the great enterprise and on his own heroism in making the adventure successful. He alludes (quite falsely) to the fierce opposition which he encountered from Night and from Chaos. He claims with catastrophic foolishness to have purchased a Universe with a bruise and an apple, and having held God up as an object for laughter he is greeted appropriately with a 'universal hiss'. The punishment which descends is terrible but justified. As we leave the humiliated powers of Hell, tormented by the fruits of their imagined victory, the contrast makes more reassuring the repentance of Adam and Eve and their reconciliation to the good which Satan denies.

During these last few paragraphs I have tried to suggest that what Satan is depends on his circumstances, and how his behaviour and implied stature are determined by his functions. I hope I have not suggested that he is nothing more than a collection of abstract properties, properties which can be irresponsibly shuffled to meet the demands of varying situations. But, if he is more than this, he is also more than a theological exercise, or a means of illustrating a preconceived theory of evil. He is, in short, a poetic representation, and Milton's special problem is to take those qualities which the general imagination associates with Satan and work them into a stable poetic whole. Those qualities are by no means interdependent and in juxtaposition may often seem contradictory. They can be brought together in poetry, or poetic prose, in the emotions kindled by antithesis and paradox. But, in the more spacious economy of a narrative poem, such lyrical insights are neither proper nor possible. The truth must be revealed in action, not reflection, and so the qualities which the poem portrays are most convincing when they are made to emerge from the situations in which they are presented. If Satan is heroic, he should be heroic in Hell. If he is melodramatic, he is best so in the serene peace of Eden. If he combines weakness in understanding with subtlety in debate, that combination is best revealed in circumstances which Milton's contemporaries would associate with Christian warfare. The qualities, then, are harmonized by their relationship to a fable which is constructed to imply them. They can be brought together still more closely by the disposition of that fable, that is by the divergence between the chronological and the reading order. Chronologically Satan's deterioration is neither continual nor consistent : before his fall from Heaven he is far less impressive than he is immediately after it. But the difference (made unavoidable by Satan's function in Heaven) is one submerged in the unity which the reading order stipulates, the inexorable law of Satan's degeneration which is exercised so evenly from the first books to the last.

Satan's history therefore is meant to be read poetically. You may bring to it (and indeed it is essential that you should bring to it) the preconceptions of an established moral outlook. But such preconceptions are no more than an equipment, an accepted means of reacting to the poem. They are what Milton assumes rather than what he demonstrates. Given the organization of sensibility they imply, the function of the poem is to play upon it, to use it as far as possible as a medium through which its own character is created and known. To vary the metaphor a little, the poem imposes its perspective on your feelings. The great figure of Satan and its inexorable decline confirms and yet insensibly rearranges the mass of beliefs and sentiments which you bring to it. You see it as a sermon on the weakness of evil and you learn more clearly than you can from any philosophy that evil must die by the logic of its being. But it is also a sermon on the strength of evil; because you see Satan created as he is, huge in the magnificence with which the first books surround him, you are compelled to know him as the Prince of Darkness and to admit his dominion over the forces of history. When two facts so apparently opposed are reconciled in one figure a poetic synthesis has been effected. Add to that synthesis the emotions which it orders, fear of the marauder and contempt for the liar, with wary admiration of the orator's resources, add to these the dramatic insights of soliloquy, and the result must make Satan symbolically alive within the universe which Milton's epic operates. In defining or interpreting this life, 'hero' and 'fool' are inadequate alternatives. They are descriptions, not so much of the poetry, as of the moral system which the poetry is said to recommend, or else of the intellectual convictions which Milton's imagination is taken to deny.

In opposition I have tried to maintain that Milton's heart was not at war with his head and that his Satan is on the whole what he intended to make him. Here and there Milton's execution may falter. But if we look at his picture through seventeenth century eyes, if we try not to impose upon it the deceptions of our own historic and personal perspectives, its implications should be plain and unmistakable. The failure lies not in the depiction of Satan but in that of the heavenly values which should subdue him. Those values are only imperfectly realized. So, though one half of the picture may be painted convincingly, the other half is sketched rather than painted. Milton's God is what his Satan never is, a collection of abstract properties, or, in his greatest moments, a treatise on free-will. The Son moves us more deeply, particularly in the quiet, firm monosyllables in which he announces his sacrifice. But the spare precision of the language Milton gives him is lit only seldom by the ardour which should inform it. Clothed in the language of Ezekiel's vision his triumph over Satan must have its moments of majesty, but it remains a moral rather than a poetic victory.

It is I think the barrenness of this victory which makes some misunderstanding of Satan's function inevitable. His regression faces us with a sort of vacuum and though the values which triumph over him are everywhere announced they are never brought to the foreground of our assent. Milton can describe pride, and in doing so condemn it; but love is to him never much more than loyalty, and humility teaches him only to 'stand and wait'. He may justify God's ways but he does not celebrate them. His sense of responsibility is too contractual, too persistently concerned with the mechanics of crime and punishment, for good-

ness or mercy to come into being within it. Because such goodness is so seldom real within the limits of Milton's poetry it becomes possible to claim that the poet was interested predominantly
in evil, or even that evil was unconsciously his good. Such
conclusions are to my mind untenable. Milton knows his Satan
well enough to reject him and to make that rejection a poetic
fact. If that dismissal is never stabilized in its transformation by
a higher poetic acceptance, the failure should not blind us to
the poverty of the values Milton condemns or to the reality and
force of his depiction of evil.

SOURCE : Paradise Lost *and the Seventeenth Century Reader*
(1947).

NOTES

1. Raleigh, *Milton* (London, 1915), p. 133.
2. Especially Landor, who, in a well-known passage, asserts that
'there is neither wit nor truth however in saying that Satan is hero
of the piece, unless, as is usually the case, he is the greatest hero
who gives the widest sway to the worst passions'. From 'Imaginary
Conversations : Southey and Landor', *Works*, ed. C. G. Crump
(London, 1891), IV, 201. The comment is given to Southey.
3. *The English Poems of John Milton*, ed. Charles Williams
(London, 1940), introduction, p. xv.
4. C. S. Lewis, *Preface to 'Paradise Lost'* (London, 1942),
pp. 92–100.
5. E. E. Stoll, 'Give the Devil his Due', *RES*, xx (1944),
pp. 108–24.
6. G. Rostrevor Hamilton, *Hero or Fool: A Study of Milton's
Satan* (London, 1944).
7. Notably S. Musgrave's 'Is the Devil an Ass?' (*RES*, xxi,
1945), pp. 302–15. I have not had access to Professor Waldock's
'Mr C. S. Lewis and *Paradise Lost*' (Australian English Association,
1943).
8. Calvin, *Institutes*, I, xiv, 13. Norton's translation.
9. Defoe, *The Political History of the Devil* (London, 1726),
p. 52.
10. Addison in Todd, I, 302.
11. Addison, op. cit.

12. Jeremy Taylor, XXVIII *Sermons* (London, 1651), p. 343.

13. Burton, *The Anatomy of Melancholy*, pt. 3, mem. 1, sec. 4, subs. 2.

14. William Ames, *The Marrow of Sacred Divinity* (London, 1638), p. 324. Similarly Calvin comments on *Gen.* 2 : 18 : 'Many think that celibacy conduces to their advantage, and, therefore, abstain from marriage, lest they should be miserable . . . To these wicked suggestions of Satan, let the faithful learn to oppose this declaration of God, by which he ordains the conjugal life for man, not to his destruction but to his salvation.'

15. See, e.g., *Paradise Lost*, VI 398, 742, 767, 801, 882 : X 614.

16. The ideas which Satan here misuses (IX 99 ff.) remind us of Raphael's words to Adam (VIII 91 ff.). At IX 718 ff. Satan again misuses the idea that the sun, otherwise barren, is fruitful only as it serves the earth and man. This time he quotes in order to challenge (and significantly at the climax of the temptation) Raphael's opening words to Adam on degree (V 469 ff.).

E. M. W. Tillyard

THE CRISIS OF *PARADISE LOST* (1951)

It was Walter Raleigh who spoke of the crisis of *Paradise Lost* in the tone of greatest assurance. After setting forth the vast range of topics comprised in the poem he went on :

> All these are exhibited in the clearest and most inevitable relation with the main event, so that there is not an incident, hardly a line of the poem, but leads backwards or forwards to those central lines in the Ninth Book :
>
> > So saying, her rash hand in evil hour
> > Forth reaching to the fruit, she plucked, she ate.
> > Earth felt the wound, and nature from her seat
> > Sighing through all her works gave signs of woe,
> > That all was lost. (IX 780–4)
>
> From this point radiates a plot so immense in scope, that the history of the world from the first preaching of the gospel to the Millennium occupies only some fifty lines of Milton's epilogue.

And Raleigh's assurance has been compelling. When studying *Paradise Lost* for my *Milton* I accepted his statement as axiomatic; and this seems to have been a common experience. Hanford, for instance, in *A Milton Handbook*, describing how the poem evolves, assumes Book Ten to be of less moment than Book Nine, an appendage in subservience to it. Grierson in his *Milton and Wordsworth* assumes the same :

> If there is a falling off of interest in the later books it was inherent in the subject. Who could make an heroic poem of Adam and Eve tempted to transgress a tabu? Milton has done his best in the ninth book, the varied decorative material of which is all that it should

be. But it is not until the Fall is accomplished that the two characters grow human and winning.

Note how Grierson assumes that the one place where there
should be heroic action is the story of eating the fruit : for Adam
and Eve to grow interesting after the Fall is to do so too late;
the idea that it is then that they find scope in noble doings simply
does not arise.[1]

Now if you go to the bare story and seek a point from which
all events radiate you can hardly choose otherwise than Raleigh.
It might indeed be argued that the first entrance of pride into the
heart of Lucifer was even more significant than the eating of the
fruit, since without Lucifer's defection there would have been no
gap in heaven, no need to find recruits for it from a second
creation; in fact no world and no world history. And as a subject
for a Miracle Play, where no elaboration of incident or of motivation is required, it does well enough. We cannot ask for better
than Lucifer's unmotivated boastings at the beginning of the
Towneley Cycle :

> For I am lord of blis
> Over all the world, I wis,
> My myrth is moot of all;
> Therefor my will is this,
> Master ye shall me call.
>
> And ye shall see full soon onone
> How that me semys to sit in trone
> As King of blis;
> I am so semely, blode and bone,
> My sete shall be there as was his.
>
> Say, felows, how semys now me
> To sit in seyte of Trynyte?
> I am so bright of ich a lym,
> I trow me seme as well as hym.

But to make Lucifer the main figure, as the centralizing of his
fall would dictate, could not possibly square with Milton's final
choice of the human theme of Everyman. Once Lucifer's fall is
ruled out, only Eve's can be considered the logical centre of the

plot: for Adam's fall was conditioned by Eve's and is hence sub-ordinate; and without Eve's fall there would have been no anticipatory offer by the Son to be a ransom, no effusion of heavenly Grace after, and no world history. In her fall Heaven and Hell meet in conflict. So, as far as the plot goes, Raleigh ought to be right.

But abstracted plot and actual poetry are different things, and we should not assume that they must each evolve with the same emphasis. And if we read *Paradise Lost* rightly, opening ourselves to the poetry, we shall find that Eve's eating the apple is by no means the one, exclusive, centre of the poem. There are reasons why in actual practice a poet would find it hard to make it so.

In the bare story Eve was sinless till the precise moment when she reached out her rash hand and plucked the fruit.[2] Milton may have intended to substantiate the story. He does indeed say that she was still sinless when she had so far yielded to the serpent's blandishments as to follow him to the tree whose fruit he had been advertising so skilfully. But intentions could be of no avail against the terms to which Milton submitted himself by offering to present in ample narrative the transition from a state of innocence to a state of sin. Under the terms of the story these two realms must be separated by a definite but dimensionless frontier: there cannot be a no-man's-land between; in the passage, time must not count. Such a lightning-quick change might be effective in a film; as mentioned above, it showed itself to be possible in the simple form of the Miracle Plays; but in a narrative poem it could only be ridiculous, and in his heart Milton knew that well enough.

In Book Four of *Paradise Lost* Milton pictured his state of innocence, and it is one of the most lovely and thrilling pictures in all poetry. But he could not possibly have conducted his account of the Fall with that picture for sole starting-point; the effect would have been sudden and violent and would have carried no conviction. And he makes no such attempt. Instead he resorts to some faking: perfectly legitimate in a poem, yet faking never-theless. He anticipates the Fall by attributing to Eve and Adam feelings which though nominally felt in the state of innocence are actually not compatible with it.[3] The first stage is Eve's dream

at the beginning of Book Five, an episode which, it is recognized,
duplicates in its small way the greater temptation in Book Nine.
Here Satan insinuates the insidious (and characteristically
Cavalier) sentiment of 'suffer thyself to be admired', urging her
to walk out in the night so that all heaven's eyes may admire her
beauty. She is then made to imagine herself seeking Adam and
finding herself suddenly by the 'Tree of interdicted Knowledge'.
She sees to her horror an angelic shape eat the fruit, boast of its
virtue, and make her eat too, on the plea that she will become a
goddess. Having eaten, she seems to fly up to heaven and see the
earth beneath her. In her wonder at her flight her dream ends.
Adam does his best to comfort Eve, giving her a reassuringly
academic account of the way dreams happen and ending with the
general principle that *should* clear Eve of all offense:

> Evil into the mind of god or man
> May come and go, so unapproved, and leave
> No spot or blame behind ... (v 117–19)

This means[4] that into the mind of angel or man evil may enter,
and, if it is repudiated, fail to incriminate. In the abstract the
doctrine may be tenable, but it cannot work in concrete literary
presentation. No human being can conceive or represent evil
entering a mind quite alien to it. Dramatically, the mere fact of
entrance implies some pre-existing sympathy. And, in actual
dramatic truth, Eve, though not approving the implication of her
dream, does by her symptoms imply that it has touched her, that
it is far from alien; for Adam, waking out of the light sleep of
perfect innocence, is surprised

> to find unwakened Eve
> With tresses discomposed, and glowing cheek,
> As through unquiet rest (v 9–11)

And if the dream has disturbed Eve so much, she has really
passed from a state of innocence to one of sin. This is not to
blame Milton. He is confronted with an impossibility; and to
achieve dramatic poetry at all he has to fake. And he has succeeded as well as a man, in the circumstances, can. We do accept,

as we read, Milton's specious plea that Adam and Eve satisfy the conditions of nominal innocence required by the story; and with another part of our mind we know that Eve is really, even if only a little way, on the far side of the line that divides innocence from experience.

Eve having made the transition, it was necessary for Adam to do the same. And he does it at the end of Book Eight when he confides to Raphael how Eve's beauty is apt to affect his mind in a way that is dangerous to the sovereignty there of the Reason. Not that Adam denies this sovereignty, but by speaking of his transport of love for Eve as 'commotion strange', he has admitted to feelings alien to the angelic and akin to Eve's sleeping perturbation. Technically, he is still innocent, but in our hearts we recognize him as just across the frontier. Nor is he straightforward in his dealings with Raphael. When rebuked by Raphael for allowing Eve's physical charms to create in him the illusion of her wisdom, he neither answers nor admits the rebuke but merely shifts his ground and says that it is rather her delightful manners that have this effect. He then, with something near impudence, counterattacks and asks if the angels love too.[5] Adam shows great charm and mental dexterity. The irony was that Eve was to treat him, her superior, exactly as Adam here treats his superior, Raphael, when they argue about separate or joint garden-work in the next book. My main point is that both are virtually fallen before the official temptation has begun.

A further advance into the realm of experience is effected by means of the smoke-screen generated by the great prologue to Book Nine. Having there announced that he is changing his notes to tragic, Milton can risk presenting us with an Adam and Eve more human still than the two episodes just mentioned could dictate. Although ignorant as yet of the more violent human passions, Adam and Eve conduct their dispute about separate or joint gardening as evolved human beings such as we know.

The Fall, then, must be extended back in time; it has no plain and sensational beginning; and the actual eating of the apple becomes no more than an emphatic stage in a process already begun, the stage when the darker and stormier passions make their entry into the human heart.

The same is true of what happens after Eve has eaten the apple. The process of falling continues. It takes time for it to work itself utterly out. Indeed it could be maintained that the Fall is not accomplished, does not in deepest verity take place, till Adam's great despairing speech late in Book Ten (720), ending :

> O conscience ! into what abyss of fears
> And horrors hast thou driven me; out of which
> I find no way, from deep to deeper plunged ! (x 842–4)

By that time indeed Adam's education in the knowledge of good and evil is complete.

Raleigh's point of radiation, then, turns out in the poem itself not to be a point at all but an inseparable item in a substantial area of the whole poem. But once this is granted, it will be found that another theme has been added to, or intertwined with, the theme of the Fall; intertwined so firmly as to be inextricable : the theme of regeneration. Long before the effects of the Fall have made themselves fully felt, the process of regeneration has begun. It begins, although the characters in whom it operates are not conscious of it, when, early in Book Ten, the Son, having pronounced his judgment on the actors in the Fall, pities Adam and Eve and clothes their nakedness. And it reaches obvious fruition when, at the end of the book, Adam and Eve make peace with each other and confess their errors to God.

It comes then to this. Instead of a small spot in Book Nine for a watershed you have to take the whole great area of Books Nine and Ten. That Milton intended these to go together is evident from the way he concludes them : one end is the pendant of the other. Book Nine ends with the unresolved quarrelling of Adam and Eve :

> Thus they in mutual accusation spent
> The fruitless hours, but neither self-condemning,
> And of their vain contest appeared no end. (IX 1187–9)

Book Ten comes to rest with the contrasted picture of Adam and Eve reconciled in mutual amity and common humility, seeking the pardon of God :

So spake our father penitent, nor Eve
Felt less remorse : they forthwith to the place
Repairing where he judged them prostrate fell
Before him reverent, and both confessed
Humbly their faults, and pardon begged, with tears
Watering the ground, and with their sighs the air
Frequenting, sent from hearts contrite, in sign
Of sorrow unfeigned, and humiliation meek. (x 1097–1104)

The habit, then, of subordinating Book Ten to Book Nine, is mistaken; and if you argue from such an assumption you may do violence to what the poetry should be telling you.

SOURCE : *Studies in Milton* (1951).

NOTES

1. On the other hand C. G. Osgood in *Poetry as a Means of Grace* (Princeton, 1941), p. 100, sees that the drama extends uninterrupted till Adam and Eve repent in Book Ten.

2. With the argument that follows compare Waldock, *Paradise Lost and its Critics* (Cambridge, 1947), p. 61 : 'Adam and Eve must already be fallen (technically) before they can begin to fall.'

3. Milton does the same with Mammon in 1 680–4. Even in Heaven, while yet unfallen, Mammon was more interested in the gold of Heaven's pavement than in the beatific vision. Such an interest in the heart of one of the principal angels shows him already fallen. But who minds in the reading or blames Milton for faking to the advantage of the poetry?

4. See Maurice Kelley, *This Great Argument* (Princeton, 1941), p. 77.

5. See the excellent analysis of these speeches by Paul Turner in *English Studies* (1948), pp. 1–5, where he disagrees with Waldock's contention that it is Raphael who misunderstands Adam (A. J. A. Waldock, *'Paradise Lost' and its Critics*, pp. 43–4. But Turner underrates Adam's loverlike fervour as Waldock overrates it. Surely the poetic virtue lies in the ambivalence : Raphael's rebuke was just. Adam's love (in a man virtually fallen) was also good up to a point. Just so the loves of Paolo and Francesca were noble up to a point. Yet they merited their infernal punishment.

R. J. Zwi Werblowsky

ANTAGONIST OF HEAVEN'S ALMIGHTY KING (1952)

Milton's Satan has often been compared to Prometheus, and practically every critic has at least once used the epithet 'Promethean' to describe some of Satan's qualities. Already Newton had noted the affinity in his note to *Paradise Lost*, i 94 ff. : 'Milton in this and other passages, where he is describing the fierce and unrelenting spirit of Satan, seems very plainly to have copied after the picture that Aeschylos gives of Prometheus.' He and the other commentators have pointed out various references which will in part be mentioned here. Again, Shelley[1] was greatly affected by the similarity of the two characters, clearly identifying them to a certain extent. Amongst the moderns, the best-known statement is that in Raleigh's *Milton* :

Satan unavoidably reminds us of Prometheus, and although there are essential differences, we are not made to feel them essential. His very situation as the fearless antagonist of Omnipotence makes him either a fool or a hero, and Milton is far indeed from permitting us to think him a fool. The nobility and greatness of his bearing are brought home to us in some half-dozen of the finest poetic passages in the world.

More recently, Mr G. R. Hamilton distinguishes between the two,[2] precisely because he feels their strong affinity. '. . . behind the tragic darkness of Satan, powerful and boasting in his own power, we catch the vision, not quite eclipsed, of an ardent Lucifer in a Heaven more truly harmonious, giving glory to Love and a world of Light.'[3]

. . . To my knowledge the comparison has so far never been taken seriously and in a literal sense, in fact I doubt whether it was ever meant to be taken so. All that was implied by the analogy was a vague sense of the heroic at its limits : fighting not against heavy odds but against divine omnipotence itself. As a dramatic necessity, and to prevent the heroism from turning into folly,[4] the absoluteness of this omnipotence must somehow be mitigated, but this does not detract essentially from the hero's glory. Moreover, we are supposed to see in Prometheus merely a hero, the idealized struggle of mankind, and not a sinner. Says Mr Hamilton : 'The rebellion . . . of a Prometheus, not of a Satan : a rebellion founded on the principle of love, not of self-seeking and personal ambition.'[5] The comparison thus carries a very dangerous *sous-entendu*, a critical shift of emphasis. It tends to slur over the heinous wickedness and abysmal evil of Satan, by throwing into relief his heroic virtues. Shelley, like Mr Hamilton, was clearly aware of this, and consequently tried to delimit the two characters from each other. For that reason, too, the anti-Satanists have always rejected the comparison, which has thus become the sole property of the 'romantic' school.[6]

I doubt whether this conventional account is correct, although it is extremely revealing. It shows that we have reached a stage where the most 'unromantic' critics, while strictly adhering to the orthodox condemnation of Satan, nevertheless exhibit a markedly positive and 'romantic' response to the figure of Prometheus.[7] I almost feel certain that Hesiod himself, in contrast to Mr Lewis or Professor Musgrove, would not have taken exception to the comparison. But he would have been deeply shocked by the words of Mr Hamilton. Quite simply because in his eyes Prometheus would be as sinful as Satan is in the eyes of Mr Lewis. I therefore think it worth our while to push the analogy a little further and to investigate beyond the superficial resemblance the possibility of profounder mythical i.e. archetypal identities. I suggest that we may discover some distinctly Promethean features in the Satan of *Paradise Lost*, and that these may go a long way to explain some of the poem's major difficulties.

I do not assert, of course, that Milton consciously thought of Prometheus when describing his Satan, or that he worked Aeschylean references into his text in the way he did with Scripture. The actual quotations from and references to

Aeschylos are relatively negligible, and certainly do not excel in quantity or significance the far more numerous allusions to Homer, Vergil, Ovid, Tasso and the like. The literal parallels[8] pointed out by the various commentators and editors such as Thyer, Richardson, Todd, Newton, Mitford and others are of small or no account here, and there is no reason to suppose any special 'influence' on Milton of Aeschylos' *Prometheus.* Fortunately so, one almost feels tempted to add, as these influences, so dear to research scholars all over the world, are usually more exact than significant. As the great Swiss scholar, the late Professor Fehr of Zürich, once put it :[9] '. . . *nachweisbare Einflüsse deuten immer nur auf das Nebensächliche, nie auf das Wesentliche hin*'. Milton owes little to Aeschylean mythology,[10] but the comparison is interesting because their myths are similar and the same archetypes seem active with both of them.

More interesting, though often too obvious to be of value, are those similarities which give us something of a common atmosphere. Such are e.g. the identification of a God who excels mainly by his more powerful thunder

> . . . so much the stronger proved
> He with his thunder (*P.L.* 1 92–3)

> . . . he
> Whom thunder hath made greater (257–8)

with Zeus :

> .The Father's thunder-clap and lightning-flame (*Prom,* 1049)

> So now let him cast, if it please him, the two-
> Edged curl of his lightning (1075–6)

> The reverberant thunder is heard from the deep,
> And the forked flames flares of the lightning (1116–17)

(though this parallel is not confined to the Zeus of Aeschylos), and the belief in the possibility of beating God at his own game :

> . . . when to meet the noise
> Of his almighty engine he shall hear
> Infernal thunder, and for lightning see
> Black fire and horror shot with equal rage (*P.L.* II 64–7)

> Such is the wrestler he now trains against
> Himself, a prodigy unconquerable,
> Whose strength shall battle down the lightning blast
> And master the mighty roar of heaven's thunder (*Prom.* 952–5)

and similar points of contact.

There are however a few passages in Aeschylos which, whether sources or not, certainly evince a related pattern of emotive reaction and dramatic attitude. To these belong in the first place those passages which have been primarily responsible for the making of the comparison, those namely which express indomitable courage and unshakeable resolve. Thus Newton's note quoted above was prompted by *Paradise Lost*, I 94 ff., as compared with

> . . . and dost thou think that I
> In fear of these new gods will cower and quake?
> Far, far am I from that. (*Prom.* 991–3)

> So, let him hurl his sulphurous flames from heaven,
> With white-winged snow and subterranean thunder
> Make chaos and confusion of the world!
> Not thus will he constrain my tongue to tell
> By whose hand he from tyrrany shall fall. (1024–8)

and by

> . . . To bow and sue for grace
> With suppliant knee, and deify his power,
> Who from the terror of this arm so late
> Doubted his empire, that were low indeed,
> That were an ignominy and shame beneath
> This downfall (*P.L.* I 111–16)

as compared with

> Or dost thou deem that I, fearing the purpose
> Of Zeus, will, woman-hearted, supplicate
> My hated adversary with bow abased
> And abject inclination of my palms,
> To free me from my bondage? (*Prom.* 1034–8)

The satanic solution of the problem of liberty and service . . . has its counterpart in *Prom.* 998–9

> I have no wish to change my adverse fortune,
> Be well assured, for thy subservience

and Newton was probably right in suggesting that Milton intended to answer this with Abdiel's Christian

> Reign thou in hell thy kingdom, let me serve
> In heaven God ever blest, and his divine
> Behests obey, worthiest to be obeyed (*P.L.* vi 183–5)

What greatly strengthens the resemblance is the divine, or rather semi-divine, nature of the protagonists in both cases. The contest is inflated to enormous dimensions by the fact that none of the parties can, properly speaking, be annihilated. The knowledge of at least the possibility of immortality is a decisive factor of Satan's resistance :

> . . . since by fate the strength of gods
> And this empyreal substance cannot fail (*P.L.* i 116–17)

> . . . laid thus low,
> As far as gods and heavenly essences
> Can perish (i 137–9)

> Since now we find this our empyreal form
> Incapable of mortal injury
> Imperishable (vi 433–5)

even as with Prometheus

> What should I fear, predestined not to die (*Prom.* 965)

> For with death I cannot be stricken. (1086)

With this impossibility of dying should be compared *P.L.* II 95 ff. and the idea of death as a desirable impossibility *P.L.* x 775 ff. and 783 ff., together with the fragment of the *Prometheus Lyomenos* preserved by Cicero[11]

> amore mortis terminum anquirens mali.

Here the sufferings of Prometheus have reached such a pitch of intensity, that immortality, instead of being a source of hope, has become hell

> ... where peace
> And rest can never dwell, hope never comes
> That comes to all ... (*P.L.* I 65–7)

to him that had brought hope to all :

> First I implanted in his heart blind hopes, (*Prom.* 266)

Equally underlying both actions is the assumed possibility of overthrowing Jove's order. For Satan

> ... endangered heaven's perpetual king;
> And put to proof his high supremacy (*P.L.* I 131–2)

God himself being gravely concerned about his omnipotence.

> Let us advise, and to this hazard draw
> With speed what force is left, and all employ
> In our defence, lest unawares we lose
> This is our high place ... (*P.L.* v 729–32)

Prometheus, suffering his time

> Decreed till Zeus from tyranny hath fallen (*Prom.* 782)

is sustained by the knowledge that even

> He [Zeus] could not alter that which is ordained (534)

> And yet shall Zeus, so obstinate of spirit,
> Be humbled.... (939 ff)

These are, I believe, all the external resemblances between the *Prometheus Desmotes* and *Paradise Lost*. Individually they are not astounding, nor is their cumulative evidence in any way telling. Even the points of resemblance mentioned last, although they go deeper, do not reveal their significance at a mere visual inspection. It is necessary first to state who Prometheus is and what the Promethean myth may mean, before one can hope to extract the full value of the comparison. Only with a right understanding of this myth is it possible to read the texts with their full resonance. I do not suggest that by then we shall have discovered an identity of the Lucifer and Prometheus myths, or that the Satan of *Paradise Lost* is simply a blend of the two. I merely claim at present that the Promethean myth shows a harmonious development which overlaps to a great extent that of the Christian Satan, and that by looking closer into the meaning of the former, we shall understand many things about Milton and his *Paradise Lost*.

As has already been remarked, the Promethean myth can also be read romantically, that is with an antinomian attitude. But the Prometheus of Goethe,[12] Shelley and Spitteler is not the classical one. Although the romantic readings may thus have to be discarded when we want to analyse the Greek Prometheus in a scientifically responsible manner, yet, even so, they can claim legitimate consideration. The fact alone that the original myth showed itself capable of so vital and strong a development[13] is at least as interesting as the exegesis of the Greek texts. In trying first to give a short outline of the Promethean myth, I shall therefore limit myself to a statement of the essential facts and data, in so far as they seem to me of direct relevance to our present inquiry, without going into technical detail such as, e.g., a comparison of the Hesiodic and Aeschylean versions.[14] In the first place it should be noted that the Promethean world lacks the sense of creation. Man's creatureliness, as we have it in biblical tradition, is unknown. Men and gods are coeternal and of common origin; both are children of Gaia, in spite of all their fundamental differences.[15] They are two poles of existence. *Prima facie* man is therefore neither creature nor rebel.

Secondly, Prometheus himself is a god, like Zeus. The fact that somehow he comes to stand for mankind as their suffering champion, and possibly as their type and symbol, must not make us oblivious to his essentially divine nature. As Kerényi says, Prometheus is first and foremost a god. The paradox here lies in the fact that he undergoes insult and suffering in a typically human manner. This distinguishes him both from Christ and from the romantic Prometheus. Jesus is primarily a man. In his case the paradox comes through the faith that the man Jesus is also God. The romantic Prometheus, Goethe's for instance, is man claiming the rank and dignity of God. His suffering is that of mankind, but his protest is that of outraged divinity, or rather of the divine quality of his humanity. The only parallel to Prometheus would therefore be a gnostic *Urmensch, anthropos* or *Adam Kadmon*.[16] In the mythological sphere Prometheus is thus the divine representative of the non-olympic, the human pole of the world.

Thirdly, the fact should be noted that Prometheus suffers during daytime. With sunrise the eagle of Zeus, itself an obvious symbol for the sun (which is actually apostrophized once by Prometheus as 'bird of Zeus'), comes to feed on his liver. Now the liver of Prometheus grows again during night. But also generally speaking the liver belongs to the night as the traditional seat of the passions, partly also because of its dark colour, and last but not least in its function as a means of divination.[17] The unbinding of Prometheus and his liberation from daylight suffering therefore correspond to an important step forward in the evolution of the human image in man. He has now become a daylight being, and is accepted as such by the gods.

This brings us . . . to the problem of the development of consciousness . . . The *hubris* problem [is] essentially one of the evolution of the human *psyche* to consciousness. The connection with the Promethean myth, based on the same problem, though dealing with it in a more inclusive and existential way, is obvious.

Already Prometheus' first and original act, as told by Hesiod,[18] is one of differentiation. His second act, that to which he chiefly owes his fame, the bringing of fire, equally points to a *prise de conscience* symbolism. It is unnecessary, indeed it would be impossible here, to mention all the evidence and literature on the subject. The best-known example probably is the descent of the Holy Ghost, visible as 'cloven tongues like as of fire'. But also in Greek philosophy, from Heraclitus to the Stoics, fire and its qualities were a favourite subject of speculation. Empedocles ascribed to fire consciousness, thought and knowledge, qualities which Heraclitus thought were a divine prerogative, whilst Aristotle allowed them to men also, though admitting their divine provenance.[19] For if there is anything divine in man, it is undoubtedly his consciousness of himself, whether we call it soul, spirit, reason or thought. Its most prominent symptom is the loss of man's original unity, or even identity with the world. The primitive *participation mystique* has given way to a new distance of man not only towards nature, but also towards himself. Man has ceased to exist as a mere piece of nature, something has emerged within him in virtue of which he now stands over and above himself and the world. Life in its specifically human sense, as thought, speech, purposeful and creative activity, is the expression of man's new status and dignity. But every light has its shadow – even as every shadow has its light – and to every medal there is a reverse. *Homo sapiens* is not only given mastery over the world as *homo faber*[20] and exercising dominion over 'the fish of the sea, and over the fowl of the air, and over every living thing that moveth upon earth'. He is also harassed by a new uneasiness and a new sense of guilt and danger. Original unity and *participation mystique* may be characteristic of a low level of psychic evolution, but at any rate they imply living in a stable and integrated community with a greater and more embracing, albeit less conscious whole. The way of individuation, however, and the growth towards consciousness and freedom is a process of severance from this original unity, and is attended accordingly by feelings of uneasiness and loneliness. The image that obtrudes itself is, of course, that of human birth and of the embryonic organism exchanging the security of the motherly body for a more individual existence, exposed to greater dangers. This image is more than a comparison. It is, as experience has shown, a real archetype. To speak here figuratively of a birth-trauma may therefore be misleading. Perhaps it would be better to regard the birth-trauma as the most concrete and obvious example and therefore also the most ready-at-hand symbol of this aspect of the pattern of life. Every dimension stretches into two directions, and every 'birth' opens a new dimension of life. It is only appropriate that man's new sensibilities should also give him the possibility of negative experiences,[21] and that anxiety, care, unhappiness, injustice and spiritual suffering should rear their ugly heads in the newly opened vista.

Another danger of increasing consciousness is that it may lead to a feeling of equality with the gods through the awareness that one shares their knowledge, freedom and power. Together with consciousness there emerges thus a sense of guilt and sin. The double consequence is that on the one hand man himself does not want to be free,[22] and on the other, that the gods too look askance at every human attempt to reach out towards higher levels of personality. A third corollary is the rather queer position of religion in this scheme : it is a system of behaviour where man respects and serves his jealous gods, carefully avoiding offence by anything that might look like independence, freedom, or self-consciousness. Literary illustrations are legion; but one thinks in the first place of Nietzsche, though one may also cite Spitteler's *Prometheus*, Quinet's trilogy[23] *Prometheus*, Dostoievski's Great Inquisitor, and, for a modern variation on the same theme, Jean-Paul Sartre's play *Les Mouches*. The hybridic shadow of every new progress of knowledge makes it a boon and a bane at the same time, a victory and a punishment, a double-edged sword – like that mysterious element, fire. It is a blessing, but can also be destruction if it is not carefully limited and kept down. But significantly enough it is also the only element whose natural tendency is upwards. Moreover, like the spirit, it confers might and mastery, and with the fire at his disposal, nature becomes mere raw-material in the hands of man, who in his turn becomes shaper and creator. Fire is the appropriate symbol for the spirit and knowledge which is in man and by which he 'aspires to divinity' and becomes a god.[24] It is therefore quite in order that the bringer of fire is called – *nomen est omen* – Prometheus, the 'knower', or, to be more precise, the 'foreknower', although in his relations with Zeus he proved himself an Epimetheus :

> Falsely we named thee the Foresighted One,
> Prometheus – thine the need of foresight now,
> How from this art to extricate thyself! (*Prom.* 85–7)

It is of course possible that the two brothers were originally one undifferentiated being. But more important for our present purpose than his probably different and less transparent original name or names, is the fact that he ended as a *Prometheus*. It is his knowledge which determines his actions, which made him side with Zeus in the Titan war and which gave him security in his perseverance against Zeus.

But Prometheus has more than knowledge. He has cunning. He is astute and clever, and Zeus himself had profited from his 'smartness' not less than mankind.[25] But this astuteness implies, as Kerényi points out,[26] a certain crookedness of mind, ranging from deceitfulness to inventiveness. Prometheus is *ankulometes*, that is, his thinking is *ankulos*, crooked – the mark of a basic deficiency which wants to be overcome. Zeus, the god, whose being knows no inherent defections, *per definitionem* lacks this crookedness, and may thus well need at times the help of a Prometheus.

The order of Zeus is perfect, regulated and static. His world has measure and limits, and every being is assigned its place. But, and here the trouble starts, the human pole of the universe, as soon as it becomes aware of itself at all, becomes aware of fatal deficiencies. Man's attempt to cope with this situation by remedying these deficiencies, presupposes a mental make-up foreign to Zeus. Cleverness is a compensatory function of defectiveness, and man's resourcefulness is thus the means by which he evades and oversteps the rules and bounds set by Zeus, whilst Zeus, like Milton's God, may ironically look on. Kerényi's comment on *Theogony*, 550–2:[27] '*Durchschauend den Trug lässt er* [Zeus] *sich belisten, doch nicht überlisten. . . . Er enthält das Sein impliziert und unbeweglich, die Taten und Untaten mit ihren Folgen, kennt daher auch gar kein Wünschen und Aendernwollen*' might be equally said of Milton's God, and almost sounds like a paraphrase of *P.L.* III 77 ff., but particularly of God's words :

... be not dismayed,
Nor troubled at these tidings from the earth,
Which your sincerest care could not prevent,
Foretold so lately what would come to pass,
When first this tempter crossed the gulf from hell.
I told ye then he should prevail and speed
On his bad errand.... (*P.L.* x 35–41)

Prometheus thus betrays some essentially human characteristics. In fact, he is the founder of human existence as specifically human : he invented the sacrifice and brought the fire. The latter raised the fireless animal existence to the level of the human. Everything now changes into the specifically human, even man's vulnerability. He no longer suffers dumbly, anonymously, as a part of nature, but existentially, as a human. He questions himself and the universe, he calls the world to witness, he measures reality against another ideal order, in short, he can suffer unjustly. His suffering is doubled by becoming the direct source of a further suffering, that of the spirit : man suffers from the injustice of his suffering, because, from *his* standpoint, his actions were necessary and unavoidable. In the case of Prometheus, his actions were prompted by his adopting the human point of view, by his love and friendship for mankind :

Yet of my present state I cannot speak
Cannot be silent. The gifts I gave to man
Have harnessed me beneath this harsh duress.

.   .   .   .   .

Such the transgressions which I expiate,
A helpless captive.... (*Prom.* 106 ff.)

Herein lies the daring of the Greek tragedian, which in many respects even outdoes that of the author of the book of Job.

O majestical mother, O heavenly Sky,
In whose region revolveth the Light of the World,
Thou seest the Wrongs that I suffer![28] (*Prom.* 1125–7)

are the words with which Prometheus disappears in Tartaros.

It is this aspect of the Promethean drama which so strongly appeals to us that we forget that Prometheus is actually trespassing, violating Zeus' order, the *dike*. For if we recognize in Prometheus our own existential suffering, we must equally recognize that this is due primarily to his specifically human sin. *Sin* is the violation of Zeus' order in an attempt to supplement a deficiency, and specifically *human* in the sense that both the awareness of this deficiency and the idea and resolve to overcome it, are peculiar to human existence, that is consciousness. Prometheus has been guilty of *hubris* by ignoring his limits in a very profound sense. He is accused that

> A god, thou didst defy the wrath of gods,
> On men their powers bestowing *beyond due.* [Literally :
> > beyond their *dike*] (*Prom.* 29–30)

and himself admits as much in similar, though at the same time vitally different words :

> For my *too* great love of the children of men. (*Prom.* 124)

But this 'beyond measure' is, humanly speaking, a bare minimum. For what the original *dike* of Zeus would have meant to men, has been made clear by Hesiod[29] and Aeschylos :

> No sooner was he on his father's throne
> ... but held the hapless race of man
> Of no account, resolving to destroy
> All human kind and sow new seed on earth.
> And none defied his will in this save me,
> I dared to do it, I delivered man
> From death and steep destruction. (*Prom.* 244 ff.)

The *basso continuo* of the Promethean drama is thus given : the inevitability of trespassing. Trespassing, because no one thinks of denying Zeus' exclusive right to dispose of the fire at his own discretion ; inevitable, because without Prometheus' theft the human race would have perished.[30]

We are now far enough to summarize the main implications

of the Promethean myth as presented by Aeschylos or as inter-
preted later, often in variance to, but always in organic
development from, the Aeschylean meaning. These are :

In the first place a sense of deficiency, even of fatal deficiency,
inherent in human existence, and consequently a constitutive
factor of the human *prise de conscience.*

Secondly, man's attempt to remedy this state of affairs is a
manifestation of dynamism which violates the static harmony,
order and *dike* of the cosmic household, whose norm and law is
the will of Father Zeus.

Thirdly, human suffering is conceived as the inevitable concomitant of the equally inevitable wrongdoing. It gains moreover a specifically human depth of agony by being doubled in the
sufferer's consciousness by becoming a suffering of injustice, if not
yet a suffering for the sake of righteousness. Existence is seen as the
tragic equation of 'action is suffering', though not yet of 'suffering
is action'.

Fourthly, the idea of transcendence, by which I mean the extra-
human reality, the 'other' pole : heaven and the gods, is necessarily conceived as personified world-order, impersonal fate, a
cold and hard omnipotence.[31]. It is essential to keep this in mind.
For in spite of his anthropomorphic behaviour, his irascibility
and revengefulness, Zeus is here rather impersonal, cold and
aloof. For our appreciation of the character of Zeus in his relations with Prometheus, i.e. mankind, it is immaterial to define
his precise relation to Fate and

.The three-formed Moires and the remembering Erinies.
                                        (*Prom.* 532)

Actually this relation changes and develops in the drama, and
one of the main interests of Aeschylos is the evolution of Zeus
and of his manner of government, and the final consolidation of
his order. But all this is outside the scope of our present purpose.
What matters here is the fact that Zeus whom Prometheus
opposes is dangerously near the Father of *Paradise Lost*, or rather
that the God of *Paradise Lost* is dangerously near the Zeus of
the Greek drama.[32] The difference between the two lies not with

God, but with his opponents: Prometheus suffers in his own sphere

See what I suffer from the gods, a god! (*Prom.* 92)

whilst Satan sets himself up as a sort of anti-god.

These observations bring us back to the considerations central to our theme. Even as the Greek *hubris* is a dynamic movement of man, by definition conceived as inordinate and as an encroachment, so the action of Prometheus too is an encroachment on the limits imposed on man. Bertrand Russell's definition of *hubris* should be recalled here: 'Where there is vigour, there is a tendency to overstep just bounds.' The punishment that follows *hubris* (*nemesis*) 'restores the eternal order which the aggressor sought to violate'.[33] *Human* consciousness, and its consequence, *human* action, are as such inordinate, a 'too much', a sinful aspiration and rebellious trespass. We are at the point where civilization and culture, which are human consciousness, resourcefulness and power in action, inevitably take on the character of hybridic trespass. The archetypal structure is given which, in certain circumstances and under the influence of certain ideas, can lead to the rather quietistic attitude which we shall find to be inherent in Christianity.

There is of course still another way, which is, however, apt to become a full-fledged antinomianism. It is the way of making a virtue of necessity, and has been chosen by the so-called romantics. Prometheus is now recognized as the prototype of humanity and its few heroes. On this premise it matters little whether the Promethean action and suffering are bewailed as a tragic necessity or exultingly glorified as the apotheosis of heroism. In any case the borderline into the Satanic has been crossed. This can be done with the naïve and ardent idealism of a Shelley, which tries to put itself at ease by distinguishing between Satan's heinous wickedness and Prometheus' virtuous self-sacrifice for humanity; as well as with Blake's thoroughly perverse glorification of passionate energy and his hybridic repudiation of all bounds and limits. Equally characteristic is Saint-Victor's rapturous rhapsody on the history of civilization as a perpetuation of the

Promethean crime.[34] For him, as for all romantics, Prometheus incarnates the genius of mankind. He lives in all the great moments of human progress. He is Roger Bacon, Averroës, Galileo and Giordano Bruno, always victim of the jealousy of the gods and the ingratitude of men. *Le Titan est puni de ses bienfaits, châtié de ses dons; il expia sa science par la souffrance et son génie par la dérision.*[35] Man's agony, victory and despair in his struggle against the iron laws of a superior fate, indifferently dispensing good and evil, is symbolized by Prometheus who is *le prophète permanent, la voix inextinguible de ses cris de l'âme.*[36] The stage of his efforts may have outwardly changed but *ses bourreaux le torturent sous d'autres masques et par d'autres fers; d'autres aigles se relaient sur sa plaie incessamment élargie. Mais Eschyle reconnaitrait encore son Titan dans ce Prométhée transformé qui n'est autre que l'homme éternel.*[37]

I have quoted at some length not only because these passages seem fairly representative of the romantic mind, but mainly because of the conclusions they lead up to. It is the refusal, already to be found in Shelley, to agree to the traditional solution of the drama, and to accept the 'sham peace' imposed on Aeschylos by Greek religious tradition. No, Prometheus perseveres in his revolt and suffering. *Le temps, en détruisant le Prométhée Délivré, a revoqué sa grâce souscrite par Eschyle. Il ne connaît que le Prométhée Enchaîné, il n'admire et il ne comprend que lui seul . . .*[38] Curiously enough, this attitude (Goethe's, Shelley's) recoils from an all-round identification with Satan. Whether this is due to an intuition of the evitability of this identification, or to mere fear, I would not decide here. Suffice it to note that there were others who did not recoil: Blake, Byron and Nietzsche, and that the accusation of devil-worship addressed to the romantics is not quite without foundation.

But the case of Shelley and his similars shows that there is another side to the picture. Mention has already been made of differences between Prometheus and Christ. But these also imply the existence of resemblances: the god who throws in his lot with mankind, who takes upon himself the existential suffering of a humanity otherwise doomed to perdition, or at least to a hopeless impasse, and therefore in vital need of succour, liberation and salvation. *Prometheus* lines 702–74 are unique in classical Greek literature. They are the expectation of a saviour! The analogy becomes still more significant when we consider the role of vicarious suffering in the unbinding of Prometheus. Heracles, sheer male strength, liberates the 'foreknower' Prometheus; but also wounds with his arrow, aimed at the centaur Elatos, Cheiron, another centaur, the good and wise physician. The saviour who disappears in the underworld, taking upon himself the Promethean suffering, is the half-divine, half-animal physician, the healer who bears pain in all eternity. No wonder, then, that in spite of the many profound differences between the two myths, the early Fathers could point to Prometheus as the symbol of Christ.[39] Tertullian[40] speaks of the *crucibus Caucasorum* and exclaims: *Verus Prometheus, deus omnipotens, blasphemiis lancinatus*, whilst others found god-and-man in a bold anagram (*Protheus*), or dilated on the similarities of the sufferings of Prometheus and the passion of Christ, comparing Zeus' eagle to the lance, the Oceanides to the disciples, Cheiron's descent to Hades with that of Christ to hell, the virgin conception of Io and of Mary, and more fond similarities of this sort.[41]

The Promethean myth thus betrays an interesting ambivalence, and shows itself capable of developing in two directions. As a typical Lucifer, 'bringer of light', Prometheus shares the full ambivalence of this archetypal image. He has a light and a dark side, which can either differentiate into two sharply distinguished figures (as has happened with the original Lucifer) or else remain a multivalent, amorphous whole, lending itself, at the bid of occasion, to absorption by and amalgamation with other, more clear-cut and determined images. The Promethean myth can thus point towards Christ as well as towards Satan, according to our susceptibilities and our views about man, as imposed on us by our civilization and the exigencies of our psychic situation.

. . . Early Biblical thought is relatively unconcerned with these problems. Human activity as such is essentially god-willed, nay, even commanded, as long as the right attitude and the right proportions are guarded. To illustrate this one would have to give a phenomenological analysis of the various Biblical stories, laws, ordinances and rites connected with human activity. But even the Jewish *homo faber* lacks all Promethean emotion. As the Rabbis said in the Talmud,[42] God himself created the first pair of tongs just before Sabbath eve, i.e. at the end of his six days' work, and gave them to man, because 'to make tools a first tool is needed'. This is the same God who clothed Adam and Eve[43] and instructed them further,[44] Adam qualifying in the end Cain's posterity as

> . . . inventors rare,
> Unmindful of their maker, though his Spirit
> Taught them, but they his gifts acknowledged none.
> (*P.L.* xi 610–12)

It seems not too much to say that in the question of human progress and self-assertion the pagan i.e. Greek in Milton got the upper hand over the Hebrew. One feels that in Milton's scheme Prometheus is nearer to Satan than to Christ. After all, he is a bringer of light and as such a *lucifer*, like Satan.[45] The circumstances in which Christianity was born made it inevitable that every *lucifer* should be vehemently rejected (except, of course *ille* . . . *Lucifer qui nescit occasum*), and that the bringing of light and fire, in fact every human surge forwards, should be abandoned for that other 'light of the world' whose passion, death, and resurrection were to supplement the dramatic 'action is suffering' with the messianic, or rather Christian, 'suffering is action'.[46] Moreover, the fact that the Son has to mediate between God the Father and mankind, tends to give the former the inhuman remoteness of Zeus, turns him into Raleigh's 'whimsical tyrant', and is also responsible for Blake's equation that with Milton 'the Father is Destiny'. M. Saurat, who heartily agrees with this,[47] quotes in support :

> As they would confine th' interminable,
> And tie him to his own prescript,
> Who made our Laws to bind us, not himself
> (*Samson Agonistes,* 307–9)

lines remarkably similar to Aeschylos'

> None is free but Zeus. (*Prom.* 50)

Although the Biblical Satan, even the post-Biblical and patristic Lucifer, is the product of a very different psychic constellation than the one that produced Prometheus, there are enough inherent similarities to make contaminations and amalgamations possible. The initial development depends on the sort of 'fatherhood' ascribed to God. It can be that of Zeus, the Olympian *pater familias,* guardian of custom, law and the present order; in other words the father-image functioning as the mediator of the (conservative) collective conscience. But it can also be that of the Biblical God, which is the transpersonal imperative for a creative change and movement towards new levels. This is the God of Abraham who said : 'Get thee out of thy country, and from thy kindred, and from thy father's house, unto the land that I will show thee'.[48] Appropriately enough, rabbinical legend tells that as a true revolutionary, Abraham, before leaving, destroyed all his father Terah's idols.[49] Historical Christianity, one must conclude, has chosen the former. The Christian acceptance of the ambivalent Greek *hubris*-complex, combined with a Hebrew sense of a calling by and relation to a personal God, could easily create a situation where every human act must be a sinful trespass, and where in fact there can be no escape except the intervention of divine grace. Not only is this very different from the old Jewish idea of God, to whom the people have direct and immediate contact and who, in spite of occasional outbursts, nevertheless loves his people and yearns for them. It is tantamount to saying that every human act, as long as it is merely *human,* is hybridic, Promethean, and of the devil. In other words, every human move is condemned. The only thing that matters is Christ's move towards us, and (possibly) our response. Implicitly this contains a condemnation of civilization of which the Greek myth in itself can hardly be said to be guilty in this form, but into which its archetypal meaning could develop and be intensified, when absorbed into the Christian climate. Professor Grierson is certainly right when saying that the 'pessimism' ascribed by Dr Tillyard to Milton personally, is actually inherent in the Evangelicism of Milton's time and 'indeed . . . in Christianity in any form that is historical'.

SOURCE : *Lucifer and Prometheus* (1952).

NOTES

1. Preface to *Prometheus Unbound*. See also Macaulay's essay.
2. G. Rostrevor Hamilton, *Hero or Fool? A Study of Milton's Satan* (1944), p. 37.
3. Ibid., p. 41.
4. The problem of heroism and folly actually deserves a special study. It seems as if heroism, at least a certain very widespread conception of it, can never be far away from folly. That is also why the unheroic attitude is at times not cowardly but realistic.
5. Hamilton, op. cit., p. 37.
6. To which we should also reckon Schiller. See the highly interesting quotations in Mario Praz, *The Romantic Agony* (Oxford, 1933), p. 57. On the Promethean aspect see also Rex Warner's introduction to his translation of the *Prometheus Bound* (The Bodley Head, London, 1947), pp. 8–10.
7. A good example of the 'romantic' interpretation of Prometheus can be found in P. de Saint Victor's *Les Deux Masques* (3rd ed., 1883), vol. I, chaps. 9 and 10.
8. E.g. 'adamantine chains', *P.L.* I 48 with *Prom.* 6; 'Arimaspian', *P.L.* II 945 with *Prom.* 831; 'flaming sun', *P.L.* VIII 162 with *Prom.* 817. Phrases and similes like the 'proud steed reined', *P.L.* IV 858–60 with *Prom.* 1041–2 (almost literally translated); 'spite with spite', *P.L.* IX 178 with *Prom.* 1002; etc.
9. 'Typologische Literaturbetrachtung', *Englische Studien*, LXIV (1929).
10. Cf. C. G. Osgood, *The Classical Mythology of Milton's English Poems* (1900), pp. xlii–xliii.
11. *Tusc. Disp.* ii, 10.
12. *Vermischte Gedichte. Prometheus.*
13. For the evolution of the Prometheus figure in literature, see Karl Heinemann, *Die tragischen Gestalten der Griechen in der Weltliteratur* (1920), vol. I, chap. 2, which, though mainly concentrating on European drama (Calderon, Goethe, Shelley, Edgar Quinet, etc.), also discusses Byron, Spitteler and others; and Margarete Ostrowski-Sachs, 'Die Wandlungen des Prometheus-Mythus' in *Der Psychologe*, II 7–8 (Sonderheft zum 75. Geburtstag von C. G. Jung, 1950), pp. 334–43, a rather short but readable survey of the trend of the development of the myth.
14. On Prometheus, see Roscher's *Lexicon*, 3.2, 3032–110, and, for a recent very profound study, Karl Kerényi, *Prometheus*

(Zürich, 1946), which is a further elaboration of the interpretation given by the same author in his *Die Antike Religion*, pp. 157–62.

15. 'Of one race, one only, are men and gods; both of one mother's womb we draw our breath : but far asunder is all our power divided and parts us – here there is nought and there is strength of bronze, a seat unshaken, eternal, abides the heaven above.' (Pindar, *Nemea*, VI 1–5). The same is said by Hesiod, *Works and Days*, 108. See also Kerényi, op. cit., pp. 1A–15.

16. Kerényi, op. cit., pp. 9 and 54–5.

17. Ibid., pp. 22–3.

18. *Theogony*, 535 ff.

19. See Ostrowski-Sachs, art. cit., p. 335.

20. On intelligence and the *homo faber* see Henri Bergson, *L'Evolution Créatrice*, 62nd ed. (1946), pp. 138 ff.

21. For the relation of this profound psychological ambivalence to cultural and sociological problems, and in particular to our modern crisis, see E. Fromm, *The Fear of Freedom* (1945).

22. Cf. Fromm, op. cit.

23. 1883. A short account of the two last mentioned can be found in Heinemann, op. cit., pp. 37 and 32.

24. The other alternative for man would be to conceive of himself *a priori* as created in God's image. In the biblical sphere man's protection against the danger of hybridic inflation and arrogated god-like mastery over nature, would be the institution of the Sabbath. That the commandment not only of rest, but negatively of abstention from work (Exod. 20 :10; Deut. 5 :14; Exod. 31 :13–15, 35 :2) is a literally 'religious' self-limitation before the Lord of All, is clearly brought out by the juxtaposed motivations : because God is the creator of the world (Exod. 20 :11, 31 :17) and because Israel was a servant in the land of Egypt whence they were brought out through a mighty hand and a stretched-out arm (Deut. 5 :15), the corollary obviously being that 'unto me the children of Israel are servants; they are my servants whom I have brought forth out of the land of Egypt : I am the Lord your God' (Lev. 25 :55). For the rest all the learned critical disquisitions on the double motivation of the Sabbath-law are completely beside the point. As further evidence of the relation of the Sabbath to the Promethean problem, one might add that the prohibition of work is always couched in general terms without any detail : 'Thou shalt not do any work', with but one notable exception : 'Ye shall kindle no fire throughout your habitations upon the sabbath day' (Exod. 35 :3).

25. Hesiod, *Theogony*, 540, 546, 701, etc., Aesch., *Prom.* 251 ff.

26. Op. cit., pp. 20–1 and 56.

27. Op. cit., p. 30.

28. Or : 'Thou seest how unjustly I suffer.'

29. *Works and Days*, 42–6.

30. This was clearly the intention of Zeus. It should be noted, however, that according to one possible interpretation, Prometheus' solicitude for mankind, which overlooked its essential limitations, frustrated the purpose of Zeus which was (Hesiod) to create another, more permanent race after this one had passed away. (Aesch. *Prom.* 247–9.) Because of Prometheus, humanity survives in permanent and irreparable limitations. The myth might consequently be described as a sort of theodicy.

31. *Prom.* 156–9, 173–4.

32. See also Grierson, *Milton and Wordsworth*, pp. 105 ff. It should be noted in this connection that the 'divine irony' so much talked about by Milton critics is actually the same thing as the 'homeric' laugh of the Greek gods. On the latter see Kerényi, *Die Antike Religion*, pp. 163 ff.

33. *History of Western Philosophy* (1946), pp. 134–5.

34. Op. cit., pp. 339–42.

35. Ibid., p. 340.

36. Ibid., p. 342.

37. Ibid., p. 342.

38. Ibid., p. 345.

39. Cf. also Shelley, *Prometheus Unbound*, Act I, 578–85, and Heinemann's account of Quinet's trilogy (op. cit., pp. 32–3) and of Siegfried Lipiner's epic, *Der Eintfesselte Prometheus* (1875) (ibid., pp. 34–5).

40. *Adv. Marc.* I, I.

41. Saint Victor, op. cit., pp. 335–7.

42. Aboth 5 :9.

43. Gen. 3 :21.

44. Cf. also *P.L.* x 1056–62 ff.

45. The identification of Lucifer (Isa. 14:12) with Satan, though a notorious historical error, is nevertheless a genuine and profound psychological intuition.

46. It is the redemptive i.e. active character of suffering which constitutes the great contribution of the Servant chapters of *Isaiah*, and which gives them that messianic quality on which later christology could legitimately draw, in spite of the orthodox exegetical nonsense which it entailed. It is this same quality which is just outside the reach of the Greek dramatist.

47. Denis Saurat, *Milton Man and Thinker* (1925), pp. 105 and 130 ff.

48. Gen. 12 : 1.

49. Of course even the Jewish God, once having given laws and commandments, could not help becoming a conservative *pater familias* himself. Like Abraham, Jesus had to be an iconoclast and revolutionary. In due course the time came for his so-called successors to be the pillars of reactionary conservatism. Nevertheless, the emergence of the revolutionary, prophetic, 'calling' God, out of the Jewish unconscious, and the relatively high number of Jews in revolutionary movements of all sorts, not only partly substantiates some of the stock antisemitic contentions, but also throws a new light on their springs and basic motives.

Stanley Fish

THE HARASSED READER IN
PARADISE LOST (1965)

I

I would like to suggest something about *Paradise Lost* that is not
new except for the literalness with which the point will be made :
(1) the poem's centre of reference is its reader who is also its
subject; (2) Milton's purpose is to educate the reader to an
awareness of his position and responsibilities as a fallen man, and
to a sense of the distance which separates him from the innocence
once his; (3) Milton's method is to recreate in the mind of the
reader (which is, finally, the poem's scene) the drama of the
Fall, to make him fall again exactly as Adam did, and with
Adam's troubled clarity, that is to say, 'not deceived'. In a
limited sense few would deny the truth of my first two statements;
Milton's concern with the ethical imperatives of political and
social behavior would hardly allow him to write an epic which
did not attempt to give his audience a basis for moral action; but
I do not think the third has been accepted in the way that I intend
it.

A. J. Waldock, one of many sensitive readers who have confronted the poem since 1940, writes that '*Paradise Lost* is an
epic poem of singularly hard and definite outline, expressing itself (or so at least would be our first impressions) with unmistakable clarity and point'.[1] In the course of his book, Waldock ex-
pands the reservation indicated by his parenthesis into a reading
which predictates a disparity between Milton's intention and his
performance :

In a sense Milton's central theme denied him the full expression of
his deepest interests. It was likely, then, that as his really deep
interests could not find outlet in his poem in the right way they

may find outlet in the wrong way. And to a certain extent they do; they find vents and safety-valves often in inopportune places. Adam cannot give Milton much scope to express what he really feels about life : but Satan is there, Satan gives him scope. And the result is that the balance is somewhat disturbed; pressures are set up that are at times disquieting, that seem to threaten more than once, indeed, the equilibrium of the poem.[2]

The 'unconscious meaning' portion of Waldock's thesis is, I think, as wrong as his description of the reading experience as 'disquieting' is right. If we transfer the emphasis from Milton's interests and intentions which are available to us only from a distance, to our responses which are available directly, the disparity between intention and execution becomes a disparity between reader expectation and reading experience; and the resulting 'pressures' can be seen as part of an intelligible pattern. In this way we are led to consider our own experience as a part of the poem's subject.

By 'hard and definite outline' I take Waldock to mean the sense of continuity and direction evoked by the simultaneous introduction of the epic tradition and Christian myth. The 'definiteness' of a genre classification leads the reader to expect a series of formal stimuli – martial encounters, complex similes, an epic voice – to which his response is more or less automatic; the hardness of the Christian myth predetermines his sympathies; the union of the two allows the assumption of a comfortable reading experience in which conveniently labelled protagonists act out rather simple roles in a succession of familiar situations. The reader is prepared to hiss the devil off the stage and applaud the pronouncements of a partisan and somewhat human deity who is not unlike Tasso's 'il Padre eterno'. But of course this is not the case; no sensitive reading of *Paradise Lost* tallies with these expectations, and it is my contention that Milton ostentatiously calls them up in order to provide his reader with the shock of their disappointment. This is not to say merely that Milton communicates a part of his meaning by a calculated departure from convention; every poet does that; but that Milton consciously wants to worry his reader, to force him to doubt the correctness of his responses, and to bring him to the realization that his inability to read the poem with any confidence in his own perception is its focus.

Milton's programme of reader harassment begins in the opening lines; the reader, however, may not be aware of it until line 84 when Satan speaks for the first time. The speech is a powerful one, moving smoothly from the *exclamatio* of 'But O how fallen' (84) to the regret and apparent logic of 'till then who knew/The force of those dire arms' (93–4), the determination of 'courage never to submit or yield' (108) and the grand defiance of 'Irreconcilable, to our grand foe,/Who now triumphs, and in the excess of joy/Sole reigning holds the tyranny of heaven' (122–4). This is our first view of Satan and the impression given, reinforced by a succession of speeches in Book I, is described by Waldock : 'fortitude in adversity, enormous endurance, a certain splendid recklessness, remarkable powers of rising to an occasion, extraordinary qualities of leadership (shown not least in his salutary taunts)'.[3] But in each case Milton follows the voice of Satan with a comment which complicates, and according to some, falsifies, our reaction to it :

> So spake the apostate angel, though in pain,
> Vaunting aloud, but racked with deep despair. (125–6)

Waldock's indignation at this authorial intrusion is instructive :

If one observes what is happening one sees that there is hardly a great speech of Satan's that Milton is not at pains to correct, to damp down and neutralize. He will put some glorious thing in Satan's mouth, then anxious about the effect of it, will pull us gently by the sleeve, saying (for this is what it amounts to) : 'Do not be carried away by this fellow : he *sounds* splendid, but take my word for it . . .' Has there been much despair in what we have just been listening to? The speech would almost seem to be incompatible with that. To accept Milton's comment here . . . as if it had a validity equal to that of the speech itself is surely very naive critical procedure . . . in any work of imaginative literature at all it is the demonstration, by the very nature of the case, that has the higher validity; an allegation can possess no comparable authority. Of course they should agree; but if they do not then the demonstration must carry the day. (pp. 77–8)

There are several assumptions here: (1) There is a disparity between our response to the speech and the epic voice's evaluation of it. (2) Ideally, there should be no disparity. (3) Milton's intention is to correct *his* error. (4) He wants us to discount the effect of the speech through a kind of mathematical cancellation. (5) The question of relative authority is purely an aesthetic one. That is, the reader is obliged to harken to the most dramatically persuasive of any conflicting voices. Of these I can assent only to the first. The comment of the epic voice comes as a shock to the reader who at once realizes that it does not tally with his experience. It is not enough to analyze, as Lewis and others have, the speciousness of Ṣatan's rhetoric. It is the nature of sophistry to lull the reasoning process; logic is a safeguard against a rhetorical effect only after the effect has been noted. The deep distrust, even fear, of verbal manipulation in the seventeenth century is a recognition of the fact that there is no adequate defense against eloquence at the moment of impact. (Thus the insistence in the latter half of the century on the complete absence of rhetoric. The Royal Society, Sprat promises, will 'separate the knowledge of Nature from the colours of Rhetorick, the devices of Fancy, or the delightful deceit of Fables.)[4] In other words one can analyze the process of deception only after it is successful. The reader who is stopped short by Milton's rebuke (for so it is) will, perhaps, retrace his steps and note more carefully the inconsistency of a 'tyranny' that involves an excess of joy, the perversity of 'study of revenge, immortal hate' (a line that had slipped past him sandwiched respectably, between will and courage), the sophistry of the transfer of power from the Potent Victor of 95 to the Fate of 116, and the irony, in the larger picture, of 'that were *low* indeed' and 'in *foresight* more advanced'. The fit reader Milton has in mind would go further and recognize in Satan's finest moment – 'And courage never to submit or yield' – an almost literal translation of *Georgic IV*, 84, 'usque adeo obnixi non cedere'. Virgil's 'praise' is for his bees whose heroic posturing is presented in terms that are at least ambiguous:

ipsi per medias acies insignibus alis
ingentis animos angusto in pectore versant,

usque adeo obnixi non cedere, dum gravis aut hos
aut hos versa fuga victor dare terga subegit.
hi motus animorum atque haec certaimina tanta
pulveris exigui iactu compressa quiescunt. (82–7)[5]

If we apply these verses to Satan, the line in question mocks him
and in the unique time scheme of *Paradise Lost* looks both backward (the Victor has already driven the rebel host to flight) and
forward (in terms of the reading experience, the event is yet to
come). I believe that all this and more is there, but that the complexities of the passage will be apparent only when the reader has
been led to them by the necessity of accounting for the distance
between his initial response and the *obiter dictum* of the epic
voice. When he is so led, the reader is made aware that Milton
is correcting not a mistake of composition, but the weakness all
men evince in the face of eloquence. The error is his not Milton's;
and when Waldock invokes some unidentified critical principle
('they should agree') he objects to an effect Milton anticipates
and desires.

But this is more than a stylistic trick to assure the perception
of irony. For, as Waldock points out, this first epic interjection
introduces a pattern that is operative throughout. In Books I and
II these 'correctives' are particularly numerous and, if the word
can be used here, tactless. Waldock falsifies his experience of the
poem I think, when he characterizes Milton's countermands as
gentle; we are not warned ('Do not be carried away by this
fellow'), but accused, taunted by an imperious voice which says
with no consideration of our feelings, 'I know that you *have been*
carried away by what you have just heard; you should not have
been; you have made a mistake, just as I knew you would'; and
we resent this rebuke, not, as Waldock suggests, because our
aesthetic sense balks at a clumsy attempt to neutralize an unin-
tentional effect, but because a failing has been exposed in a context that forces us to acknowledge it. We are angry at the epic
voice, not for fudging, but for being right, for insisting that we
become our own critics. There is little in the human situation more
humiliating in both senses of the word, than the public acceptance of a deserved rebuke. Arnold Stein writes, 'the formal

perspective does not force itself upon Satan's speech, does not label and editorialize the impressive willfulness out of existence; but rather sets up a dramatic conflict between the local context of the immediate utterance and the larger context of which the formal perspective is expression. This conflict marks . . . the tormented relationship between the external boast and the internal despair'.[6] Stein's comment is valuable, but it ignores the way the reader is drawn into the poem not as an observer who coolly notes the interaction of patterns (this is the mode of Jonsonian comedy and masque), but as a participant whose mind is the locus of that interaction. Milton insists on this since his concern with the reader is necessarily more direct than it might be in any other poem; and to grant the reader the status of the slightly arrogant perceiver-of-ironies Stein invents would be to deny him the full *benefit* (I use the word deliberately, confident that Milton would approve) of the reading experience. Stein's 'dramatic conflict' is there as are his various perspectives, but they are actualized, that is translated into felt meaning, only through the more pervasive drama (between reader and poem) I hope to describe.

The result of such encounters is the adoption of a new way of reading. After I, 125–6 the reader proceeds determined not to be caught out again; but invariably he is. If Satanic pronouncements are now met with a certain caution, if there is a new willingness to search for complexities and ironies beneath simple surfaces, this mental armour is never quite strong enough to resist the insidious attack of verbal power; and always the irritatingly omniscient epic voice is there to point out a deception even as it succeeds. As the poem proceeds and this little drama is repeated, the reader's only gain is an awareness of what is happening to him; he understands that his responses are being controlled and mocked by the same authority, and realizes that while his efforts to free himself from this rhetorical bind are futile, that very futility becomes a way to self-knowledge. *Control* is the important concept here, for my claim is not merely that this pattern is in the poem (it would be difficult to find one that is not), but that Milton (*a*) consciously put it there and (*b*) expected his reader to notice it. Belial's speech in Book II is a

case in point. It is the only speech that merits an introductory
warning :

> On the other side up rose
> Belial, in act more graceful and humane;
> A fairer person lost not heaven; he seemed
> For dignity composed and high exploit :
> But all was false and hollow; though his tongue
> Droppt manna, and could make the worse appear
> The better reason, to perplex and dash
> Maturest counsels : for his thoughts were low;
> To vice industrious, but to nobler deeds
> Timorous and slothful : yet he pleased the ear,
> And with persuasive accent thus began. (II 108–18)

The intensity of the warning indicates the extent of the danger :
Belial's apparent solidity, which is visible, must be contrasted to
his hollowness, which is not, the manna of his tongue to the low-
ness of mind it obscures; and the 'yet' in 'yet he pleased the ear',
more than a final admonition before the reader is to be left to
his own resources, is an admission of wonder by the epic voice
itself (*yet*, he pleased . . .) and one of the early cracks in its
façade of omniscience. Belial's appeal is a skilful union of logical
machinery ('*First*, what revenge?') and rhetorical insinuation.
The easy roll of his periods literally cuts through the contortions
of Moloch's bluster, and the series of *traductio*-s around the word
'worse' are an indirect comment on the 'what can be worse' of
the 'sceptred king's' desperation. The ploys are effective, and since
in the attempt to measure the relative merits of the two devils we
forget that their entire counsel is baseless, the return of the epic
voice yields one more slight shock at the inevitability of our
susceptibility :

> Thus Belial with words clothed in reason's garb
> Counselled ignoble ease, and peaceful sloth,
> Not peace : (II 226–8)

Waldock complains, 'Belial's words are not only "clothed in
reason's garb"; they *are* reasonable'.[7] Belial's words are *not*
reasonable, although a single uncritical reading will yield the

appearance of reason rather than the reality of his ignoble ease. Again the flaw in the speech is to be located precisely at its strongest point. Belial cries at line 146: 'for who would lose,/ Though full of pain, this intellectual being,/Those thoughts that wander through eternity,/To perish rather, swallowed up and lost/In the wide womb of uncreated night'. In other words, do we wish to give up our nature, our sense of identity? The rhetorical question evokes an emphatic 'no' from the assembled devils and the reader. Yet at line 215 Belial offers his final argument, the possibility of adapting to their now noxious environment: 'Our purer essence then will overcome/Their noxious vapour, or enured not feel,/Or changed at length, and to the place conformed/In temper and in nature, will receive/Familiar the fierce heat, and void of pain'. If this is less spectacular than the question posed at 146, it is still a direct answer to that question, Belial *is* willing to lose 'this intellectual being'. The choice is not, as he suggests, between annihilation and continued existence, but between different kinds of annihilation – Moloch's suicidal thrust at the Almighty or his own gradual surrender of identity, no less suicidal, much less honest. This will be obvious on a second reading. My intention is not to refute Waldock, but to suggest that while his reaction to the epic voice ('they *are* reasonable') is the correct one, Milton expects his reader to go beyond it, to see in the explicitness of the before and after warnings an immediate challenge to his own assessment of the speech.

It is almost a laboratory demonstration, especially since the case is an easy one; Belial's rhetoric calls attention to itself and is thus less dangerous than other lures the reader has met and will continue to meet throughout the poem. The whole is reminiscent of Spenser's technique in the *Faerie Queene,* 1 9. There the approach to Despair's cave is pointedly detailed and the detail is calculated to repel; the man himself is more terrible than the Blatant Beast or the dragon of 1 12, for his ugliness is something we recognize. Spenser's test of his reader is less stringent than Milton's; he makes his warning the experience of this description rather than an abstract statement of disapproval. It is, of course, not enough. Despair's adaptation of Christian rhetoric (guilt, grace) is masterful and the Redcross Knight (along with the reader) allows the impression of one set of appearances (the old man's ugliness) to be effaced by another (the Circean lure of his rhetoric): 'Sleepe after toyle, port after stormie seas,/Ease after warre, death after life does greatly please' (40). Spenser eases us along by making it impossible to assign stanza 42 to either the knight or Despair. At that point the syntactical ambiguity is telling; the dialogue is over, and we have joined them both in a three part unanimity that leads inexorably to the decision of 51 :

> At last, resolv'd to worke his finall smart
> He lifted up his hand that backe again did start.

Una's exhortation and accusation – 'Come, come away, fraile, feeble, fleshly wight' – is for us as well as her St George, and we need the reminder that she brings to us from a context *outside* the experience of the poem : 'In heavenly mercies hast thou not a part?' Without this *deus ex machina* we could not escape; without Milton's 'snubs' we could not be jolted out of a perspective that is after all *ours*. The lesson in both poems is that the only defense against verbal manipulation (or appearances) is a commitment that stands above the evidence of things that are seen, and the method of both poems is to lead us beyond our perspective by making us feel its inadequacies and the necessity of accepting something which badly contradicts it. The result is instruction, and instruction is possible only because the reader is asked to observe, analyze, and *place* his experience, that is to think about it.

II

The wariness these encounters with demonic attraction make us feel is part of a larger pattern in which we are taught the hardest of all lessons, distrust of our own abilities and perceptions. This distrust extends to all the conventional ways of knowing that might enable a reader to locate himself in the world of any poem. The questions we ask of our reading experience are in large part the questions we ask of our day to day experience. Where are we, what are the physical components of our surroundings, what time is it? And while the hard and clear outline of *Paradise Lost* suggests that the answers to these questions are readily available to us, immediate contexts repeatedly tell us that they are not. Consider, for example, the case of Satan's spear. I have seen responsible critics affirm, casually, that Satan's spear is as large as the mast of a ship; the poem of course affirms nothing of the kind, but, more important, it deliberately encourages such an affirmation, at least temporarily :

> His spear, to equal which the tallest pine
> Hewn on Norwegian hills to be the mast
> Of some great ammiral, were but a wand. (1 292–4)

Throughout *Paradise Lost*, Milton relies on the operation of three truths so obvious that many critics fail to take them into account : (1) the reading experience takes place in time, that is, we necessarily read one word after another; (2) the childish habit of moving the eyes along a page and back again is never really abandoned although in maturity the movement is more mental than physical, and defies measurement; therefore the line as a unit is a resting place even when rhyme is absent; (3) a mind asked to order a succession of rapidly given bits of detail (mental or physical) seizes on the simplest scheme of organization which offers itself. In this simile, the first line supplies that scheme in the overt comparison between the spear and the tallest pine, and the impression given is one of equality. This is not necessarily so, since logically the following lines could assert any number of things about the relationship between the two objects; but because they are objects, offering the mind the convenience of focal points that are concrete, and because they are linked in the reading sequence by an abstract term of relationship (equal), the reader is encouraged to take from the line an image, however faint and wavering, of the two side by side. As he proceeds that image will be reinforced, since Milton demands that he attach to it the information given in 293 and the first half of 294; that is, in order to maintain the control over the text that a long syntactical unit tends to diminish, the reader will accept 'hewn on Norwegian hills' as an adjunct of the tallest pine in a very real way. By providing a scene or background (*memoria*) the phrase allows him to strengthen his hold on what now promises to be an increasingly complex statement of relationships. And in the construction of that background the pine frees itself from the hypothetical blur of the first line; it is now real, and through an unavoidable process of association the spear which stood in an undefined relationship to an undefined pine is seen (and I mean the word literally) in a kind of apposition to a conveniently visual pine. (This all happens very quickly in the mind of the reader who does not have time to analyze the cerebral adjustments forced upon him by the simile.) In short the equation (in size) of the two objects, in 292 only a possibility, is posited by the reader in 292–4 because is simplifies his task; and this movement towards simplification will be encouraged, for Milton's fit reader, by the obvious reference in 'to be the mast/Of some great ammiral' to the staff of the Cyclops Polyphemus, identified in the *Aeneid* as a lopped pine[8] and likened in the *Odyssey* to 'the mast of some black ship of twenty oars'.[9]

The construction of the image and the formulation of the relationship between its components are blocked by the second half of line 294, 'were but a wand'. This does several things, and I must resort to the mechanical aid of enumeration : (1) in the confusion that follows this rupture of the reading sequence, the reader loses his hold on the visual focal points, and is unable to associate firmly the wand with either of them. The result is the momentary diminution of Satan's spear as well as the pine, although a second, and more wary reading, will correct this; but, corrected, the impression remains (in line 295 a miniature Satan supports himself on a wand-like spear) and in the larger perspective, this aspect of the simile is one of many instances in the poem where Milton's praise of Satan is qualified even as it is bestowed.

(2) The simile illustrates Milton's solution of an apparently insoluble problem. How does a poet provide for his audience a perspective that is beyond the field of its perception? To put the case in terms of *Paradise Lost*, the simile as it functions in other poems will not do here. A simile, especially an epic simile, is an attempt to place persons and/or things, perceived in *a* time and *a* space, in the larger perspective from which their significance

must finally be determined. This is possible because the components of the simile have a point of contact – their existence in the larger perspective – which allows the poem to yoke them together without identifying them. Often, part of the statement a simile makes concerns the relationship between the components and the larger perspective in addition to the more obvious relationship between the components themselves; poets suggest this perspective with words like smaller and greater. Thus a trapped hero is at once like and unlike a trapped wolf, and the difference involves their respective positions in a hierarchy that includes more than the physical comparison. A complex and 'tight' simile then can be an almost scientific description of a bit of the world in which for 'the immediate relations of the crude data of experience' are substituted 'more refined logical entities, such as relations between relations, or classes of relations, or classes of classes of relations'.[10] In Milton's poem, however, the components of a simile often do not have a point of contact that makes their comparison possible in a meaningful (i.e. relatable or comprehensible) way. A man exists and a wolf exists and if categories are enlarged sufficiently it can be said without distortion that they exist on a comparable level; a man exists and Satan (or God) exists, but any statement that considers their respective existences from a human perspective, however inclusive, is necessarily reductive, and is liable to falsify rather than clarify; and of course the human perspective is the only one available. To return to Book 1, had Milton asserted the identity of Satan's spear and the tallest pine, he would not only have sacrificed the awe that attends incomprehensibility; he would also have lied, since clearly the personae of his extra-terrestrial drama are not confined within the limitations of our time and space. On the other hand, had he said that the spear is larger than one can imagine, he would have sacrificed the concreteness so necessary to the formulation of an effective image. What he does instead is grant the reader the convenience of concreteness (indeed fill his mind with it) and then tell him that what he sees is not what is there ('there' is never located). The result is almost a feat of prestidigitation: for the rhetorical negation of the scene so painstakingly constructed does not erase it; we are relieved of the necessity of believing the image true, but permitted to retain the solidity it offers our straining imaginations. Paradoxically, our awareness of the inadequacy of what is described and what we can apprehend provides, if only negatively, a sense of what cannot be described and what we cannot apprehend. Thus Milton is able to suggest a reality beyond this one by forcing us to feel, dramatically, its unavailability.

(3) Finally, the experience of reading the simile tells us a great deal about ourselves. How large is Satan's spear? The answer is, we don't know, although it is important that for a moment we think we do. Of course, one can construct, as James Whaler does, a statement of relative magnitudes (spear is to pine as pine is to wand)[11] but while this may be logical, it is not encouraged by the logic of the reading experience which says to us: If one were to compare Satan's spear with the tallest pine the comparison would be inadequate. I submit that any attempt either to search out masts of Norwegian ships or determine the mean length of wands is irrelevant, however attractive the prospect to a certain kind of mind.

Another instance may make the case clearer. In Book III, Satan lands on the Sun:

> There lands the fiend, a spot like which perhaps
> Astronomer in the sun's lucent orb
> Through his glazed optic tube yet never saw. (588–90)

Again in the first line two focal points (spot and fiend) are offered the reader who sets them side by side in his mind; again the detail of the next one and one half lines is attached to the image, and a scene is formed, strengthening the implied equality of spot and fiend; indeed the physicality of the impression is so persuasive that the reader is led to join the astronomer and looks with him through a reassuringly specific telescope ('glazed optic tube') to see – nothing at all ('yet never saw'). In both similes the reader is encouraged to assume that his perceptions extend to the object the poet would present, only to be informed that he is in error; and both similes are constructed in such a way that the error must be made before it can be acknowledged by a surprised reader. (The parallel to the rhetorical drama between demonic attraction and authorial rebuke should be obvious.) For, however many times the simile is reread, the 'yet never saw' is unexpected. The mind can not perform two operations at the same time, and one can either cling to the imminence of the disclaimer and repeat, silently, ' "yet never saw" is coming, "yet never saw" is coming', or yield to the demands of the image and attend to its construction; and since the choice is really no choice at all -- after each reading the negative is only a memory and cannot complete with the immediacy of the sensory evocation – the tail-like half line always surprises.

Of course Milton wants the reader to pull himself up and re-read, for this provides a controlled framework within which he is able to realize the extent and implication of his difficulty, much like the framework provided by the before and after warnings surrounding Belial's speech. The implication is personal; the similes and many other effects, say to the reader : 'I know that you rely upon your senses for your apprehension of reality, but they are unreliable and hopelessly limited'. Significantly, Galileo is introduced in both similes; the Tuscan artist's glass represents the furthest extension of human perception, and that is not enough. The entire pattern, of which the instances I analyze here are the smallest part, is, among other things, a preparation for the moment in Book VIII when Adam responds to Raphael's astronomical dissertation : 'To whom thus Adam cleared of doubt'. Reader reaction is involuntary : cleared of doubt? by that impossibly tortuous and equivocal description of two all too probable universes?[12] By this point, however, we are able to place our reaction, since Adam's experience here parallels ours in so many places (and a large part of the poem's meaning is com-municated by our awareness of the relationship between Adam and ourselves). He *is* cleared of doubt, not because he now knows how the universe is constructed, but because he knows that he can not know; what clears him of doubt is the certainty of self-doubt, and as with us this certainty is the result of a superior's willingness to grant him, momentarily, the security of his per-spective. Milton's lesson is one that twentieth century science is just now beginning to learn :

Finally, I come to what it seems to me may well be from the long range point of view the most revolutionary of the insights to be derived from our recent experiences in physics, more revolutionary than the insights afforded by the discoveries of Galileo and Newton, or of Darwin. This is the insight that it is impossible to transcend the human reference point . . . The new insight comes from a realization that the structure of nature may eventually be such that our processes of thought do not correspond to it sufficiently to permit us to think about it at all.[13]

In *Paradise Lost,* our sense of time proves as illusory as our sense of space and physicality. Jackson Cope quotes with approval Sigfried Giedion and Joseph Frank who find in modern literature a new way of thinking about time :

The flow of time which has its literary reflection in the Aristotelian development of an action having beginning, middle and end is . . . frozen into the labyrinthe planes of a spatial block which . . . can only be perceived by travelling both temporally and physically from point to point, but whose form has neither beginning, middle, end nor center, and must be effectively conceived as a simultaneity of multiple views.[14]

And Mrs Isabel MacCaffrey identifies the 'simultaneity of multiple views' with the eternal moment of God, a moment she argues that Milton makes ours :

The long view of time as illusory, telescoped into a single vision, had been adopted in fancy by Christian writers . . . Writing of Heaven and the little heaven of Paradise, Milton by a powerful releasing act of the imagination transposed the intuitive single glance of God into the poem's mythical structure. Our vision of history becomes for the time being that of the Creator 'whose eye/ Views all things at one view' (ii 189–90); like him, we are stationed on a 'prospect high/Wherein past, present, future he beholds'. (iii 77–8)[15]

The experience of every reader, I think, affirms the truth of these statements; Milton does convince us that the world of his poem is a static one which 'slight chronology in favor of a folded structure which continually returns upon itself, or a spiral that circles about a single center'.[16] The question I would ask is how does he so convince us? His insistence on simultaneity is easily documented. How many times do we see Christ ascend, after the war in Heaven, after the passion, after Harrowing Hell, after giving Satan his death wound, after the creation, after the final conflagration, at the day of final judgment? How many times do our first parents fall, and how many times are they accorded grace? The answer to all these questions is, 'many times' or is it all the time (at each point of time) or perhaps at one, and the same, time. My difficulty with the preceding sentence is a part of my point : I cannot let go of the word 'time' and the idea of sequence; timelessness (I am forced to resort to a question-begging negative) is an interesting concept, but we are all of us trapped in the necessity of experiencing in time, and the attempt even to conceive of a state where words like day and evening measure space rather than duration is a difficult one; Chaucer's Troilus, among others, is defeated by it. Mrs MacCaffrey asserts that 'spatial imagining' is part of Milton's 'mental climate' and the researches of Walter Ong, among others, support her; but if Milton has implanted the eternal moment 'into the poem's mythical structure', how does the reader, who, in Cope's words, must travel 'temporally and physically from point to point', root it out? Obviously many readers do not; witness the critics who are troubled by contradictory or 'impossible' sequences and inartistic repetitions. Again the reactions of these anti-Miltonists are the surest guide to the poet's method; for it is only by encouraging and then 'breaking' conventional responses and expectations that Milton can point his reader beyond them. To return to Waldock, part of the poem's apparently 'hard and definite' outline is the easy chronology it seems to offer; but the pressures of innumerable local contexts demand adjustments that give the lie to the illusion of sequence and reveal in still another way the inability of the reader to consider this poem as he would any other.

In the opening lines of Book 1 chronology and sequence are suggested at once in what is almost a plot line : man disobeys, eats fruit, suffers woe and awaits rescue. It is a very old and simple story, one that promises a comfortable correlation of plot station and emotional response: horror and fear at the act, sorrow at the result, joy at the happy ending, the whole bound up in the certain knowledge of cause and effect. As Milton crowds more history into his invocation the reader, who likes to know what time it is, will attempt to locate each detail on the continuum of his story line. The inspiration of the shepherd, Moses, is easily placed between the fall and the restoration; at this point many readers will feel the first twinge of complication, for Moses is a type of Christ who as the second Adam restores the first by persevering when he could not; as one begins to construct statements of relationship between the three, the clarity of lines 1–3 fades. Of course there is nothing to force the construction of such statements, and Milton thoughtfully provides in the very next line the sequence establishing phrase, 'In the beginning'. Reassured both by the ordering power of 'beginning' and by the allusion to Genesis (which is, after all, the original of all once-upon-a-times), the reader proceeds with the invocation, noting no doubt, all the riches unearthed by generations of critical exegesis, but still firmly in control of chronology; and that sense of control is reinforced by the two-word introduction to the story proper: 'Say first', for with the first we automatically posit a second and then a third, and in sum, a neat row of causal statements leading all the way to an end already known.

The security of sequence, however, is soon taken away. I have for some time conducted a private poll with a single question. 'What is your reaction when the second half of Line 54 – "for *now* the thought" – tells you that you are *now* with Satan, in Hell?' The unanimous reply is, 'surprise', and an involuntary question: how did I come to be here? Upon re-reading, the descent to Hell is again easy and again unchartable. At line 26 the time scheme is still manageable: there is (*a*) poem time, the *now* in which the reader sits in his chair and listens, with Milton, to the muse, and (*b*) the named point in the past when the story ('our grand-parents . . . so highly to fall off') and our understanding of it ('say first what cause') is assumed to begin. At 33, the 'first' is set back to the act of Satan, now suggested but not firmly identified as the cause of 27, and a third time (*c*) is introduced, further from (*a*) than (*b*), yet still manageable; but Satan's act also has its antecedent: 'what time his pride/Had cast him out from heaven' (36–7); by this point, 'what time' is both an assertion and a question as the reader struggles to maintain an awkward, backward-moving perspective. There is now a time (*d*) and after (that is, before) that an (*e*) 'aspiring . . . He trusted to have equalled the most high' (38, 40). Time (*f*) breaks the pattern, returning to (*d*) and providing, in the extended description of 44–53, a respite from sudden shifts. To summarize: the reader has been asked repeatedly to readjust his idea of 'in the beginning' while holding in suspension two plot lines (Adam and Eve's and Satan's) that are eventually, he knows, to be connected. The effort strains the mind to its capacity, and the relief offered by the vivid and easy picture of Satan falling is more than welcome.[17] It is at this time, when the reader's attention has relaxed, that Milton slips by him the 'now' of 54 and the present tense of 'torments', the first present in the passage. The effect is to alert the reader both to his location (Hell) and to his inability to retrace the journey that brought him there. Re-reading leads him only to repeat the mental operations the passage demands, and while the arrival in Hell is anticipated, it is always a surprise. The technique is of course the technique of the spot and spear similes, and of the clash between involuntary response and authorial rebuke, and again Milton's intention is to strip from us another of the natural aids we bring to the task of reading. The passage itself tells us this in lines 50–1, although the message may pass unnoted at first: 'Nine times the space that measures day and night'. Does space measure day and night? Are day and night space? The line raises these questions, and the half-line that follows answers them, not 'to mortal men' who think in terms of duration and sequence, not to us. In this poem we must, we will, learn a new time.

The learning process is slow at first; the reader does not necessarily draw the inferences I do from this early passage; but again it is the frequency of such instances, that makes my case. In Book II, when the fallen Angels disperse, some of them explore 'on bold adventure' their new home. One of the landmarks they pass is 'Lethe the river of oblivion', and Milton pauses to describe its part in God's future plans: 'At certain revolutions all the damned/. . . They ferry over this Lethean sound/Both to and fro, their sorrow to augment,/And wish and struggle, as they pass, to reach/The tempting stream, with one small drop to lose/In sweet forgetfulness all pain and woe,/All in one moment and so near the brink;/But fate withstands' (597–8, 604–10). At 614 the poet continues with 'Thus roving on/In confused march forlorn', and only the phrase 'adventurous bands' in 615 tells the reader that the poet has returned to the fallen angels. The mistake is a natural one: 'forlorn' describes perfectly the state of the damned, as does 'confused march' their movements 'to and fro': indeed a second reflection suggests no mistake at all; the fallen angels *are* the damned, and one drop of Lethe would allow them to lose their woe in the oblivion Moloch would welcome. Fate *does* withstand. What Milton has done by allowing this momentary confusion is point to the identity of these damned and all damned. As they fly past Lethe the fallen angels are all those who will become them; they do not stand for their successors (the word defeats me), they *state* them. In *Paradise Lost*, history and the historical sense are denied and the reader is forced to see events he necessarily perceives in sequence as time-identities. Milton cannot recreate the eternal moment, but by encouraging and then blocking the construction of sequential relationships he can lead the reader to accept the necessity of, and perhaps even apprehend, negatively, a time that is ultimately unavailable to him because of his limitations.

This translation of felt ambiguities, confusions, and tautologies into a conviction of timelessness in the narrative is assured partially by the uniqueness of Milton's 'fable'. 'For the Renaissance', notes Mrs MacCaffrey, 'all myths are reflections, distorted or mutilated though they may be, of the one true myth'.[18] For Milton all history is a replay of the history he is telling, all rebellions, one rebellion, all falls, one fall, all heroism the heroism of Christ. And his readers who share this Christian view of history will be prepared to make the connection that exists potentially in the detail of the narrative. The similes are particularly relevant here. The first of these compares Satan to Leviathan, but the comparison, to the informed reader, is a tautology; Satan *is* Leviathan and the simile presents two aspects of one, rather than the juxtaposition of two, components. This implies that Satan is, at the moment of the simile, already deceiving 'The pilot of some small night-foundered skiff'; and if the reader has attended to the lesson of his recent encounter with the epic voice he recognizes himself as that pilot, moored during the speech of 1, 84–126 by the side of Leviathan. The contests between Satan and Adam, Leviathan and the pilot, rhetoric and the reader – the simile compresses them, and all deceptions, into a single instant, forever recurring. The celebrated falling-leaves simile moves from angel form to leaves to sedge to Busiris and his Memphian Chivalry, or in typological terms (Pharaoh and Herod are the most common types of Satan) from fallen angels to fallen angels. The compression here is so complex that it defies analysis: the fallen angels as they *lie* on the burning lake (the Red Sea) are already *pursuing* the Sojourners of Goshen (Adam and Eve, the Israelites, the reader) who are for the moment on the safe shore (Paradise, the reader's chair). In Book xii, 191, Pharaoh becomes the River-Dragon of Leviathan (*Isaiah* 27 : 1), pointing to the ultimate unity of the Leviathan and falling leaves similes themselves. As similes they are uninformative; how numberless are the falling angels? they are as numberless as Pharaoh's host, that is, as fallen angels, and Pharaoh's host encompasses all the damned who have been, are, and will be, all the damned who will fly longingly above Lethe. As vehicles of perception they tell us a great deal, about the cosmos as it is in a reality we necessarily distort, about the ultimate subjectivity of sequential time, about ourselves.

There are many such instances in the early books and together they create a sensitivity to the difficulties of writing and reading this particular poem. When Milton's epic voice remarks that pagan fablers err relating the story of Mulciber's ejection from Heaven (1 747), he does not mean to say that the story is not true, but that it is a distorted version of the story he is telling, and that any attempt to apprehend the nature of the angels' fall by comparing it to the fall of Mulciber or of Hesiod's giants involves another distortion that can not be allowed if *Paradise Lost* is to be read correctly. On the other hand the attempt is hazarded

(the reader cannot help it), the distortion is acknowledged along
with the unavailability of the correct reading, and Milton's point
is made despite, or rather because of, the intractability of his
material. When Satan's flight from the judgment of God's scales
(IV 1015) is presented in a line that paraphrases the last line
of the *Aeneid,* the first impulse is to translate the allusion into a
comparison that might begin, 'Satan is like Turnus in that . . .';
but of course, the relationship as it exists in a reality beyond that
formed by our sense of literary history, is quite the opposite.
Turnus' defiance of the fates and his inevitable defeat are significant and comprehensible only in the light of what Satan did in
the past that our time signatures can not name and is about to do
in a present (poem time) that is increasingly difficult to identify.
Whatever the allusion adds to the richness of the poem's texture
or to Milton's case for superiority in the epic genre, it is also one
more assault on the confidence of a reader who is met at every
turn with demands his intellect cannot even consider.

III

Most poets write for an audience assumed fit. Why is the fitness of
Milton's audience a concern of the poem itself? One answer to
this question has been given in the preceding pages: only by
forcing upon his reader an awareness of his limited perspective
can Milton provide even a negative intuition of what another
would be like; it is a brilliant solution to the impossible demands
of his subject, enabling him to avoid the falsification of anthropomorphism and the ineffectiveness of abstraction. Another answer
follows from this one: the reader who fails repeatedly before the
pressures of the poem soon realizes that his difficulty proves its
major assertions – the fact of the fall, and his own (that is
Adam's) responsibility for it, and the subsequent woes of the
human situation. The reasoning is circular, but the circularity
is appropriate to the uniqueness of the poem's subject matter;
for while in most poems effects are achieved through the manipulation of reader response, this poet is telling the story that *created*
and still creates the responses of its reader and of all readers. The
reader who falls before the lures of Satanic rhetoric displays again

the weakness of Adam, and his inability to avoid repeating that fall throughout indicates the extent to which Adam's lapse has made the reassertion of right reason impossible. In short, the reader's difficulty is the result of the act that is the poem's subject. The reading experience becomes the felt measure of man's loss, and since Milton always supplies a corrective to the reader's errors and distortions, what other critics have seen as the 'disquieting' aspect of that experience can be placed in a context that makes sense of it.

The ultimate assault is on the reader's values. The fifth inference I drew from Waldock's criticism of the intrusive epic voice was that for him the question of relative authority is a purely aesthetic one. 'Milton's allegations clash with his demonstrations . . . in any work of imaginative literature at all it is the demonstration . . . that has the higher validity : an allegation can possess no comparable authority.' In his brilliantly perverse *Milton's God* William Empson asserts 'all the characters are on trial in any civilized narrative'[19] and Waldock would, I think, include the epic voice in this statement. The insistence on the superiority of showing as opposed to telling is, as Wayne Booth has shown, a modern one, and particularly unfortunate in this case since it ignores the historical reality of the genre.[20] When Homer names Achilles wrathful, do we search the narrative for proof he is not; is Odysseus' craft on trial or do we accept it because we accept the authority of the epic voice? Do we attempt to make a case for Aeneas' *im*piety? There is an obvious retort to all this: the authority of epic voices in other epics is accepted because their comments either confirm or anticipate the reading experience; Milton invites us to put his epic voice on trial by allowing the reading experience to contradict it. (Waldock: 'Of course they should agree'.) I agree that the reader can not help but notice the clash of authorities; his familiarity with the genre would lead him to look to the epic voice for guidance and clarification. But I do not think that any fit reader would resolve the problem, as Waldock does, and decide immediately and happily for the poem (and for himself) and against the prescience of its narrator. Milton assumes a predisposition in favour of the epic voice rather than a modern eagerness to put that voice on trial; he expects his reader to worry about the clash, to place it in a context that would resolve a troublesome contradiction and allow him to re-unite with an authority who is a natural ally against the difficulties of the poem. The reader who does this gains more than a clarifi-cation of perspective. Although re-reading does reveal the incon-sistencies and sophistries of the Satanic party line, it does not deny the reality of the values inherent in the Satanic stance. Waldock's summary of these values will serve again : 'fortitude in adversity, enormous endurance, a certain splendid recklessness'. In a word, heroism, or at least a form of heroism most of us find easy to admire because it is visible and flamboyant. Satan's initial attractiveness owes as much to a traditional and accepted idea of what is heroic as it does to our weakness before the rhetorical lure. Waldock complains there is not 'much despair in what we have just been listening to'. Just so ! Despair and courage are sometimes indistinguishable, and the example of Moloch will sug-gest that one can shade into the other. True courage or heroism is often physically unimpressive and as beings who operate on the basis of appearances we require special instruction before we can recognize it. The lesson Milton would teach us here is a subtle one, and we have learned it when we see that Satan is indeed heroic and that heroism, or what we are taught to recognize as heroism, is on trial. If this poem does anything to its reader it forces him to make finer and finer discriminations. Perhaps the most important aspect of the process I have been describing – the creation of a reader who is fit because he knows and under-stands his limitations – begins here at i 125 when Milton's authorial correctiveness casts the first stone at the concept of epic heroism, and begins to educate us toward the meaningful accept-ance of something better.

That something is, of course, Christian heroism; and as it emerges from *Comus, Lycidas, Samson Agonistes,* and ultimately in *Paradise Regained* Christian heroism is more an attitude than an abstraction, more a stance than a program for action. The attitude is called faith, and the stance is characterized by pro-visionality. The sign of Christian heroism is a willingness to move in a world where moral decision is imperative, but where moral guidelines are obscure. It is the heroism of Abraham who 'when he was called . . . obeyed; *and he went out, not knowing whither he went'* (*Hebrews* 11 :8). This is a difficult heroism for its tentativeness involves a burden the conventional hero could not bear, the burden enjoined by the simultaneous awareness of uncertainty and the necessity of action. The explanation of this 'unfair' situation lies of course in the fact of original sin; what makes the situation tolerable and finally joyful for the Christian hero is his belief (which is itself an act of faith) in the benignancy of the prime mover.[21] Abraham and the other heroes of faith in *Hebrews* 11 go out because they trust in an all-seeing deity who observes their blindness with compassion. 'These all died in faith, not having received the promises, but having seen them afar off, and were persuaded of them, and embraced them, and confessed that they were strangers and pilgrims on the earth' (*Hebrews* 11 : 13). In *Paradise Lost* the definition of Christian heroism is still another aspect of the relationship between the poem and a reader who must move between his immediate experience of a poetic effect and the authority of a 'hard and definite outline'. He must remain open to the first and await (not demand) the guidance of the second. He must, in other words, attune the operations of his mind (and of his eyes) to the demands of the poem's universe, and forge for himself a *modus vivendi* that will allow him to proceed, however uncertainly. When he does this successfully (tentatively), that is when he learns how to read the poem, he will himself become the Christian hero who is, after all, the only fit reader. In the end, the education of Milton's reader, the identification of his hero, and the description of his style, are one.[22]

SOURCE : *Critical Quarterly* (1965).
(See also Acknowledgements, p. 7.)

NOTES

1. *Paradise Lost And Its Critics* (Cambridge, 1961), p. 15. I consider Waldock's book, first published in 1947, to be the most forthright statement of an anti-Miltonism that can be found in the criticism of Leavis and Eliot, and more recently of Empson and John Peter. Indeed, Mr Peter, in his *A Critique of Paradise Lost* (Columbia, 1960), says of Waldock's essay, 'I have wondered

whether the agreements between it and some of my own chapters might not have passed the point where such things cease to be comforting', and Empson records his agreement with Waldock at several points. Bernard Bergonzi concludes his analysis of Waldock with this statement : 'no attempt has been made to defend the poem in the same detailed and specific manner in which it has been attacked' (*The Living Milton*, ed. Frank Kermode, London, 1960, p. 171). This essay is such an attempt. Bergonzi goes on to assert that 'a successful answer to Waldock would have to show that narrative structure of *Paradise Lost does* possess the kind of coherence and psychological plausibility that we have come to expect from the novel. Again, there can be no doubt that it does not' (p. 174). I shall argue that the coherence and psychological plausibility of the poem are to be found in the relationship between its effects and the mind of its reader. To some extent my reading has been anticipated by Joseph Summers in his brilliant study, *The Muse's Method* (Harvard, 1962). See especially pp. 30–1 : 'Milton anticipated . . . the technique of the "guilty reader" . . . The readers as well as the characters have been involved in the evil and have been forced to recognize and to judge their involvement.' See also Anne Ferry's *Milton's Epic Voice: The Narrator in Paradise Lost* (Harvard, 1963), pp. 44–66.

2. Ibid., p. 24.

3. Ibid., p. 77.

4. Quoted by Basil Willey in *The Seventeenth Century Background* (New York : Doubleday Anchor Books, 1955), p. 211.

5. As David Harding points out (*The Club of Hercules*, Urbana, 1962, pp. 103–8), this passage is also the basis of the bee-simile at line 768. The reader who catches the allusion here at line 108 will carry it with him to the end of the book and to the simile.

6. *Answerable Style* (Minneapolis, 1953), p. 124.

7. Op. cit., p. 79.

8. III 659. Harding insists that 'if this passage does not conjure up a mental picture of Polyphemus on the mountaintop, steadying his footsteps with a lopped pine . . . it has not communicated its full meaning to us' (*The Club of Hercules*, p. 63). In my reading the 'full meaning' of the passage involves a recognition of the inadequacy of the mental picture so conjured up.

9. The translation is E. V. Rieu's in the Penguin Classic edition (Baltimore, 1946), p. 148.

10. A. N. Whitehead in *The Limits of Language* (New York, 1962), pp. 13–14. In classical theory metaphor is that figure of

speech whose operation bears the closest resemblance to the operations of dialectic and logic. Aristotle defines it in the *Poetics* as 'a transference either from genus to species or from species to genus, or from species to species'.

11. See 'The Miltonic Simile', *PMLA,* xlvi (1931), 1064.

12. Milton clearly anticipates this reaction when he describes the dialogue in the 'argument'; 'Adam inquires concerning celestial Motions, is *doubtfully* answered'.

13. Percy Bridgeman, in *The Limits of Language,* p. 21.

14. *The Metaphoric Structure of Paradise Lost* (Baltimore, 1962), pp. 14–15.

15. Op. cit., p. 53.

16. Ibid., p. 45.

17. The technique is reminiscent of Virgil's 'historical present', which is used by the Roman poet to bring the action of his epic before the reader's eyes.

18. Op. cit., p. 14.

19. Norfolk, 1961, p. 94.

20. *The Rhetoric of Fiction* (Chicago, 1961), p. 4. '. . . even Homer writes scarcely a page without some kind of direct clarification of motives, of expectations, and of the relative importance of events. And though the gods themselves are often unreliable, Homer – the Homer we know – is not. What he tells us usually goes deeper and is more accurate than anything we are likely to learn about real people and events.'

21. Faith can not help us make the decisions forced on us by a difficult and obscure universe; but it can make the necessity of deciding more bearable.

22. An obvious objection to this way of resolving the contradictions so many have seen in *Paradise Lost* is the excessively self-conscious reader it posits, a reader who continually makes discriminations of incredible delicacy, a reader who is able to accept, even use, reproof and confusion, a reader who is, in sum, the detachedly involved observer of his own mental processes. Could Milton have assumed such a reader? I believe that he could have and did, and that my reading is true not only to the poem but to its historical context, although the remarks that follow are intended to be the barest outline of an argument presented in *Surprised by Sin* (Macmillan). My argument is based on the opposition of rhetoric, the art of appearances, to dialectic, the pursuit of a scientific-mathematical truth. Aristotle locates the power of rhetoric in the 'defects of our hearers' (*Rhetoric* 3 : 1); the pressures of Christian-

ity transforms the vagueness of the 'defects of our hearers' into the precision of 'original sin'. Each text presents a problem for the Christian reader who must learn to resist the impulse to dwell on the niceties of rhetoric and attend only to the moral doctrine contained therein. Of course a rhetorical stimulus can be resisted if it is first recognized, that is felt. The crucial moment, in the reading experience then is the moment between the first response to the lure and its rejection or acceptance. That moment is analogous to the crucial stage in the progress of sin, that moment between the consideration of sin and assent or rejection. The three stages of sin – suggestion–delectation–consent find their analogies in the reading experience – response to the pull of the rhetorical, the moment of decision (whether or not to surrender to it), the abandonment of one's intellectual awareness to it. In practical terms this results in a program of Christian reading, one that involves referring all appeals to the repository of Christian morality a reader must bring to a poem if it is to be read 'properly'. Boccaccio writes : 'But I repeat my advice to those who would appreciate poetry, and unwind its difficult involutions. You must read, you must persevere, you must sit up nights; you must inquire, and exert the utmost power of your mind' (*Boccaccio on Poetry,* ed. C. G. Osgood, Princeton, 1930, p. 62.) In Milton's poem the epic voice acts as surrogate for the 'power of mind' that has defected to the lures the poem offers. What Milton does then is translate a philosophical-religious commonplace into a method of procedure. The method is possible and successful because the reader is taught by his theology to see in its operation the evidence of his own weakness or sin. In other words, rhetoric becomes the object attacked, and since rhetoric is firmly attached in the poem to the psychology of fallen man, the attack is finally on the reader who is forced by an inspired epic voice to acknowledge its success. The entire pattern is framed in the seventeenth century by an epistemology that stresses analysis and precision, and preaches a distrust of the rhetorical and emotional, and by an aesthetic that regards a poem as a potential instrument of conversion.

Frank Kermode

ADAM UNPARADISED (1960)

Miss Rosemond Tuve, in her magnificent and too brief book, has persuasively expounded Milton's treatment in the minor poems of certain great central themes. They lie at the heart of each poem and govern its secondary characteristics of imagery and diction; given the theme, the poet thinks in the figures appropriate to it, and in every case the theme and the figures have a long and rich history. 'The subject of *L'Allegro* is every man's Mirth, our Mirth, the very Grace herself with all she can include';[1] the *Hymn on the Morning of Christ's Nativity* proliferates images of harmony because its theme is the Incarnation. I now take a step of which Miss Tuve would probably not approve, and add that beneath these figures and themes there is Milton's profound and personal devotion to an even more radical topic, potentially co-extensive with all human experience: the loss of Eden. In the *Hymn* there is a moment of peace and harmony in history – the 'Augustan peace', which looks back to human wholeness and incorruption, as well as forward to a time when, after generations of human anguish, the original harmony will be restored. The same moment of stillness, poised between past and future, is there in 'At a Solemn Musick', for music remembers as well as prefigures. In *Comus* too there is presented that moment of harmony, of reunion and restitution, that prefigures the final end, and in *Comus* as in the others there is an emphasis on the long continuance of grief and suffering; for in the much misunderstood Epilogue Adonis is still not cured of his wound and Venus 'sadly sits'. Only in the future will Cupid be united with Psyche and the twins of Paradise, Youth and Joy, be born. *Lycidas* tells of disorder, corruption, false glory as incident to life here and now, with order, health, and the perfect witness of God to come. All of them speak of something that is gone.

Paradise Lost deals most directly with this basic theme, the recognition of lost possibilities of joy, order, health, the contrast between what we can imagine as human and what is so here and now; the sensuous import of the myth of the lost Eden. To embody this theme is the main business of *Paradise Lost*; thus will life be displayed in some great symbolic attitude and not by the poet's explanations of the how and the why. His first task is to get clear the human experience of the potency of delight, and its necessary frustration, and if he cannot do that the poem will fail no matter what is added of morality, theology or history.

My difficulty in establishing this point is that some will think it too obvious to be thus laboured, and others will think it in need of much more elaborate defence. What is rare is to find people who read *Paradise Lost* as if it were true that the power of joy and its loss is its theme; and though it is true that for certain well-known and important reasons Milton's poem is not accessible to the same methods of reading as Romantic literature, it is also true that this is the theme of *The Prelude*, and that we can do some harm by insisting too strongly upon differences at the expense of profound similarities. Anyway, I think I can make my point in a somewhat different way by a reference to Bentley, and in particular to his observations on the last lines of *Paradise Lost*, stale as this subject may seem.

Adam, hearing Michael's promise of a time when 'earth/Shall all be paradise, far happier place/Than this of Eden' (xɪɪ 463–5) is 'replete with joy and wonder' (468) and replies with the famous cry of *felix culpa*:

> Full of doubt I stand,
> Whether I should repent me now of sin
> By me done and occasioned, or rejoice
> Much more, that much more good thereof shall spring . . .
>   (xɪɪ 473–6)

Michael says that the Comforter will watch over and arm the faithful; Adam, benefiting by Michael's foretelling of the future (in which 'time stands fixed' as it does in the poem) has now

all possible wisdom (575–6); and Eve is well content with her
lot. And thus matters stand when Eden is closed, and Adam and
Eve move away

> The world was all before them, where to choose
> Their place of rest, and providence their guide :
> They hand in hand with wandering steps and slow,
> Through Eden took their solitary way. (XII 646–9)

'Why' asks Bentley, 'does this distich dismiss our first parents in
anguish, and the reader in melancholy? And how can the expression be justified, *with wandering steps and slow*? Why
wandering? Erratick steps? Very improper, when, in the line
before, they were *guided by Providence*. And why slow? even
when Eve has professed her readiness and alacrity for the journey :

> but now lead on;
> In me is no delay (XII 614–15)

And why their *solitary way*? All words to represent a sorrowful
parting? when even their former walks in Paradise were as
solitary as their way now; there being nobody besides them two
both here and there. Shall I therefore, after so many prior pre-
sumptions, presume at last to offer a distich, as close as may be to
the author's words, and *entirely agreeable to his scheme*?

> Then hand in hand with *social* steps their way
> Through Eden took, *with heavenly comfort cheered.*'

Bentley assumes that he has exact knowledge of Milton's
'scheme', and quarrels with the text for not fitting it. He seems
to be forgetting God's instructions to Michael – 'so send them
forth, though sorrowing, yet in peace' (XI 117), and also Adam's
knowledge of the events leading up to the happy consummation;
yet it remains true that if Milton's 'scheme' was simply to show
that everything would come out right in the end, and that this
should keenly please both Adam and ourselves, Bentley is not at
all silly here; or if he is, so are more modern commentators who,

supported by all that is now known about the topic *felix culpa*, tend to read the poem in a rather similar way though without actually rewriting it, by concentrating on Milton's intention, somewhat neglected in the past, to present this belated joy of Adam's as central to the whole poem. There is, of course, such an intention or 'scheme'; the mistake is to suppose that it is paramount. It is in fact subsidiary, *Paradise Lost* being a poem, to the less explicable theme of joy and woe, which has to be expressed in terms of the myth, as a contrast between the original justice of Paradise and the mess of history: between Paradise and Paradise lost. The poem is tragic. If we regard it as a document in the history of ideas, ignoring what it does to our senses, we shall of course find ideas, as Bentley did, and conceivably the closing lines will seem out of true. But our disrespect for Bentley's Milton, and in this place particularly, is proof that the poem itself will prevent our doing this unless we are very stubborn or not very susceptible to poetry. The last lines of the poem are, we *feel*, exactly right, for all that Adam has cried out for pleasure; death denounced, he has lost his Original Joy. The tragedy is a matter of *fact*, of life as we feel it; the hope of restoration is a matter of faith, and faith is 'the substance of things hoped for, the evidence of things unseen' – a matter altogether less simple, sensuous, and passionate, altogether less primitive. We are reminded that 'the conception that man is mortal, by his nature and essence, seems to be entirely alien to mythical and primitive religious thought'.[2] In the poem we deplore the accidental loss of native immortality more than we can applaud its gracious restoration.

ADAM IMPARADISED

One of the effects of mixing up Milton with the Authorized Version, and of intruding mistaken ideas of Puritanism into his verse, is that it can become very hard to see what is made absolutely plain: that for Milton the joy of Paradise is very much a matter of the senses. The Authorized Version says that 'the Lord God planted a garden' (Genesis 2 : 8) and that he 'took the man and put him into the garden of Eden to dress it and keep it' (2 : 15). But even in Genesis 2 : 8 the Latin texts usually have *in paradisum voluptatis* 'into a paradise of pleasure' – this is the reading of the Vulgate currently in use. And the Latin version of 2 : 15 gives *in paradiso deliciarum*. Milton's Paradise is that of the Latin version; in it, humanity without guilt is 'to all delight of human sense exposed' (IV 206), and he insists on this throughout. Studying the exegetical tradition on this point, Sister Mary Corcoran makes it plain that Milton pushes this sensuous pleasure much harder than his 'scheme' as Bentley and others might conceive it, required. For example, he rejected the strong tradition that the first marriage was not consummated until after the Fall, choosing to ignore the difficulty about children conceived before but born after it. For this there may be an historical explanation in the Puritan cult of married love; but it could not account for what has been called Milton's 'almost Dionysiac treatment'[3] of sexuality before the Fall; Sister Corcoran is sorry that she can't even quite believe the assertion that 'in those hearts/Love unlibidinous reigned (V 449–50).[4]

In fact Milton went to great trouble to get this point firmly made; had he failed no amount of finesse in other places could have held the poem together; and it is therefore just as well that nothing in the poem is more beautifully achieved.

Why was innocent sexuality so important to Milton's poem? Why did he take on the task of presenting an Adam and an Eve unimaginably privileged in the matter of sensual gratification 'to all delight of human sense expos'd'? There is a hint of the answer in . . . his view of the function of poetry. Believing as he did in the inseparability of matter and form, except by an act of intellectual abstraction, Milton could not allow a difference of kind between soul and body; God

> created all
> Such to perfection, one first matter all,
> Indued with various forms, various degrees
> Of substance, and in things that live, of life;
> But more refined, more spirituous, and pure,
> As nearer to him placed or nearer tending
> Each in their several active spheres assigned,
> Till body up to spirit work, in bounds

> Proportioned to each kind. So from the root
> Springs lighter the green stalk, from thence the leaves
> More airy, last the bright consummate flower
> Spirits odorous breathes : flowers and their fruit
> Man's nourishment, by gradual scale sublimed
> To vital spirits aspire, to animal,
> To intellectual, give both life and sense,
> Fancy and understanding, whence the soul
> Reason receives, and reason is her being,
> Discursive or intuitive ; discourse
> Is oftest yours, the latter most is ours ... (v 471–89)

An acceptance of Raphael's position involves, given the cosmic scale of the poem, a number of corollaries which Milton does not shirk. Matter, the medium of the senses, is continuous with spirit; or 'spirit, being the more excellent substance, virtually and essentially contains within itself the inferior one; as the spiritual and rational faculty contains the corporeal, that is, the sentient and vegetative faculty' (*De Doctrina Christiana* I vii). It follows that the first matter is of God, and contains the potentiality of form;[5] so the body is not to be thought of in disjunction from the soul, of which 'rational', 'sensitive' and 'vegetative' are merely aspects. Raphael accordingly goes out of his way to explain that the intuitive reason of the angels differs only in degree from the discursive reason of men; and Milton that there is materiality in angelic spirit. It is a consequence of this that part of Satan's sufferings lie in a deprivation of sensual pleasure. Milton's thought is penetrated by this doctrine, which, among other things, accounts for his view of the potency of poetry for good or ill; for poetry works through pleasure, by sensuous delight; it can help 'body up to spirit work' or it can create dangerous physiological disturbance. Obviously there could be no more extreme challenge to the power and virtue of his art than this : to require of it a representation of ecstatic sensual pleasure, a *voluptas* here and only here not associated with the possibility of evil : 'delight to reason joined' (IX 243). The loves of Paradise must be an unimaginable joy to the senses, yet remain 'unlibidinous'.

If we were speaking of Milton rather than of his poem we

might use this emphasis on materiality, on the dignity as well as the danger of sense, to support a conclusion similar to that of De Quincey in his account of Wordsworth : 'his intellectual passions were fervent and strong; but they rested upon a basis of preter-natural animal sensibility diffused through *all* the animal passions (or appetites); and something of that will be found to hold of all poets who have been great by original force and power . . .' (De Quincey was thinking about Wordsworth's facial resemblance to Milton). And it would be consistent with such an account that Milton also had, like Wordsworth, a constant aware-ness of the dangers entailed by a powerful sensibility. This gives us the short reason why, when Milton is representing the enor-mous bliss of innocent sense, he does not do so by isolating it and presenting it straightforwardly. He sees that we must grasp it at best deviously; we understand joy as men partially deprived of it, with a strong sense of the woeful gap between the possible and the actual in physical pleasure. And Milton's prime device for ensuring that we should thus experience his Eden is a very sophisticated, perhaps a 'novelistic' one : we see all delight through the eyes of Satan.

POINTS OF VIEW

I shall return to this, and to the other more or less distorting glasses that Milton inserts between us and the voluptuousness of Eden; but first it seems right to say a word in general on a neglected subject, Milton's varying of the point of view in this poem. He uses the epic poet's privilege of intervening in his own voice, and he does this to regulate the reader's reaction; but some of the effects he gets from this device are far more complicated than is sometimes supposed. The corrective comments inserted after Satan has been making out a good case for himself are not to be lightly attributed to a crude didacticism; naturally they are meant to keep the reader on the right track, but they also allow Milton to preserve the energy of the myth. While we are hearing Satan we are not hearing the comment; for the benefit of a fallen audience the moral correction is then applied, but its force is calculated lower; and the long-established custom of claiming

that one understands Satan better than Milton did is strong
testimony to the tact with which it is done. On this method the
devil can have good tunes. Not only does his terrible appearance
resemble an eclipse which 'with fear of change/Perplexes Mon-
archs' (1 598–9), but his oratory can include sound republican
arguments – God is 'upheld by old repute,/Consent or custom'
(639–40). This sort of thing makes its point before the authorial
intervention corrects it. Milton even takes the risk of refraining
from constant intervention and Satan-baiting in the first book,
where the need for magnificence and energy is greatest. It is in the
second that the intense persuasions of the angelic debaters are
firmly qualified; the speech of Belial is a notable case, for it is
poignantly and humanly reasonable, but hedged before and
behind by sharp comments on its hollowness and lack of nobility.
We may find this argument attractive, but we ought to know that
it has a wider moral context, and this the comment provides.
At the other extreme, when God is laying down the law or
Raphael telling Adam what he needs to know, the presentation is
bare and unambiguous not because there is nothing the author
wants to draw one's attention to but because these are not the
places to start on the difficult question of how the reader's senses
enhance or distort the truth; it is when the fallen study the
deviousness of the fallen that corrective comment is called for,
but even there sense must be given its due.

Of all the feats of narrative sophistication in the poem the most
impressive is the presentation of the delights of Paradise under
the shadow of Satan. He approaches out of chaos and darkness;
a warning voice cries 'Woe to the inhabitants on earth' (IV 5);
he is 'inflamed with rage' (9) as he moves in on calm and joy;
and the consequences of the coming encounter are prefigured in
the terminal words of lines 10–12 : *mankind . . . loss . . . hell.*
Before him Eden lies 'pleasant' (28); but we are not to see the
well-tempered joys of its inhabitants before we have studied, with
Uriel in the sun, the passionate fact of Satan, marred by 'distempers foul' (118), a condition possible only to the fallen. He
fares forward to Eden, 'delicious Paradise' (132); distemper and
delight are about to meet. A good deal is made of the difficulty
of access to Eden; not, I think, because Satan would find it

difficult – he 'in contempt/At one slight bound high overleaped all bound' (180–1) – but because *we* must find it so; we are stumbling, disorientated, with Satan into an unintelligible purity :

> and of pure now purer air
> Meets his approach, and to the heart inspires
> Vernal delight and joy, able to drive
> All sadness but despair : now gentle gales
> Fanning their odoriferous wings dispense
> Native perfumes, and whisper whence they stole
> Those balmy spoils. As when to them who sail
> Beyond the Cape of Hope, and now are past
> Mozambic, off at sea north-east winds blow
> Sabean odours from the spicy shore
> Of Arabie the blest, with such delay
> Well pleased they slack their course, and many a league
> Cheered with the grateful smell old Ocean smiles.
> So entertained those odorous sweets the fiend
> Who came their bane, though with them better pleased
> Than Asmodeus with the fishy fume,
> That drove him, though enamoured, from the spouse
> Of Tobit's son, and with a vengeance sent
> From Media post to Aegypt, there fast bound. (IV 152–71)

This passage is preceded by praises of the colours of Paradise, and of delights directed at the senses of hearing, touch and taste; here the sense of smell is predominant, and Milton provides a remarkable association of fallen and unfallen odours. What becomes of the scents of Eden? They decay, and another smell replaces them, as Death himself will describe :

> a scent I draw
> Of carnage, prey innumerable, and taste
> The savour of death from all things there that live . . .
> So saying, with delight he snuffed the smell
> Of mortal change on earth. (X 267 ff.)

At first Milton uses a lot of force to establish a situation lacking entirely this evil smell. 'Of pure now purer air' – we are moving into the very centre of purity, delight and joy, where no sadness

could survive save irredeemable hopelessness (a hint that even
this purity cannot repel Satan). The breezes carry scents which
betray their paradisal origin : 'balmy' is a key-word in the life-
asserting parts of the poem, being used in the sense in which
Donne uses it in the 'Nocturnall', as referring to the whole principle of life and growth; compare 'virtue', meaning natural
vitality, in the same parts. The simile of the perfumes drifting out
to sea from Arabia Felix refers to this breeze-borne odour, but
also, with a characteristic and brilliant syntactical turn, to its
effect upon Satan, the next topic treated; 'as when' seems at first
to refer back, then to refer forward. This effect is helped by the
Miltonic habit of boxing off formal similes with fullstops before
and after. Satan checks himself at this influx of sensual delight;
but we are reminded, with maximum force, of the difference
between Satan and the sailors, by the emphatic 'Who came their
bane'. And this dissonance prepares us for the fuller ambiguities
introduced by the reference to Asmodeus, a lustful devil who was
driven away from Sarah by the stink of burning fish-liver. Why
does Milton go about to fetch Asmodeus into his verses? The
point is not the one he explicitly makes, that Satan liked the smell
of Eden better than Asmodeus the smell of fish-liver; anybody
who believes that will believe all he is told about Milton's sacrific-
ing sense to sound, and so forth. The point is partly that Satan
is also going to be attracted by a woman; partly that he too will
end by being, as a direct consequence of his attempt upon her,
'fast bound'; but the poet's principal intention is simply to get
into the context a bad smell. The simile offers as an excuse for
its existence a perfunctory logical connection with what is being
said; but it is used to achieve a purely sensuous effect. As soon
as we approach Eden there is a mingling of the good actual odour
with a bad one, of Life with Death.

Another rather similar and equally rich effect is produced by
another very long sentence, IV, 268–311. From the dance of
'universal *Pan*/Knit with the *Graces*' (266–7) we pass on to
negative comparisons between Eden and other gardens. All the
negations work at an unimportant level of discourse; they are
denials of similarity which would not be worth making if they
did not imply powerful resemblances. Eden is not the vale of

Enna, nor Eve Prosperine, nor Satan Dis, nor Ceres Christ. Though Daphne was saved from a devil by a divine act, her grove was not Eden, and though 'old *Cham*' protected in another garden the 'florid son' of Amalthea, this does not mean that the garden of Bacchus was the same paradise as that in which another lover of pleasure, almost divine, was, though inadequately, protected. In their unlikeness they all tell us more about the truth of Eden; yet it is upon their unlikeness that Milton is still, apparently, dwelling when his Satan breaks urgently in; they are all

> wide remote
> From this Assyrian garden, where the fiend
> Saw undelighted all delight.... (IV 284–6)

Whereupon, having included the undelighted Satan in the enormous, delighted scene, Milton goes on, still without a full period, to an elaborate account of Adam and Eve.

THE GARDEN OF LOVE

The degree of literary sophistication in Milton's treatment of the biblical account of Adam and Eve in Paradise is a reasonably accurate index of his whole attitude to what I have called the myth. I have already mentioned the incorporation of other literary and mythological gardens in this Eden; they are significant shadows of it. But the full exploration of the literary context of Milton's Paradise would be a very large inquiry, and here there is occasion only for a brief and tentative sketch of it, touching only upon what affects the present argument.

When Milton comes to treat of the inhabitants of the garden he plunges us at once into a dense literary context. The Bible says: 'And they were both naked, the man and his wife, and were not ashamed' (Genesis 2 : 25). According to Milton, however, they were 'with native honour clad/In naked majesty' (289–90); and a little later he moralizes this:

> Nor those mysterious parts were then concealed,
> Then was not guilty shame, dishonest shame

Of nature's works : honour dishonourable,
Sin-bred, how have ye troubled all mankind
With shows instead, mere shows of seeming pure ...

(IV 312–16)

This is in open allusion to a literary topic so often treated in Renaissance and seventeenth-century writing as to be unwieldy in its complexity. First one needs to understand the general primitivistic position which held that custom and honour were shabby modern expedients unnecessary in a Golden Age society, with all its corollaries in Renaissance 'naturalism'. Then one has to consider the extremely complex subject of literary gardens and their connection with the Earthly Paradise and the Golden Age, not only in Renaissance, but also in classical and mediaeval literature. Of the first of these I now say nothing. The easy way to approach the second is through the *locus classicus,* the chorus *O bella étà de l'oro* in Tasso's *Aminta.* In the Golden Age, as in Eden, the earth bore fruit and flowers without the aid of man; the air was calm and there was eternal spring. Best of all, there was continual happiness because – in the translation of Henry Reynolds –

Because that vain and ydle name,
That couz'ning Idoll of unrest,
Whom the madd vulgar first did raize,
And call'd it Honour, whence it came
To tyrannize o're ev'ry brest,
Was not then suffred to molest
Poore lovers hearts with new debate. ...
The Nymphes sate by their Paramours,
Whispring love-sports, and dalliance. ...

It was Honour that ruined Pleasure,

And lewdly did instruct faire eyes
They should be nyce, and scrupulous ...
         (*Torquato Tassos Aminta Englisht,* 1628)

This is the Honour, a tyrant bred of custom and ignorant opinion, which inevitably intrudes into Milton's argument when he uses the word in forcible oxymoron, 'honour dishonourable'. But he is not using the idea as it came sometimes to be used in poetry Milton would have called dishonest; his Honour is 'sin-bred', a pathetic subterfuge of the fallen, and not, as it is in libertine poems, an obstacle to sexual conquest that must yield to primitivist argument.[6] Of these ambiguities Milton must have been fully aware, since the poetry of his time contains many libertine attacks on Honour which imply that reason and 'native Honour' will be satisfied only by an absolute surrender to pleasure. Furthermore, many of these poems are set in gardens, and we should not overlook the difficulties Milton had to overcome before he could be reasonably satisfied that his garden of love was the right kind. The garden of love has a long history, and the topic nowadays called the *locus amoenus*[7] is as old as the garden of Alcinous in the *Odyssey*; the expression *locus amoenus* meant to Servius 'a place for lovemaking', and *amoenus* was derived by a false etymology from *amor*. This tradition, mingling with the continuous traditions of the Earthly Paradise, and modified by the allegorical skills of the Middle Ages, sometimes conformed and sometimes conflicted with the garden of Genesis; gardens could be the setting for all kinds of love, just as Venus herself could preside over all kinds of love and all kinds of gardens. Milton needed a *paradisus voluptatis*, but it must not be the same as a 'naturalist' or libertine garden, and it must not be connected with 'courtly love' – hence the disclaimers in iv 744 ff. and iv 765 ff. Whatever the dishonest and sophisticate, or for that matter the falsely philosophical, might do with imaginary Edens, he was dealing with the thing itself, and must get innocent delight into it. So he uses these conventions, including the usual attack upon Honour, with his customary boldness, as if his treatment, though late, were the central one, and all the others mere shadows of his truth; the same method, in fact, as that used for pagan mythology. In Book ix, having risked all the difficulties of his contrast between love unlibidinous and love libidinous by showing them both in the experience of Adam and Eve, he is able to enlarge upon the oxymoron 'honour dishonourable', saying that

> innocence, that as a veil
> Had shadowed them from knowing ill, was gone,
> Just confidence, and native righteousness
> And honour from about them. . . . (IX 1054–7)

And Adam sees that the fruit of knowledge was bad, 'if this be to know,/Which leaves us naked thus, of honour void' (1073–4); here the fig-leaves are assimilated to the literary tradition. As for *locus amoenus*, Milton also contrives to give two versions of it : in Book IV it is worked into the account of 'unreproved' love-making (see especially IX 1034 ff.) as the scene of the first fallen act of love. Pope first saw another link between these two passages, and Douglas Bush has recently written upon this link a brilliant page of commentary :[8] each derives a good deal, and the manner of derivation is ironical, from a single episode in the *Iliad*, the lovemaking of Zeus and Hera in Book XIV.

So erudite and delicate, yet so characteristic a device might find, among fit audience, someone to value it for itself; but Milton's object was to exploit, with what force all the literature in the world could lend, the contrast between the true delight of love and the fallacious delight which is a mere prelude to woe; between possible and actual human pleasure. And however complex the means, the end is simply to show Adam and Eve as actually enjoying what to us is a mere imagination, and then explain how they lost it, and what was then left. In this sense their simple experience contains the whole of ours, including that which we feel we might but know we cannot have; and in this sense they include us, they are what we are and what we imagine we might be. This inclusiveness is given remarkably concrete demonstration in lines so famous for their unidiomatic English that the reason for the distorted word-order has been overlooked :

> the loveliest pair
> That ever since in love's embraces met,
> Adam the goodliest man of men since born
> His sons, the fairest of her daughters Eve. (IV 321–4)

The syntax may be Greek, but the sense is English, and inclusiveness could hardly be more completely presented; Adam and Eve here literally include us all. The illogic of the expression serves the same end as the illogic of those mythological parallels inserted only to be denied, or of those continuous reminders that the whole of history 'since created man' is somehow being enacted here and now in the garden. What must never be underestimated is the sheer absorbency of Milton's theme; everything will go into it, and find itself for the first time properly placed, completely explained. Todd has a note on the passage (IV 458 ff.) in which Milton adapts, to the awakening of Eve, Ovid's account of Narcissus first seeing himself in the pool: he cites one commentator who enlarges upon Milton's enormous improvement of Ovid's lines, and another who adds that 'we may apply to Milton on this occasion what Aristotle says of Homer, that he taught poets how to lie properly'. Lying properly about everything is a reasonable way of describing the poet's achievement in *Paradise Lost*, if a proper lie is one that includes the *terra incognita* of human desires, actual love and possible purity.

That is why we see Adam and Eve in the garden of love not directly, but through many glasses; and the darkest of these is the mind of Satan. He looks at his victims with passionate envy and even regret:

> Ah gentle pair, ye little think how nigh
> Your change approaches, when all these delights
> Will vanish and deliver ye to woe,
> More woe, the more your taste is now of joy;
> Happy, but for so happy ill secured
> Long to continue, and this high seat your heaven
> Ill fenced for heaven to keep out such a foe
> As now is entered (IV 366–73)

He is reluctant to harm them; he pleads necessity (Milton calls this 'The tyrant's plea' (394) and neatly gives it to Adam in X 131 ff.). But what he must take away from them is *delight*, physical pleasure in innocence; his dwelling in Hell 'haply may not please/Like this fair Paradise, your sense' (IV 378–9). They are to 'taste' something other than Joy; and one remembers how frequently, at critical moments, the word 'taste' occurs in *Paradise Lost*, from the second line on. The shadow of Satan falls most strikingly over the pleasures of the garden when he watches Adam and Eve making love. It is not merely that the absolutely innocent and joyous act is observed as through a peep-hole, as if the lovers had been tricked into a bawdy-house; Satan himself acquires some of the pathos of an old *voyeur*. Pursuing his equation of delight with innocence, Milton boldly hints that the fallen angel is sexually deprived. He has forfeited the unfallen delights of sense. There is, we are to learn, lovemaking in heaven, but not in hell; the price of warring against omnipotence is impotence.

> Sight hateful, sight tormenting ! Thus these two
> Imparadised in one another's arms
> The happier Eden, shall enjoy their fill
> Of bliss on bliss, while I to hell am thrust,
> Where neither joy nor love, but fierce desire,
> Among our other torments not the least,
> Still unfulfilled with pain of longing pines . . . (IV 505–11)

Satan is so sure of their sexual joy that he anticipates later love poetry in making the body of the beloved a paradise in itself – his 'happier Eden' is not the same as that promised later to Adam (XII 587) – and he uses a word, 'imparadises' which was to have its place in the vocabulary of fallen love. But at this moment only Satan can feel desire without fulfilment, and Milton reminds us that he resembles in this fallen men; thus he actualizes the human contrast between innocence and experience, and between love and its counterfeits – the whole 'monstruosity of love', as Troilus calls it.

Milton, in short, provides an illogical blend of purity and impurity in the first delightful lovemaking. He does not present an isolated purity and then its contamination, as the narrative might seem to require, but interferes with this order just as he does with word-order, and for similar reasons. Not only does he show us the unfallen Adam and Eve in such a way that we can never think of their delight without thinking of its enemies; he also establishes such links between the fourth and ninth books that we can never think of his account of unfallen love without remembering the parallel passages on lust. It is here relevant to emphasize the unpraised brilliance of one of the linking devices,

Milton's use of the theme of physiological perturbation. At the opening of Book IV Uriel observes that Satan is affected by unregulated passions, as the unfallen Adam and Eve cannot be; he is the first person on earth to experience this. But by the end of the Book he has established by an act of demonic possession that Eve is physiologically capable of such a disturbance (IV 799 ff; V 9–11); and the effect of the Fall in Book IX can be measured by the degree to which the humours of the lovers are distempered by the fruit:

> Soon as the force of that fallacious fruit,
> That with exhilarating vapour bland
> About their spirits had played, and inmost powers
> Made err, was now exhaled, and grosser sleep
> Bred of unkindly fumes, with conscious dreams
> Encumbered, now had left them, up they rose
> As from unrest. . . . (IX 1046–52)

We happen to know what Milton, as theologian, believed to be the significance of the eating of the fruit. He regarded the tree of the knowledge of good and evil as merely 'a pledge, as it were, and memorial of obedience'. The tasting of its fruit was an act that included all sins: 'it comprehended at once distrust in the divine veracity, and a proportionate credulity in the assurances of Satan; unbelief, ingratitude; disobedience; gluttony; in the man excessive uxoriousness, in the woman a want of proper regard for her husband, in both an insensibility to the welfare of their offspring, and offspring the whole human race; parricide, theft, invasion of the rights of others, sacrilege, deceit, presumption in aspiring to divine attributes, fraud in the means employed to attain the object, pride, and arrogance, (*De Doctrina Christiana* I XI, Sumner's translation). But none of this stemmed from the intoxicating power of the fruit; God was testing fidelity by forbidding 'an act of its own nature indifferent'. In other words Milton the poet establishes the theme of perturbation as a structural element in the poem, using it as an index of fallen nature, of the disaster brought upon Joy by Woe, by means which must have earned the disapproval of Milton the theologian, namely the attribution of intoxicating powers to the forbidden fruit. Joy and Woe in the poem take precedence over theological niceties; Milton's theology is in the *De Doctrina*, not in *Paradise Lost.*

ADAM UNPARADISED

Joy and Woe, the shadow of one over the other, the passage from one to the other, are the basic topic of the poem. We turn now to Adam unparadised, to Joy permanently overshadowed by Woe, light by dark, nature by chaos, love by lust, fecundity by sterility. Death casts these shadows. It is not difficult to understand why a very intelligent Italian, reading *Paradise Lost* for the first time, should have complained to me that he had been curiously misled about its subject; for, he said, 'it is a poem about Death'.

> For who would lose
> Though full of pain, this intellectual being? (II 146–7)

Belial asks the question, as Claudio had done; it is a human reaction, and most of the time we do not relish the thought of being without 'sense and motion' (II 151); nor can we help it if this is to be called 'ignoble' (II 227). In the same book, Milton gives Death allegorical substance, if 'substance might be called that shadow seemed' (669); for it is all darkness and shapelessness, a 'phantasm' (743), all lust and anger, its very name hideous (788). The only thing it resembles is Chaos, fully described in the same book; and it stands in relation to the order and delight of the human body as Chaos stands to Nature. So, when Satan moved out of Chaos into Nature, he not only 'into Nature brought/Misery' (VI 267), but into Life brought Death, and into Light (which is always associated with order and organic growth) darkness. At the end of Book II he at last, 'in a cursed hour' (1055), approaches the pendent world, having moved towards it from Hell through Chaos; and the whole movement of what might be called the *sensuous* logic of the poem so far – the fall into darkness and disorder, the return to light and order – is triumphantly halted at the great invocation to Light which opens Book III. But the return is of course made with destructive intent. We see the happiness of a man acquainted with the notion of Death but having no real knowledge of it – 'So near grows death to life, whate'er death is,/Some dreadful thing no doubt' (IV 425–6); and then, after the long interruption of Books V–VIII, which represent the everything which stretched between life and death, we witness the crucial act from which the real knowledge of Death will spring, when Eve took the fruit, 'and knew not eating death' (IX 792). The syntax, once again, is Greek; but we fill it with our different and complementary English senses: 'she knew not that she was eating death'; 'she knew not death even as she ate it'; 'although she was so bold as to eat death for the sake of knowledge, she still did not know – indeed she did not even know what she had known before, namely that this was a sin'. Above all she *eats* Death, makes it a part of her formerly incorruptible body, and so explains the human sense of the possibility of incorruption, so tragically belied by fact. The function of Death in the poem is simple enough; it is 'to destroy, or unimmortal make/All kinds' (X 611–12). There is, of course, the theological explanation to be considered, that the success of Death in this attempt is permissive; but in terms of the poem this is really no more than a piece of dogmatic cheering-up, and Milton, as usual, allows God himself to do the explaining (X 616 ff.). From the human point of view, the intimation of unimmortality takes priority over the intellectual comfort of God's own theodicy, simply because a man can feel, and can feel the possibility of immortality blighted.

Milton saw the chance, in Book IX, of presenting very concretely the impact of Death on Life; and it would be hard to think of a fiction more completely achieved. The moment is of Eve's return to Adam, enormously ignorant and foolishly cunning, 'with countenance blithe . . . But in her cheek distemper flushing glowed' (IX 886–7). This flush is a token of unimmortality; and then, since 'all kinds' are to be affected, the roses fade and droop in Adam's welcoming garland. He sees that Eve is lost, 'Defaced, deflowered, and now to death devote' (901). He retreats into Eve's self-deception; but all is lost.

The emphasis here is on *all*; from the moment of eating the fruit to that of the descent of 'prevenient grace' (end of Book X and beginning of XI) Adam and Eve have lost everything, and are, without mitigation, to death devote. If one bears this steadily in mind the tenth book is a lot easier to understand; it seems often to be misread. Adam, 'in a troubled sea of passion tossed' (718) cries out 'O miserable of happy!' (720) and laments the end of the 'new glorious world' (721). He feels particularly the corruption of love :

> O voice once heard
> Delightfully, 'Increase and multiply',
> Now death to hear ! (x 729–31)

and sums up in a couplet using the familiar pseudo-rhyme : 'O fleeting joys/Of Paradise, dear bought with lasting woes!' (741–2). He has knowledge of the contrast between then and now, but of nothing else. Deprived of Original Justice, he is now merely natural; hence the importance of remembering that he is here simply a human being in a situation that is also simple, and capable of being felt naturally, upon our pulses. Deprived as he is, Adam finds life 'inexplicable' (754); knowing nothing of the great official plan by which good will come of all this, his speculations are by the mere light of nature. Rajan made something of this in his explanation of how Milton got his heterodox theology into the poem – mortalism, for example, is not very tendentious if proffered as the opinion of a totally corrupt man.[9] But, much more important, Adam is here for the first time true kindred to the reader. The primary appeal of poetry is to the natural man; that is why it is called simple, sensuous and passionate. When Eve proposes that they should practise a difficult abstinence in order not to produce more candidates for unimmortality, or Adam considers suicide (x 966 ff.), we should be less conscious of their errors than of their typicality. Whatever the mind may make of it, the sensitive body continues to feel the threat of unimmortality as an outrage :

> Why is life given
> To be thus wrested from us? Rather why
> Obtruded on us thus? Who, if we knew
> What we receive, would either not accept
> Life offered, or soon beg to lay it down,
> Glad to be so dismissed in peace. (xi 502–7)

Michael's treatment of the same topic that the Duke inflicts upon
Claudio in *Measure for Measure* can only strengthen such sentiments :

> thou must outlive
> Thy youth, thy strength, thy beauty, which will change
> To withered weak and gray; thy senses then
> Obtuse, all taste of pleasure must forego,
> To what thou hast, and for the air of youth
> Hopeful and cheerful, in thy blood will reign
> A melancholy damp of cold and dry
> To weigh thy spirits down, and last consume
> The balm of life. (xɪ 538–46)

Whatever the consolation offered by Death – no one would wish
to 'eternize' a life so subject to distempers of every kind – it is
not pretended that this makes up for the loss of the 'two fair
gifts . . . happiness/And immortality, (x 56–8). Most criticism
of the verse of Books x and xɪ amounts to a complaint that it is
lacking in sensuousness; but this is founded on a misunderstanding of the poem. *Paradise Lost* must be seen as a whole; and who-
ever tries to do this will see the propriety of this change of tone,
this diminution of *sense* in the texture of the verse.

A striking example of this propriety is the second of the formal
salutations to Eve, Adam's in xɪ 158 ff. Here Adam sees that Eve
is responsible not only for death but for the victory over it; as
she herself says, 'I who first brought death on all, am graced/
The source of life' (xɪ 168–9). This paradox, considered as part
of the whole complex in which Milton places it, seems to me
much more central to the mood of the poem than the famous
felix culpa, because it is rooted in nature, and related to our
habit of rejoicing that life continues, in spite of death, from
generation to generation. Yet Adam is still under the shadow of
death, and his restatement of the theme Venus–Eve–Mary is very
properly deprived of the sensuous context provided for Raphael's
salutation; and since the second passage cannot but recall the
first, we may be sure that this effect was intended.

There is, indeed, another passage which strongly supports this
view of the centrality of the paradox of Eve as destroyer and giver

of life, and it has the same muted quality, casts the same
shadow over the power and delight of love. This is the curious
vision of the union between the sons of Seth and the daughters
of Cain (xi 556–636). The Scriptural warrant for this passage
is extremely slight, though there were precedents for Milton's
version. Adam rejoices to see these godly men united in love with
fair women :

> Such happy interview and fair event
> Of love and youth not lost, songs, garlands, flowers,
> And charming symphonies attached the heart
> Of Adam, soon inclined to admit delight,
> The bent of nature . . . (xi 593–7)

And he thanks the angel, remarking that 'Here nature seems ful-
filled in all her ends' (602). He is at once coldly corrected; these
women, against the evidence of Adam's own senses, are 'empty
of all good' (616), and nothing but ill comes from the 'sons
of God' (622) yielding up all their virtue to them. Milton remembered how much of Pandora there was in Eve. From
women Adam is taught to expect woe; but, more important, this
change in the divine arrangements means that the evidence
of the senses, the testimony of pleasure, is no longer a reliable
guide :

> Judge not what is best
> By pleasure, though to nature seeming meet . . . (xi 603–4)

Paradise Lost is a poem about death, and about pleasure and its
impairment. It is not very surprising that generations of readers
failed to see the importance to Milton's 'scheme' of Adam's
exclamation upon a paradox which depends not upon the senses
but upon revelation; I mean the assurance that out of all this evil
good will come as testimony of a benevolent plan

> more wonderful
> Than that which by creation first brought forth
> Light out of darkness. (xii 471–3)

The senses will not recognize that out of their own destruction will come forth 'joy and eternal bliss' (XII 551). In that line Milton echoes the *Comus* Epilogue – Joy will come from the great wound the senses have suffered, but it is a joy measured by what we have had and lost. And the sense of loss is keener by far than the apprehension of things unseen, the remote promise of restoration. The old Eden we know, we can describe it, inlay it with a thousand known flowers and compare it with a hundred other paradises; throughout the whole history of loss and deprivation the poets have reconstructed it with love. The new one may be called 'happier far', but poetry cannot say much more about it because the senses do not know it. The paradise of Milton's poem is the lost, the only true, paradise; we confuse ourselves, and with the same subtlety confuse the 'simple' poem, if we believe otherwise.

Shelley spoke of Milton's 'bold neglect of a direct moral purpose', and held this to be 'the most decisive proof of the supremacy of Milton's genius'. 'He mingled, as it were', Shelley added, 'the elements of human nature as colours upon a single pallet, and arranged them in the composition of his great picture according to the laws of epic truth; that is, according to the laws of that principal by which a series of actions of the external universe and of intelligent and ethical beings is calculated to excite the sympathy of succeeding generations of mankind.'[10] This passage follows upon the famous observations on Satan, and is itself succeeded by and involved with a Shelleyan attack on Christianity; and perhaps in consequence of this has not been thought worth much attention except by those specialized opponents who contend for and against Satan in the hero–ass controversy. Theirs is an increasing quarrel, but its ground ought to be shifted; and in any case this is not the occasion to reopen it. But the remarks of Shelley I have quoted seem to me substantially true; so, rightly understood, do the much-anathematized remarks of Blake. I say 'substantially' because Milton himself would perhaps have argued that he accepted what responsibility he could for the moral effect of his poem, and that in any case he specifically desiderated a 'fit' audience, capable of making its own distinctions between moral good and evil. Yet in so far as poetry works through the pleasure it provides – a point upon which Milton and Shelley would agree – it must neglect 'a direct moral purpose'; and in so far as it deals with the passions of fallen man it has to do with Blake's hellish energies. And however much one may feel that they exaggerated the truth in applying it to Milton, one ought to be clear that Shelley and Blake were not simply proposing naughty Romantic paradoxes because they did not know enough. Indeed they show us a truth about *Paradise Lost* which later commentary, however learned, has made less and less accessible.

With these thoughts in my mind, I sometimes feel that the shift of attention necessary to make friends out of some of Milton's most potent modern enemies is in reality a very small one. However this may be, I want to end by citing Mr Robert Graves; not because I have any hope of persuading him from his evidently and irrationally powerful distaste for Milton, but to give myself the pleasure of quoting one of his poems. It is called 'Pure Death', and in it Mr Graves speculates on a theme that he might have found, superbly extended, in Milton's epic :

> We looked, we loved, and therewith instantly
> Death became terrible to you and me.
> By love we disenthralled our natural terror
> From every comfortable philosopher
> Or tall grey doctor of divinity :
> Death stood at last in his true rank and order.[11]

Milton gives us this perception, but 'according to the laws of epic truth'; which is to say, he exhibits life in a great symbolic attitude.

SOURCE : *The Living Milton* (1960).

NOTES

1. *Images and Themes in Five Poems by Milton* (1957), p. 20.
2. E. Cassirer, *An Essay on Man* (1944), pp. 83–4.
3. Harris Fletcher, *Milton's Rabbinical Readings* (1930), p. 185.

4. *Paradise Lost with reference to the Hexameral Background* (1945), pp. 76 ff.

5. See W. B. Hunter, Jr., 'Milton's Power of Matter', *Journal of the History of Ideas,* XIII (1952), 551–62.

6. I have said part of my say about this in 'The Argument of Marvell's Garden', *Essays in Criticism,* II (1952), 225–41.

7. See E. R. Curtius, *European Literature and the Latin Middle Ages* (1953), chap. 10, especially pp. 195 ff.

8. *Paradise Lost in our Time* (1948), pp. 105–6.

9. B. Rajan, *Paradise Lost and the Seventeenth Century Reader* (1947), chap. II.

10. *A Defence of Poetry,* in *Shelley's Literary and Philosophical Criticism,* ed. J. Shawcross (1909), p. 146.

11. *Collected Poems* (1959), p. 71.

Christopher Ricks

TINCTURE OR REFLECTION (1963)

Milton's magnificent lines on the creation of Light are a noble comment on his own poetry and its light:

> Of light by far the greater part he took,
> Transplanted from her cloudy shrine, and placed
> In the sun's orb, made porous to receive
> And drink the liquid light, firm to retain
> Her gathered beams, great palace now of light.
> Hither as to their fountain other stars
> Repairing, in their golden urns draw light,
> And hence the morning planet gilds her horns;
> By tincture or reflection they augment
> Their small peculiar, though from human sight
> So far remote, with diminution seen. (VII 359–69)

By far the greater part of the light of Milton's poetry acts with the noble directness of the sun itself. The Grand Style is a 'great palace now of light'. That directness ensures that we receive the rays of the sun – the sun which is like poetry in that its

> virtue on itself works no effect,
> But in the fruitful earth; there first received
> His beams, unactive else, their vigour find. (VIII 95–7)

But not all the radiance of Milton's poetry is shed in this way. Like the light, it too is liquid; and it too is both porous and firm. And just as the stars receive and transmit light by 'tincture or reflection', so too do Milton's words. If we are to see not merely the greater part of the light, but all of it, we must receive the tinctures and reflections which gild his liquid verse.

Richardson offers a good example of what I mean. He drew

attention to the suggestiveness of the placing of 'retired' in the lines

> Others apart sat on a hill retired,
> In thoughts more elevate, and reasoned high . . . (II 557–8)

'Though the Text does not Say it, the Reader will from the Words naturally be led to imagine Some were Retir'd, in Thought, as well as from the Company, and Reason'd and Debated, Discours'd within Themselves, on these Perplexing, but Important Suttleties: This gives a very Proper Image here, a very Melancholly and Touching One.' Richardson's tone, tentative yet precise, is admirable – and so is his insistence that many of Milton's images depend on what is suggested as well as on what is explicitly said. The modern critic is often accused of reading too much into works of the past, and certainly he ought to point precisely to what it is that suggested his comments. But it is interesting to find the eighteenth-century critics responding to Milton in so supple a way.

An interchange between Bentley and Pearce brings out that flexible syntax in Milton can be mistaken for careless syntax. Bentley objected to the description of Satan,

> His countenance, as the morning star that guides
> The starry flock, allured them, and with lies
> Drew after him the third part of heaven's host. (v 708–10)

'In this Reading the Construction will be, *His countenance allured and drew them with Lies*. He is the *Father of Lies* indeed, if not his Tongue, but his Countenance spoke them.' Of course this is a quibble – such a shift is easy enough, and the main meaning offers no real difficulty. But as often with a quibble by Bentley, he fastens on a boldly suggestive metaphor: 'He is the *Father of Lies* indeed, if not his Tongue, but his Countenance spoke them.' And Pearce's reply brings out very well both the straightforward sense and the metaphorical suggestion: 'By the expression *His Countenance* is meant He himself. . . . But if this will not be allow'd to be *Milton*'s meaning, yet it may be said that *Satan's Countenance* seducing his followers by disguising the foul inten-

tions of his heart, may be very properly said to *seduce with Lyes.*'
That Pearce's suggestion is plausible may be seen from the innumerable occasions when Milton makes profound and subtle use
of Satan's countenance.

At any rate, the fact that the solid and respectable eighteenth-
century editors were aware of suggestive niceties of syntax gives
one some right to proceed.

After long argument, Eve leaves Adam to go gardening on her
own :

> Thus saying, from her husband's hand her hand
> Soft she withdrew (IX 385–6)

If we had to paraphrase the lines, we would say that 'soft' was an
adverb, not an adjective : she softly withdrew her hand. This
makes admirably grim sense; *soft* ought to include 'yielding', but
Eve is firmly and unshakeably insisting on her own way. She is
stubborn but sweet :

> Eve, who thought
> Less attributed to her faith sincere,
> Thus her reply with accent sweet renewed. (IX 319–21)

Persistent, but meek :

> but Eve
> Persisted, yet submiss, though last, replied. (IX 376–7)

And she is obdurate but soft. So much for the main sense : she
softly withdrew her hand. But Milton didn't exactly say that;
and since 'soft' is the adjectival form as well, and since Milton so
often puts his adjectives after his nouns, the word 'soft' gets attracted into Eve's hand, delicately and as it were by reflection. So
that the total effect is 'her soft hand softly she withdrew', with
soft sounded much more quietly than *softly*. And with a delicate
fusion of two points of view, since the adverb has the neutrality
of an onlooker, while the adjective puts us in the place of Adam
as he feels Eve's hand. E. E. Cummings might achieve such effects
through typography and punctuation – Milton uses syntax. Mr

Lewis's remark about Milton's network is applicable to his syntax too: 'Nearly every sentence in Milton has that power which physicists sometimes think we shall have to attribute to matter – the power of action at a distance.'[1]

This is obviously open to the charge of over-ingenuity, and substantiation is scarce. (It would be likely to be, with so delicate an effect.) But, first, one might point to softness as pre-eminently the characteristic for which Eve was created:

> For contemplation he and valour formed,
> For softness she and sweet attractive grace. (IV 297–8)

Her 'soft embraces' and 'her heavenly form angelic, but more soft, and feminine' are contrasted elsewhere with Adam, 'Less winning soft, less amiably mild'.[2]

And, second, one might support this with the lines when Adam awakens Eve, which interestingly give us the 'hand' again:

> then with voice
> Mild, as when Zephyrus on Flora breathes,
> Her hand soft touching, whispered thus . . . (V 15–17)

In the eighteenth century this was seen to be ambiguous, and was tidied up with a hyphen: *soft-touching*. And again if we had to choose, the paraphrase would obviously be 'softly touching'. But the close parallel with the other line reinforces for me the idea that 'soft' once again affects our sense of Eve's hand, a tincture that is quietly beautiful, and that would certainly deserve Bagehot's praise of Milton's 'haunting atmosphere of enhancing suggestions'.

To combine clarity of stated sense with such suggestiveness is the mark of those poets who rise above divisions into Classical and Romantic. Milton's use of syntax for such purposes is often supported by alliteration, which – like rhyme – can tie together suggestively things which are not tied together in the plain statement. This was perhaps one of the many effects which Hopkins developed from Milton. Take, for instance, the alliteration in the line from 'I wake and feel the fell of dark, not day', when Hopkins says that the heart must endure more before it reaches God's peace: 'And more must, in yet longer light's delay.' Obviously a simple paraphrase would say 'While light delays even longer', but that is not what Hopkins wrote. The compression of the syntax, itself Miltonic, brings *longer* up against *light*, which furthermore alliterates. And the alliteration is stressed by the opening of the line ('and more must . . .'). So that although logically, and primarily, *longer* goes with *delay*, and not with *light*, the effect of the syntax and alliteration is to suggest that it is light which is longer. So that it is as if, thinking apparently only of the fact that it will be a long time before God's peace comes, Hopkins also remembers that when the light of eternity does come, it will be *longer* than the darkness of this life. The phrase has just that combination of strong present despair and quiet distant hope which is characteristic of his best poetry.

Milton uses syntax and alliteration in just the same way – they allow him to suggest things which he doesn't actually say. In the account of Mulciber's fall, for example, we move through 'he fell . . . he fell . . . dropped' to

> he with this rebellious rout
> Fell long before; nor aught availed him now
> To have built in heaven high towers; nor did he scape
> By all his engines, but was headlong sent . . . (I 747–50)

Alliteration and word-order tie 'heaven' and 'high' together, though the plain sense is 'high towers', enforced as it is by the rhythm as well as by the earlier reference to 'a towered structure high'. But Milton is not satisfied with the plain sense alone. The feeling of *high heaven* is important to the sense of Mulciber's fall from that height, Mulciber who fell headlong down to Hell. To say that Heaven is high would be to risk cliché; but to suggest it while saying something else is another matter.

The support for this comes in the way Milton uses 'high' elsewhere. It is used more than a hundred times; and he uses it in the immediate context of 'heaven' more than twenty times, without actually applying it, with dull predictability, to 'heaven'. Only twice does he say that Heaven is high – but the one is tinged with a moral meaning, stressed by 'lowly':

> heaven is for thee too high
> To know what passes there; be lowly wise. (VIII 172-3)

And the other is Eve's silly hopefulness:

> heaven is high,
> High and remote to see from thence distinct
> Each thing on earth (IX 811-13)

But most worth noticing is that Milton is very fond of using this same pattern elsewhere to bring 'heaven' and 'high' together while stating something else: 'heaven's high jurisdiction', or 'heaven's high behest'.[3] Perhaps the closest to the pattern of 'in heaven high towers' is this sequence:

> Had not the eternal king omnipotent
> From his strong hold of heaven high overruled
> And limited their might (VI 227-9)

'High' there is an adverb, but how finely the syntax and alliteration merge it with 'heaven'. (Or conversely, if it is taken as an adjective, how finely it suggests the moral power of the adverb.)

Yet one can bring out the point of such a merging only by leaving syntax for a moment in order to stress the crucial importance to Milton of the word 'high', partly reflected in its great frequency. Just as 'stand' is clashed against 'fall', so is 'high' clashed against 'deep': 'the deep fall of those too high aspiring' (VI 898-9).[4] Insisting on 'the height of this great argument', a height that must be worthy of Him who sits 'high throned above all height', Milton simply but powerfully plays the literal against the abstract:

> nor ever thence
> Had risen or heaved his head, but that the will
> And high permission of all-ruling heaven . . . (I 210-12)

The play is in earnest because the physical fact about Heaven has a moral significance:

> Straight knew him all the bands
> Of angels under watch; and to his state,
> And to his message high in honour rise (v 287–9)

And Milton even makes the word receive the full weight of his sardonic condemnation. Pandaemonium, 'the high capital of Satan and his peers', is down in Hell. There 'highly they raged against the highest'. And there we hear of Dagon, who 'fell flat, and shamed his worshippers', and yet 'had his temple high'.[5]

Milton uses such fluidity of syntax so that it both makes clear sense and also is suggestive. Sometimes the suggestion is of a hyperbolical beauty which it would be indecorous to state as fact – particularly in the epic. To show this at work, it is best to take one of the most powerful and consistent of the Paradisal images: the mingled beauties of sight and of scent (and of sound too). The image itself is a lovely one, but it is the mingling syntax which brings it to life, which both suggests the magically pre-lapsarian and states the matter of fact. The syntax combines the charmed subjectivity of the lyric with the grave objectivity of the epic. Macaulay thought that poetry and science were the ends of a see-saw: 'We cannot unite the incompatible advantages of reality and deception, the clear discernment of truth and the exquisite enjoyment of fiction.'[6] Milton often did, as Richardson insisted: 'When the Imagination is Rais'd as much as Possible, let it still know More is Un-conceiv'd; Let the Lark Sing after he is Lost in Air.'

When we see Eve as she

> strews the ground
> With rose and odours from the shrub unfumed (v 348–9)

we know perfectly well what is meant and find no unseemly violence of syntax. But the actual sequence – 'strews the ground with odours' – makes the scents magically visible and physical. So, too, does the superb word-order in these lines:

> So to the silvan lodge
> They came, that like Pomona's arbour smiled
> With flowerets decked and fragrant smells; but Eve
> Undecked . . . (v 377–80)

If we want simple sense, then 'decked' goes only with 'flowerets' and not with 'smells' – 'decked with smells' might be too boldly metaphorical if badly stated. But the lines do obliquely state it, and the encircling of 'fragrant smells' by *decked* and *undecked* ensures that the metaphor is not so obliquely presented as to be itself invisible. The imagination once again treats scents as if they were as solid and visible as flowers. And there is also a perfectly intelligible non-metaphorical syntax ('smiled with fragrant smells and decked with flowerets'). The lines combine the virtues of both poetry and prose. Moreover, they achieve through syntax the mingling of the senses which Keats achieves through diction : 'Nor what soft incense hangs upon the boughs.'

This particular image for the beauty of Paradise can take simpler forms. There is the syntactical stroke of describing 'cassia, nard, and balm' not – as we would expect – as 'odorous flowers', but as 'flowering odours'. Bentley found the phrase 'Affectation extravagant'; Pearce paltered; and it was left to Richardson to maintain that the phrase was a fine one. And the beautifully unexpected substantiality of the scents here is skilfully introduced by 'field' and 'groves' :

> and now is come
> Into the blissful field, through groves of myrrh,
> And flowering odours, cassia, nard, and balm (v 291–3)

Or the syntactical imagination can juxtapose 'rose' and 'odours' as if they were of equal substantiality, and then apply to them both a verb that, in its vigour, insists on the substantial :

> fresh gales and gentle airs
> Whispered it to the woods, and from their wings
> Flung rose, flung odours from the spicy shrub (viii 515–17)

The close parallel there with the first passage quoted above (v 348–9) brings out how important to Milton is this image of Paradise. (The biographical critic would justifiably make at once for Milton's blindness.) And the poet invests Eve with this image as Satan fatally finds her :

> Eve separate he spies,
> Veiled in a cloud of fragrance, where she stood,
> Half spied ... (ix 424–6)

The veil and the cloud make the roses' scent beautifully visible –
does 'Half spied' even perhaps suggest that the scent was so thick
that it almost hid her? Not really, because I have cut short the
sentence:

> Half spied, so thick the roses bushing round
> About her glowed. (426–7)

Reasonably, it is not the scent but the roses which hide her. But
the other instances of Milton's seeing a scent, and the general
fluidity of his syntax, persuade me that we are meant for a
moment to believe that 'Half spied' follows the *fragrance*, just as
it follows 'he spies'. Of course it in fact anticipates the roses, but
the deliberate 'flicker of hesitation' which Dr Davie finds elsewhere in Milton is perhaps being used here with characteristic
subtlety. Like a skilful advocate, Milton says something which
would be impermissibly far-fetched, and then has it struck from
the record. But his skill has lodged it in our minds or feelings.

Obviously such a device, to offer and then to deny (which
has much in common with the rhetorical figure *occupatio*) is very
common in Milton, above all in the allusions but also in the syntax. Bentley objected to the line 'The fellows of his crime, the
followers rather': 'This RATHER, this correction of what he had
said before, has something little and low in it. For if the Word
wanted correcting, why was it put down here.' But Bentley ought
to allow that unsaying is not the same as never having said –
and Milton makes fine use of the difference. It is on this that the
poignant aptness of the classical allusions depends: Mulciber fell,
but no – 'Thus they relate, erring.'

The 'flicker of hesitation' which Dr Davie so well defined,
and which he so well illustrated in its effects, is not as uncom-
mon in Milton as might be suggested by Dr Davie's deploring
of the average run of the syntax. Milton uses the slightly surprising compression of a double syntax to carry the weightiest
suggestions. The syntax is not usually double in that it actually

takes two paths – that would defeat narrative and sequence. But it stands for a moment uncertain which of two paths to take, and deliberately exploiting the uncertainty. Later, when we look back, we feel not only the relief of having chosen, but also a powerful sense of what the other path led to.

> Footfalls echo in the memory
> Down the passage which we did not take
> Towards the door we never opened
> Into the rose-garden. My words echo
> Thus, in your mind.

Milton can combine, through the hesitations of his syntax, the suggestiveness of vistas with the progressions of ordered narrative.

This is so when Milton tragically exclaims

> O much deceived, much failing, hapless Eve,
> Of thy presumed return ! Event perverse !
> Thou never from that hour in Paradise
> Found'st either sweet repast, or sound repose . . .
>
> (IX 404–7)

At first, one takes 'deceived' and failing' as absolute in their application to Eve – the poet's imagination is absorbing the full bitterness of the imminent Fall. But then the next line – 'Of thy presumed return !' – declares that she is *deceived in* the one present circumstance : her presumed return. So the lines are both tragically prophetic and dramatically momentary. And the hesitation, as to whether 'deceived' and 'failing' are absolute or particular, is resolved here by our realizing that there are not in fact two paths at all, but only one. For Eve to be wrong about anything (even that she would soon be back) is for her to be wrong about everything. Before the Fall, the distinction of absolute or particular failing does not exist. Once deception and failure have arrived, then they have arrived absolutely. It is the hesitating syntax which makes the point, and resolves itself.

Mr Stein has drawn attention to the delicate balance of present innocence with potential danger when Eve leaves Raphael and Adam :

> With goddess-like demeanour forth she went;
> Not unattended, for on her as queen
> A pomp of winning graces waited still,
> And from about her shot darts of desire
> Into all eyes to wish her still in sight. (VIII 59–63)

'She leaves', says Mr Stein, 'under circumstances that emphasize (and create the opportunity for emphasizing) at once her genuine charms, her potentially dangerous charms (the 'darts of desire'), and her relations (according to the scale of creation) with Adam.'[7]

It is true that the 'darts of desire' are potentially dangerous.[8] But the point about the delicate balance of danger and innocence could best be made by references, first, to the rhythm (which emphatically juxtaposes 'shot darts'), and, second, to the syntax :

> And from about her shot darts of desire
> Into all eyes to wish her still in sight.

The balance is in the hesitation. At first, *desire* seems absolute, and as such potentially dangerous and prophetic of the Fall :

> Carnal desire inflaming, he on Eve
> Began to cast lascivious eyes, she him
> As wantonly repaid (IX 1013–15)

And the hesitation is maintained by the delaying phrase 'into all eyes' – after which, and only after which, is the *desire* defined as still innocent : 'to wish her still in sight'. Richardson noticed the ambivalence of the syntax, and hurried to protect Eve's honour: 'This passage must be pointed Thus, as in *Milton*'s Editions; as Some have done it, it makes Wild work. Darts of desire but Only to Wish her Stay.'

The potential danger, then, is expressed in the potential syntax. We are shown a path which Adam and Eve might take (and which tragically we know they will take), but they have not yet taken it. Potential danger, but still actual innocence. So the syntax is resolved into innocence, with justice to Eve. But the hesitation about 'desire' is essential to the effect – if it is equivocal, that is because it thereby provides a perfect mirror for the equivocal position of Adam and Eve before the Fall (if they could fall, were they not already in some sense fallen?). The lines admirably fulfil Dr Davie's wishes for poetic syntax: 'a movement of syntax can render, immediately present, the curve of destiny through a life or the path of an energy through the mind.'[9]

How, and how admirably, the lines do so, is clear if we substitute a more usual word-order, one that does not deliberately delay:

> And from about her shot into all eyes
> Darts of desire to wish her still in sight.

The innocence of 'desire' is there established too quickly. The subtle effect depended on subtle syntax, and also on the opportunity for legitimate surprise that is offered by the line-endings. Dr Davie finds that the line-endings are poorly used. Just how effective they really are is shown by William Forde's *The True Spirit of Milton's Versification* (1831), which quaintly rearranges the verse into sense-units: 'The *Lines* will now represent the natural division of every sentence into its component Members', so that 'the reader may attend solely to the sense and the harmonious order of the words, without feeling any embarrassment from the contrariety between the linear division, and the meaning of the language'.[10] But it is exactly this 'contrariety' which Milton uses to enforce his meaning, and when this 'embarrassment' disappears, so does the precision and the emphasis. A neat modern example is Mr Whaler's observation that at one point Milton's lines may be slid along into a different iambic pattern, and with very different effect. Thus Milton wrote:

> But wherefore thou alone? Wherefore with thee
> Came not all hell broke loose? Is pain to them
> Less pain, less to be fled, or thou than they
> Less hardy to endure? Courageous chief,
> ,The first in flight from pain, had'st thou alleged
> To thy deserted host his cause of flight,
> Thou surely hadst not come sole fugitive. (iv 917–23)

Mr Whaler [11] slides the pattern along, and the result is fascinating, not so much numerologically (Mr Whaler's concern) as critically :

> But wherefore thou alone?
> Wherefore with thee came not all hell broke loose?
> Is pain to them less pain, less to be fled,
> Or thou than they less hardy to endure?
> Courageous chief, the first in flight from pain,
> Hadst thou alleged to thy deserted host
> This cause of flight, thou surely hadst not come
> Sole fugitive.

Milton's lines have become eighteenth-century Miltonics. The surge of the verse has gone, and been replaced by the dullness of three questions that fall neatly at the ends of the lines. The playing of the syntax against the metre has disappeared, and with it has gone the emphatic placing of 'Less pain' and 'Less hardy' at the opening of the lines, and above all the great weight which the last line of the speech received by being the only one where the sense-unit met and clinched the metre.

Let me return from the 'hesitations', and their dependence on the skilful use of line-endings, to the point at which it was necessary to explain them : the suggestive mingling of the senses in the harmony of Paradise. An eighteenth-century editor might well have objected to Eve's lines :

> Not distant far from thence a murmuring sound
> Of waters issued from a cave and spread
> Into a liquid plain, then stood unmoved
> Pure as the expanse of heaven . . . (IV 453–6)

We all know what this means, but it does say that the *sound* 'spread into a liquid plain . . .'. Is this just carelessness? Or is there a reason why Milton treats the water as sound?

First, we must remember Milton's recurring insistence that sound is a movement of the air, that an air is the air. We sense how all the different movements of the air, including sounds, blend together in Paradise :

> for his sleep
> Was airy light from pure digestion bred,
> And temperate vapours bland, which the only sound
> Of leaves and fuming rills, Aurora's fan,
> Lightly dispersed, and the shrill matin song
> Of birds on every bough (v 3–8)

'Sound' as 'air', then, in the lines of Eve under discussion. But what is there in the context that explains the further mingling of the air with water?

Eve awakes, and gazes like Narcissus into the lake, which is 'pure as the expanse of heaven',

> the clear
> Smooth lake, that to me seemed another sky. (IV 458–9)

Upon this mirroring of the airy sky in the lake depends the whole important episode. But perhaps 'mirroring' judges the situation more knowledgeably than Eve could – say rather, indistinguishability: 'Uncertain which, in ocean or in air' (III 76). Milton insists on the indistinguishable commingling not only by the explicit comparisons, but also by the syntactical mingling in a 'sound . . . spread into a liquid plain'. It is not entirely accidental that we might talk of the *fluidity* of such syntax.

That this is Milton's creation rather than mine is made clear if we notice how he does not rely upon the syntax and the explicit comparisons alone, but uses for the water the diction with which he elsewhere presents the creation of the airy sky – *liquid*, *pure*, and *expanse* :

> and God made
> The firmament, expanse of liquid, pure,
> Transparent, elemental air. (VII 263–5)[12]

Of course 'the liquid air' is a commonplace,[13] but it is one of great use and importance when Eve as it were regards herself as Narcissus – one of the most poignantly significant of her appearances before the Fall. Milton brings this commonplace to life by blurring the distinction between air and water in his syntax.

Bentley was shocked by the lines which I have just quoted from the opening of Book v, describing Adam waking to the vapours and sounds of Paradise. He took exception to the phrase 'the only sound of leaves and fuming rills': 'What's that which follows, *The sound of fuming rills*?' Newton followed Pearce and said sensibly: 'They do not make a noise as *fuming*, but only as *rills*.' True enough. But it is not necessary to believe that Milton was unaware of the strangely lovely suggestion which Bentley noticed.

To handle syntax with such various control is not what one would expect from a poet who was callous to the intrinsic nature of English. The syntax moves between the quiet poles of the power that can launch an 'adventurous song', and the delicacy that augments the song by tincture and reflection. 'Milton', said Hopkins, 'is the great master of sequence of phrase'; and R. W. Dixon, agreeing, offered an apt image in describing the Miltonic style as 'a deliberate unrolling as if of some vast material'.[14] The more one looks closely at Milton's word-order, the less truth there seems to be in Mr Eliot's remark[15] that 'the syntax is determined by the musical significance, by the auditory imagination, rather than by the attempt to follow actual speech or thought'.

SOURCE: *Milton's Grand Style* (1963).

NOTES

1. *A Preface*, p. 42. J. H. Hanford has two particularly interesting pages on the beauty of Milton's ambiguous syntax in *A Milton Handbook* (4th ed., 1946, pp. 300–1). And John Wain, discussing Hopkins, has deftly pointed out the suggestiveness of a verb 'that radiates both ways' (*Proceedings of the British Academy*, 1959, XLV p. 194).

2. IV 471; IX 457–8; IV 479.

3. This is the pattern at II 62, 319, 359; V 220, 467; VII 373; XI 251.

4. Mrs I. G. MacCaffrey writes interestingly on this in chapters III and IV of *P.L. as 'Myth'*. Jackson I. Cope goes through all the examples in chapter IV of *The Metaphoric Structure of P.L.* (1962).

5. I 756, 666, 461–3.
6. *Literary and Historical Essays* (1934), pp. 7–8.
7. *Answerable Style*, p. 91.
8. Adam was 'here only weak/Against the charm of beauty's powerful glance' (VIII 532–3).
9. *Articulate Energy*, p. 157.
10. pp. xxix, xxxiii.
11. *Counterpoint and Symbol,* pp. 20–1.
12. Cp. 'Nor in their liquid texture mortal wound
Receive, no more than can the fluid air' (VI 348–9)
13. John Arthos quotes thirty-eight examples from Empedocles to Genest (*The Language of Natural Description in 18th Century Poetry,* 1949, pp. 237–40).
14. Letters of 13 June and 25 Sept. 1878.
15. *On Poetry and Poets,* p. 142.

A. E. Dyson and Julian Lovelock

EVENT PERVERSE:
THE EPIC OF EXILE (1973)

> O much deceived, much failing, hapless Eve,
> Of thy presumed return! Event perverse!
> Thou never from that hour in Paradise
> Found'st either sweet repast, or sound repose;
> Such ambush hid among sweet flowers and shades
> Waited with hellish rancour imminent
> To intercept thy way, or send thee back
> Despoiled of innocence, of faith, of bliss. (IX 404–11)

Eve has had her lovers' quarrel with Adam, that marvellous last dialogue of innocence when Adam has encountered everything that is feminine and much, if Tillyard is right, that is fallen, before the Fall. Now she goes off on her own to be tempted.

In many ways it is right that she should. The younger Milton, as we know, could not 'praise a fugitive and cloistered virtue, unexercised and unbreathed, that never sallies out and sees her adversary, but slinks out of the race, where that immortal garland is to be run for, not without dust and heat' (*Areopagitica*, 1644). This militant optimism had found its apotheosis in *Comus* (1634), where the Lady's virtue held against all assaults and turned back the foe.

By the 1660s Milton was battered by life and familiar with suffering, but his faith in freedom remained intact. In *Paradise Lost* Eve's temptation is permitted both by God, Who has created her perfect and given her liberty ('Sufficient to have stood, though free to fall', III 99), and by Adam, who has received her from God in trust. In Book IX Adam treats Eve as a free being precisely in the manner of God's dealings with himself. He tries to dissuade her with lucid arguments, rational warnings, loving tenderness, but he does not constrain her against her will. In this he is surely right and acting wisely, even though Waldock has hinted that his failure to restrain Eve forcibly may be the root cause of the Fall. The whole justification of God's ways to man turns on this issue, since the reality of freedom alone makes sense of exile and death. We have always to compare God's dealings with His creatures as they are actually imaged in the poem with the various charges evolved against Him in the rhetoric of Hell. Is He indeed malign, tyrannical or inept, as is frequently asserted; is His omnipotence really cast in doubt by the fact of sin?

Milton's earliest plans for *Paradise Lost* (*circa* 1640) envisaged a tragic drama, and Alastair Fowler suggests in the Introduction to his recent edition of the poem that we 'should even, perhaps, consider it a tragical epic rather than a pure epic'. This notion of a 'tragical epic' is a useful corrective to over-rigid *genre* criticism, but is not without dangers of its own. If we accept it, we should remember also that *Paradise Lost* is a specifically Christian epic, and tragic precisely in the manner and to the degree inherent in its theme. Milton's task is not now to sing the power of Virtue, as it had been in *Comus*, but to account for man's exile from Paradise in a mortal world. While there can be no evading the ironies – so close to tragedy – in this material, there should be no overlooking the counterbalance of Christian Hope. All tragedy gravitates perhaps towards either hope or despair in its final suggestions, but only Christian tragedy is actually transformed by the assertion of hope. There is the hope of life after death, which most tragedy does not offer; more strikingly there is the hope invested in a God Who takes evil and turns it to good. So perhaps Christian 'tragedy' is more properly and accurately described as Divine Comedy, since it differs sufficiently from other tragedy in its resolution to need its own name.

For present purposes 'divine comedy' points usefully, as a label, to that aspect of the poem's Christianity which most controls its ironic effects. It is a mark of *Paradise Lost* that it echoes throughout with double or even treble ironies, deriving from the presence in time of realities located outside. These 'realities' brood over every episode in Heaven, Hell or Paradise, operating irrespective of the 'before', 'after' or 'now' of the fall. They can usefully be called 'original perfection', 'perfection lost', and 'perfection regained' – the triple perspectives haunting both angels and men. Since all three are perpetually present in God's consciousness, they are perpetually present in Milton's poetry from first to last. It follows also that they are perpetually present for Milton's readers, as the interplay of loss and hope, despair and joy in their lives. We read the poem not in alienation from its theme but through direct involvement, testing the fall and redemption of Adam in ourselves. If Milton's resonances chime in our hearts we can scarcely deny them; if we enact fall, judgment and redemption in our actual experience of reading, we go unusually far towards being convinced. Hence the key importance of Milton's relationship with his readers, which most modern critics fully acknowledge and stress. Stanley Fish had discerned Milton's formal 'intentions' in this area; Frank Kermode has testified to Milton's achieved and authentic effects. In what follows, it will be demonstrated that the poem witnesses to itself not only formally, as all art does, through beauty and structure, but with an added dimension implicit in its theme. 'Divine comedy' is a fluidity of overtone and suggestiveness, somewhere beyond tragedy, belonging to the simultaneous awareness of Paradise, Fall, Incarnation, Cross, Empty Tomb.

II

First then (with the lines quoted above in mind), we might take a hint from Fish, Kermode, and Milton's other recent critics, and try to catch the precise effect. '. . . much deceived' (we read of Eve); yes, but by whom? And when? How can we take our moral bearings, or our bearings in time? Eve is not yet 'much deceived' by Satan – who has indeed infected her dreams (IV 799–809), but has not yet confused her waking judgment or her will (V 28–128). And she is not yet' much deceived' in the timescale of human experience (except perhaps in over-confidence?), though in eternity, all is foreknown and foretold. Perhaps 'much deceived' carries chiefly the sad foreknowledge of the poet, lamenting from his own knowledge of good-through-evil as a son of Eve? Perhaps it carries that general burden of bewildered compassion, with which any tragic reversals of fortune may be viewed.

The next phrase 'much failing' adds further ambiguities, since 'failing' is the word both of sin and of mortality. There is active failing – failing God, failing oneself, failing (and falling from) reality – but also passive failing: failing health, failing flesh; the journey to death. But with 'hapless', we come to the possibility of judgment: who is responsible, at this point in time? Is Eve unlucky and unhappy, a victim of accident? Is she 'helpless' even? – the resonance half pushes us towards these clearly false views. Some readers blame God, some Satan, some Eve chiefly, some even Adam; and these seeming ambiguities ('seeming' because they are Satanic in origin) gather like clouds of the coming storm. So 'presumed return' moves us further into the mystery: 'presumed' in the sense of 'expected' (and for readers expecting no such thing, this is pure dramatic irony), but 'presumptuous' hovers in the background as well. We have already seen the possibility of over-reaching, suggested in that shade (so fatal!) of feminine arrogance in Eve. But the poem is full of potentially fallen attitudes in men and angels before they have fallen, as if to suggest that some temptation to independence from God – to nonsense – may be inseparable from freedom itself.

'Event perverse': we come with this to the pivotal phrase of the sentence, and again 'Event' is a floating word, raising more possibilities than strict syntax permits. At first (seemingly) it could refer either to this moment of parting (with 'perverse' a direct judgment against Eve, or even arguably against Adam), or it could refer to the fated outcome of the parting, the fall which we know we are shortly to see. But as the structure unfolds, we see rather that 'Event' is in fact the thing that did *not* happen, the event that Eve has been anticipating just one moment before, 'To be returned by noon amid the bower,/And all things in best order to invite/Noontide repast, or afternoon's repose'. So 'perverse' comes into its full root meaning of 'turned aside': *this* is the event destined never – or not yet, for us as readers even – to come about. It is the outcome of Eve's removal of herself, all unknowingly but for ever, from the wished-for, the expected, the taken-for-granted freedom of paradise. But 'perverse' must also suggest – as it normally does – at least some degree of censure, transferring itself (inevitably?) from the 'event' that never happened to the act of Eve's which permanently stands in its way. Certainly the poetic suggestions are all of freedom : Eve is to be the responsible agent in this last act of pure human freedom, this original perversity which will leave its permanent witness – including empathy with Eve? – in ourselves.

So the poet continues his haunting lament, blaming now (as surely a victim must blame?) the Enemy, who is already moving, intent and powerful, towards his 'purposed prey'. It is natural that a son of Eve should respond to her, and important that Milton's response is closer to tragic pity than to hate. Nothing could better suggest both the gravity of the sin, with its sequel in permanent exile, yet also the survival of some virtue – much virtue even – in man's fallen seed. 'Thou never from that hour in Paradise' . . . This searing 'never' of loss echoes, but deepens, the resonant 'No more . . .' at the start of Book IX. 'Such ambush hid' : and we are reminded again of secrecy, enmity, inner torment – all those evils which Eve has been told about and warned against, but which only initiation can make fully real for her.

At this moment, the poetry glides, with the serpent, towards its inevitable moment, which we have always known must come :

> For now, and since first break of dawn the fiend,
> Mere serpent in appearance, forth was come . . . (412–13)

'For now . . .'. First in Book II the idea was heard from Beelzebub, 'devilish counsel, first devised/By Satan, and in part proposed' (345–85). Then in Book III it was foretold by God, as a moment in all eternity, 'so will fall/He and his faithless progeny' (80–96). It has been the chief heroic stage for the testing of courage, first when Satan offers to attempt the hazardous enterprise of destroying man and all Hell falls silent (II 430–66), then when Christ offers to redeem man, as all Heaven waits (III 227–65). This moment was a datum in God's consciousness at the time of creation, and it is the great and central paradox of the Fortunate Fall. It is the point also on which the poem's central

and greatest polarity hinges. In Satan, we have the determination
to take good and turn it always to evil, 'Evil be thou my good'
(IV 110), and opposed to this, the divine power Whose operation is in the end the poem's triumph and truth:

> O goodness infinite, goodness immense!
> .That all this good of evil shall produce,
> And evil turn to good; more wonderful
> Than that which by creation first brought forth
> Light out of darkness! (XII 469–73)

But in poetic terms, too, this moment is central, since everything depends upon the resonances working for, and in, us as
we read. *Are* we as mortals mere cosmic accidents, whose lives
have no meaning; or are we indeed betrayed and exiled sons of
God? It is Milton's chief distinction as a poet – and a distinction
crucial to the justification of God, which is his avowed purpose –
that he can make us respond not only to the truths of evil (a
common gift among writers) but also, and perhaps even more
powerfully, to the truths of good. The poem does not ask (indeed
it discourages) our literal belief in its images, whether of Heaven,
Hell or Paradise, but it does ask, and need, our recognition of
its spiritual truths. And in this matter Milton habitually moves
us at some level of consciousness deeper than reason, as in those
moments when we remember childhood, experience sudden
shafts of self-knowledge, peer into the dark backward and abysm
of time. 'For now, and since first break of dawn the fiend . . .'
Yes, here it is: Evil, moving to confront the mighty opposite:
not equal with God; not the eventual winner; but always there.
Temporally, 'always there' for man, because the war in Heaven
has been prior (as far as time counts) to the creation of Earth.
But 'always there' too in our hearts and consciousnesses, at the
place where we grasp our identity as men. Though God did not
create evil, he created freedom; and perhaps the seeds of evil
exist, perhaps they *are*, in freedom, by the nature of things?
 Critics such as Tillyard have worried away, interestingly, at the
problem of how perfect beings can ever have come to have fallen
into evil; and perhaps none of us can resist the metaphysical

M.:P.L.—H

attempt. We know some problems elude us – did the universe have a beginning in time and space, or did it have no beginning? – and it is hard to accept the limits which are set for human intellect (according to Raphael, they were set even for unfallen man, VIII 1–216). On the other hand, we know that we can and indeed normally do accept apparent contradictions when both sides are vividly present in universal human experience. 'The good that I would I do not', said St Paul, 'the evil that I would not, that I do'. In just this manner, Milton sets about undercutting mere arguments, at moments when these would only confuse us, with images to which we cannot fail to respond. We recognise Satan's great rhetoric readily enough, with its denial of goodness; but we recognise equally – unless we are ourselves lost in evil – the vision which Satan himself, now, can never see. Milton will show us humanity holier, grander, more capable of joy than we normally dream of, and make us recognise realities in *these* images, with power in our souls. Naturally it is harder to 'believe in' Eden than it is to believe in the serpent; yet in the ruins of ourselves and our fellows have we never seen traces of Paradise, of the first Adam and Eve? Certainly there is something unusually compelling to the imagination, in this fated arrival of the serpent among the flowers :

> And on his quest, where likeliest he might find
> The only two of mankind, but in them
> The whole included race, his purposed prey.
> In bower and field he sought, where any tuft
> Of grove or garden-plot more pleasant lay,
> Their tendance or plantation for delight,
> By fountain or by shady rivulet
> He sought them both, but wished his hap might find
> Eve separate, he wished, but not with hope,
> Of what so seldom chanced, when to his wish,
> Beyond his hope, Eve separate he spies . . . (IX 414–24)

Critics have worried, naturally enough, about how God lets this happen. The epic apparatus and the nature of the sustained allegory of war in Heaven undeniably make Gabriel, in particular, look less efficient as a guardian angel than one could wish.

But in fact it is made clear that the wolf has been allowed to leap into the sheepfold by God's 'high sufferance' because freedom never is or will be violated from God's side. As the poetry here beautifully mimes the serpent's progress, we have to remain especially on our guard. It can seem – but subtly from Satan's viewpoint – that a kind of dark providence is helping the work of evil, or at least a devil's luck uncannily like the answer to un-offered prayer. The effect is to underline however the inevitability of this encounter. By whatever means it has come about, wherever in space or whenever in time, this moment manifestly had to be. Among the poem's many extreme ironies is the fact that at least once Satan – closely followed by most of the critics who throw in their lot with him – actually blames God for letting him get out of Hell to perform his task (IV 897–9). But God never has been the arbitrary tyrant of Satan's rhetoric; Hell never has been a maximum security prison block. In Book III (80 ff.) when God Himself notes of Satan that 'no bounds/Prescribed, nor bars of hell, nor all the chains/Heaped on him there, nor yet the main abyss/Wide interrupt can hold', He is neither confessing to inefficiency, nor being aloofly sardonic, but drawing attention to the uncancelled gift of freedom in His world. The poem takes care from the start to work through images which interact with, but in no sense constrain, its rational frame. At first Hell is flame and chains, and perpetual imprisonment; then it is a great debating chamber; then it is a gorgeous throne, where Satan sits exalted and adored. At times it is mediated through images of compulsive lust or of total vanity, with their torments that can be neither satisfied nor quenched. But Milton has always made clear that Hell exists in the mind and consciousness, and that it is no more to be identified with any one set of images than it is to be escaped by any mere shift of location in time or space. As we shortly see in Book IX, Satan carries Hell with him, though in mid-Heaven; potentially, any free being carries it in himself. The fact is that Hell is made by fallen angels and by fallen men after them; God merely permits it as an extension of freedom itself. The doors are locked from inside, not from outside; but they are indeed locked beyond any escape from within. The attendant irony is that because Hell is not created by God it is all negation and nonsense; but negation and nonsense with frightening power over *us*. So Hell is free to appear in Paradise, and at the appointed moment will appear there; it will come with its curious power of seeming wholly at home.

This brings us to another of the poem's two major polarities, which underlie its many shifts of imagery and tone. Created beings can respond to creation in numerous and varied ways locally, but in one of two ways only at the ground of response. Either they can celebrate and delight in it, in love and freedom; or they can reject and oppose it, in hatred and rage. The difficulty is that once the latter choice has been made it excludes the former; since the power to celebrate and to delight in celebration is then lost. Mammon's famous speech is, of course, the *locus classicus* (II 237–57), but this theme haunts the poem from beginning to end. Milton is the last poet to imply that Heaven or Hell are *merely* subjective, or to imply that they can in any manner exist on the same plane. Heaven is made by God, and is filled by Him; Hell is the experience of whatever consciousness is in exile from God. It follows that while Heaven and Hell are eternally separate, they are eternally free to impinge on one another, since the saved and the damned co-exist. The vision of reality operative in each is of course different, with 'freedom', 'nature' and all other concepts pulled to opposite poles. We test the realities only by looking beyond definitions to experiences: are there fruits of peace and love, or of bitter despair? In this aspect the moment in the garden again seems fated; Paradise cannot know its fullest potential until the serpent appears.

The next section moves us to Milton's especially poignant vision of Eve among the flowers, tending her Paradise for the last time:

> Veiled in a cloud of fragrance, where she stood,
> Half spied, so thick the roses bushing round
> About her glowed, oft stooping to support
> Each flower of slender stalk, whose head though gay
> Carnation, purple, azure, or specked with gold,
> Hung drooping unsustained, them she upstays
> Gently with myrtle band, mindless the while
> Her self, though fairest unsupported flower,
> From her best prop so far, and storm so nigh. (IX 425–33)

The phrase 'hung drooping unsustained' yokes together Eve's concern for the flowers and her own predicament; does her own tender care not deserve better than this? But if we ask again whether it is God's fault, or Adam's, or Eve's that she is 'unsustained' at this moment, we divert ourselves from the text. The rational answer of course is that it is Eve's fault; but Milton is now concerned with the infinite pity of the fact. If Eve *is* vulnerable (and this is not self-evident), perhaps this is partly because she takes her own tender concern for the flowers more for granted than she should? '. . . mindless the while/Her self' beautifully fuses the supreme virtue of forgetting self in the service of beauty with the supreme danger of being off guard. As Satan approaches, he is still exotic and majestic, 'not less than Archangel ruined' even now. He has indeed become a brute by his own choice and for his own bad ends, and this is ironic enough for one who aspired to be 'as a god'. But he comes freely, and in the innate beauty of the original serpent; he is not yet constrained to the brute form in punishment as he will be later (and Book x 504–47 is, even in this poem, one of the most astonishing images of Hell).

> Nearer he drew, and many a walk traversed
> Of stateliest covert, cedar, pine or palm,
> Then voluble and bold, now hid, now seen
> Among thick-woven arborets and flowers
> Embroidered on each bank, the hand of Eve :
> Spot more delicious than those gardens feigned
> Or of revived Adonis, or renowned
> Alcinous, host of old Laertes' son,
> Or that, not mystic, where the sapient king
> Held dalliance with his fair Egyptian spouse.
> Much he the place admired, the person more.
> As one who long in populous city pent,
> Where houses thick and sewers annoy the air,
> Forth issuing on a summer's morn to breathe
> Among the pleasant villages and farms
> Adjoined, from each thing met conceives delight,
> The smell of grain, or tedded grass, or kine,
> Or dairy, each rural sight, each rural sound ;
> If chance with nymph-like step fair virgin pass,

What pleasing seemed, for her now pleases more,
She most, and in her look sums all delight.
Such pleasure took the serpent to behold
This flowery plat, the sweet recess of Eve
Thus early, thus alone; her heavenly form
Angelic, but more soft, and feminine,
Her graceful innocence, her every air
Of gesture or least action overawed
His malice, and with rapine sweet bereaved
His fierceness of the fierce intent it brought :
That space the evil one abstracted stood
From his own evil, and for the time remained
Stupidly good, of enmity disarmed,
Of guile, of hate, of envy, of revenge;
But the hot hell that always in him burns,
Though in mid heaven, soon ended his delight,
And tortures him now more, the more he sees
Of pleausre not for him ordained ... (IX 434–70)

And so we are returned to Satan, in these further poetic inversions so deceptively simple that we can accustom ourselves to them almost as readily as Eve accustoms herself, now, to a talking worm. Already the serpent seems almost at home in Paradise, as if the territory he hopes to win by desecration is already his. And he admires it, at this moment, as it is with himself excluded : this is one of those classic moments when evil has to pay its tribute to good. So Iago has said of Roderigo, 'He has a daily beauty in his life/That makes me ugly' : he cannot deny the fact, though it torments him. This is the factor in human experience – so deadly for those who would see good as illusion and Paradise as fiction – to which T. S. Eliot gave memorable utterance in a single line : 'The darkness declares the glory of light' (from the final chorus of *Murder In The Cathedral*). Nowhere in our human exile perhaps is there any insight more hopeful than this one, the warding off of despair with the stuff of despair. But in *Paradise Lost*, at this moment when Evil stands lost for a moment in homage to goodness, the context gives to the hopefulness a further twist. Though the glory of light impinges on its enemy, for this one telling moment, it is now to be extinguished – at least in time – and death ushered in.

The fuller insight into Satan is approached by way of the simile, which is so reminiscent of a lot of later 'nature' poetry in its theme of escape to the country from urban pollution that we might overlook its novelty and subtlety in the context here. The situation depicted in the simile is by definition post-lapsarian, belonging to a world already despoiled. Satan's role for the moment is that of a simple peasant escaping from normal squalor into rural beauty, and enjoying the sight of a 'virgin' nymph as supreme delight. The simple image might remind us both that such nymphs are seldom symbols of innocence but, equally, that even seducers sometimes regret their success. In this setting, the description of Eve's 'heavenly form/Angelic' is beautifully poised between its inherent truth, as innocent and delighted appraisal, and its danger, as exaggeration and excess. Adam has already been warned by Raphael that true celebration can tip into idolatry, in the long passage (VIII 452 ff.) which is a key to Book IX. The notion 'Angelic' instantly shapes itself in Satan's mind towards the rhetoric of the coming temptation, but it is a genuine tribute while the moment lasts. The moment itself however transforms to Satan's sense of aberration; for him, it is a passing weakness, 'Stupidly good'. So the inverted tribute validates beauty at some level sensed by ourselves, as we read it, but it in no way eases Satan's evil – indeed the reverse. 'But the hot hell that always in him burns/Though in mid heaven, soon ended his delight,/And tortures him now more, the more he sees/Of pleasure not for him ordained . . .'. Since Satan's choice 'Evil be thou my good' has been granted, Paradise must after all torment him to the precise degree that he really sees it as it is.

Not the least of Milton's triumphs is his continual reminder that though God is omnipotent, the divine task of taking evil and bringing good from it is far harder than the satanic task of taking and despoiling good. To create (we are told) is greater than to destroy (VII 606–7): and certainly to re-create Paradise, as Christ will do later, is a more costly act than Satan's, in destroying it now ('So dearly to redeem what hellish hate/So easily destroyed . . .' III 300–1. It is costly in a manner that Satan moreover can no longer conceive : which is no doubt why his rhetoric comes so very close to convincing himself. But as readers we are invited to see that if freedom is real, love must be active, a continual fight to make its own nature prevail. This no doubt is the inner logic of the heroic images of war, even in Heaven (however incongruous, given God's love and omnipotence, these may sometimes seem). The suggestion is that there is energy, strife even, in the creation of freedom, just as there is energy and strife in remaining free.

The splendour of this particular poem is enhanced by its assertion of hedonism : Milton justifies the ways of God not by intellectual argument only but by celebrating all modes of happiness and delight. *Paradise Lost* is nothing if it is not a poem of love; and love is nothing in the poem if it is not a justification of creation in all of its parts. Books IV, V and VIII (in particular) have affirmed that one of God's supreme gifts to men is sexual happiness, surpassed in splendour only by the total mingling in love of the incorporeal angels themselves. The Fall disorders man's whole being, body, mind and spirit, but no images of its effect are more striking than those which depict the spoilation of sex. First, and obviously, there is the contrast between mutual love before the Fall, rooted in homage and ordered by ritual (IV 736–75), and compulsive eroticism after the Fall, culminating in shame and in muual distaste (IX 1011–98). There is an explicit recognition that lust can be more intoxicating, in the act, than ordered sensuality, but also that it can never be the servant of dignity and love (e.g. 'Our wonted ornaments now soiled and stained,/And in our faces evident the signs/Of foul concupiscence' IX 1076–8). But Milton's clear intention is less to denounce the lustful than to celebrate the voluptuous, and to remind that the total union of love and sexuality still exists as a possibility, however difficult and elusive, for fallen man.

A further insight, less explicit but no less powerful, is the image of sexual pleasure arousing envy and hatred in those who are excluded from it, as a deeper, and spiritual, evil arising from sin. In one remarkable passage, Adam has intuited that his sexual pleasure with Eve might be especially enraging to Satan (IX 261–4); and this is already known to us from Satan's famous outburst in Book IV 505–6 :

> Sight hateful, sight tormenting ! Thus these two
> Imparadised in one another's arms . . .

Satan's essence is captured, again, in the powerful phrase in our
present passage, 'And tortures him now more, the more he sees/
Of pleasure not for him ordained . . .'. *This* is the kind of envy
which will produce not only the sickness of sexual excess as an
end in itself, as one response to it, but still worse excesses of malice
and persecution from the sexually deprived. Satan takes on, as
Kermode has noted, something of the character of a tormented
voyeur, and his mentality is recognisably that which produces
hatred of the attractive by the unattractive, of the young by the
old, of the beautiful by the ugly, of the accepted by the rejected. It
produces men like Angelo in *Measure For Measure*, the stoners
of adulterers and of any who seem fair game to them. Milton
sees, no doubt, that among the fallen hatred of sex itself will become more 'respectable' than its celebration, in that alienation
from God leads naturally to dislike of His gifts.

But in Satan's approach to Eve, Milton manages to suggest
also the centre of fallen relationship, with egocentric need or
vanity replacing homage to people and things. It is no accident
that the lovely word 'gratulating' which Adam has applied to
Nature's delight in the first act of sexual love (vɪɪɪ 514) is used
now, in darker parody, of Satan :

> . . . then soon
> Fierce hate he recollects, and all his thoughts
> Of mischief, gratulating, thus excites . . . (ɪx 470–2)

The whole temptation after this is in one aspect a dark seduction,
as Fowler continually notes when commenting, in his edition, on
the images of Book ɪx. Eve is literally to be seduced from Adam
through the doubly inappropriate advances of a fallen angel disguised as a talking beast. Physically and powerfully phallic suggestions co-exist with the intellectual ones (e.g. 'So varied he, and
of his tortuous train/Curled many a wanton wreath in sight of
Eve,/To lure her eye . . .' ɪx 516–18). Eve, moreover, is to be
seduced away from happiness and peace by a mixture of lies
and flattery prepared by the one creature in creation most ex-

perienced in the desolation of Hell. Possibly the crowning irony, as
so often with Satan, is that he half deceives himself at such
moments – an archetypal seducer in this, as in all other ways.
From the 'bondage' of subjection to Adam and to reality, Eve
is to be 'liberated' into compulsion, need, envy and lies.

III

With this in mind, along with the terrible further reflections as
Satan turns to his work of temptation (IX 473–93), we can turn
to another passage central to our theme. Eve returns to Adam
after the fall, elated and devious, offering him a share in her
newly gained knowledge and status, but (as C. S. Lewis pointed
out) harbouring something akin to murder in her heart. The
wreath of flowers which Adam had made for her falls faded; he
knows mortality in this form as he speaks :

> O fairest of creation, last and best
> Of all God's works, creature in whom excelled
> Whatever can to sight or thought be formed,
> Holy, divine, good, amiable or sweet !
> How art thou lost, how on a sudden lost,
> Defaced, deflowered, and now to death devote ?
> Rather how hast thou yielded to transgress
> The strict forbiddance, how to violate
> The sacred fruit forbidden ! Some cursed fraud
> Of enemy hath beguiled thee, yet unknown,
> And me with thee hath ruined, for with thee
> Certain my resolution is to die ;
> How can I live without thee, how forgo
> Thy sweet converse and love so dearly joined,
> To live again in these wild woods forlorn ?
> Should God create another Eve, and I
> Another rib afford, yet loss of thee
> Would never from my heart ; no, no, I feel
> The link of nature draw me : flesh of flesh,
> Bone of my bone thou art, and from thy state
> Mine never shall be parted, bliss or woe. (IX 896–916)

By any criterion, this is one of the great 'tragic' speeches of
literature; it is also the culmination of the poem's theme, the

'mortal sin original' which lost the race. Uniquely fused, we have words expressing high and noble love as man now knows it, and the root evil, cause of 'all our woe'. Even before he eats the fruit Adam's decision is taken; he feels drawn by the link of 'nature' and chooses death. His speech certainly demonstrates every dangerous misunderstanding of hierarchy against which Raphael has warned him. Does it also include much or, given the circumstances, everything which we feel to be good?

Adam begins with tragic grief at Eve's lot, not deceived by *her* rhetoric: he knows, and laments, that all she was is now lost. He is not deceived himself (if we take the comment at IX 998–9 at face value), but he eats the fruit in the belief that Eve herself has been deceived. And, of course, he is right in this: Satan has told her nothing but lies. It is not only insidious flattery to which she has been subjected; or the specious lure of divinity; or the suggestion – so powerfully plausible, especially to readers coming after the romantic revolution and the twentieth-century psychologists – that God may actually want her to disobey Him, and so come of age. Beyond these stratagems there has been the direct lie, so important to the success of Satan's other obliquities, about the crucial question of how a serpent can talk. Satan has claimed to have eaten the fruit and come by speech in this manner: hence the tree is a magic tree. It has proved its power to make a beast rational; may it not also then make men divine? But the tree is not magic; Satan has not eaten of it; his power of speech is angelic, though disguised. The fact of this lie in no way justifies Eve (of course), any more than *her* lie (IX 877–8) justifies Adam now. But it is certainly true to see that she has been terribly tricked; and, given this, Adam's anguished loyalty will naturally seem the very essence of love. He echoes the marriage vow – 'flesh of flesh', 'never shall be parted', 'bliss or woe', omitting only (but how ironically) the notion 'Till death do us part'. And who can fail to feel the terrible poignancy of this choice now hideously forced upon him, between human love at its finest, and the commands of God? Nothing could seem more natural than that God's law should appear at this moment harsh, cold or impossible; or that Adam's impassioned words should appear the quintessence of noble love.

So the 'split' in the poem alleged by romantic critics again confronts us: *is* it 'natural' to respond as readers in this manner; and, if so, is it right? It is easy enough to conclude that while the analysis of Adam's 'uxoriousness' (as Tillyard calls it), his lack of proportion, his fatal disobedience, rings true intellectually, the tragic intensity transcends such analysis with truths of the heart. It is easy, again, to assume that when man's deepest love can earn only death, and God's cold anger, the 'ways of God' are not justified after all.

But if Satan is father of lies, and deceived Adam, is it not likely that the fallen sons of Adam will also be tricked? Indeed are we right to accept Milton's explicit assurance, already alluded to, that Adam himself is not deceived? The poetry *says* 'he scrupled not to eat/Against his better knowledge, not deceived/But fondly overcome with female charm'; but we have already heard Adam refer to God as 'threatening' (939), as inept creator (938–51), as 'fickle' (948), and we know by now where such perspectives originate and belong. Perhaps we also notice that even in his highest anguish Adam's stress has fallen even more on his own need for Eve than on her personal freedom and loveliness, as if the egocentric taint is already at work. He appears also to take for granted that his own love for Eve is much greater than God's love; and this assumption certainly strikes a new note. As C. S. Lewis pointed out we can never know now what God would have done if the unfallen Adam had presented himself to plead for her; but we do know that the future of humanity was vested in *him.* Adam's sense of Eve's uniqueness, her infinite preciousness and irreplaceability, is powerfully human; but have we any reason for thinking it less true of God? If individuals are in fact so precious that no one of them can ever replace another, then it is God's creative majesty not human need – however high and pure – that endorses this. Adam assumes that Eve must die for her sin, because God has said so; does he already doubt God's will and power to turn evil to good? It is arguable that if he does fail in authority in Book ix it is not, as Waldock assumes, when he allows Eve to go off on her own to be tempted, but when he fails, at this moment, to trust the mercy of God. And if we say: 'yes; this is coldly rational, but has no warmth for the emotions', we should remember that Milton has not yet finished his tale. There is not only the moment of the Fall, but all the time after; there is the burden of consciousness to be continued, and resumed. At the end of Book IX, Adam and Eve have their second quarrel (1119–89): how unlike the first one; and how recognisably true? Later there is the terrible moment when Adam turns on Eve with a mixture of wounding savagery and relentless self-laceration, calling the 'bond of nature' which drew him to fall with her not a blessing, but a curse (x 867–908). To this the terrified Eve can now only plead 'Forsake me not thus, Adam, witness heaven/What love sincere, and reverence in my heart/I bear thee' and, from the depth of her terror, beg Adam to honour the vow which he implied in the actual words, and images, and resonances of the Fall :

> bereave me not,
> Whereon I live, thy gentle looks, thy aid,
> Thy counsel in this uttermost distress,
> My only strength and stay : forlorn of thee,
> Whither shall I betake me, where subsist? (x 918–22)

It would be as dishonest to deny the sad familiarity of such passages, their truth to human emotions and relationships as almost any reader is likely to know them, as it would be to deny the goodness, however muddled, in Adam as he fell. Are we to assert indeed that the noble sentiments uttered by Adam in the elation and anguish of immediate sacrifice would, normally, sustain a lifetime's suffering endured, and on beliefs proved mistaken, for another's sake? Milton's poem forces on us that the antithesis between 'love' and 'law' remains a fallacy, a diabolical trick in the strictest sense, even when – and perhaps especially when – it is born of love and experienced in suffering. The satanic reading of the poem is indeed one-sided if it can enlist our dubious grasp on reality, our well-meaning but too indulgent and in the end ineffectual compassion, against a full experience and acknowledgment of life as it is. We must call to mind again the nature of Adam and Eve's love in the early books of the poem : not the sexual happiness only, beautiful though that is, but their serene delight in every moment of life. We have seen their pride in one

another – touching and pleasing, whatever its dangers; their
delight in each other's company; their daily ritual of celebration,
in work, worship and loving; their dignity even when differing
on the morning of the Fall. If these images, too, have their power;
if they too (and this is the great test for the poem) strike us as
possible, with a call on our allegiance: then we cannot afford,
at any point, to simplify the poem's truths.

IV

Frank Kermode points to Milton's subtle symbolic suggestiveness, reaching far beyond paraphrase, and to his sophisticated
understanding of myth as 'fiction', at least in his art. (Kermode
hints that Milton's understanding is close to his own, in *Sense
Of An Ending* : which in turn would make it possible to discuss
Paradise Lost, as Stanley Fish comes close to doing, in much the
way that novelists are discussed in *The Rhetoric of Fiction* by
Wayne Booth.) But Basil Willey has rightly reminded us that
Milton believed the Bible narrative to be God-given (this is far
more important than any belief or disbelief in its inspiration as
'literal'), and that his high poetic confidence rested chiefly on
this.

We can see these two views as complementary rather than as
mutually exclusive, if we remember that while Kermode is right
in his analysis of the actual effects of Milton's verse, he would be
wrong to assimilate it, even if he wished to do this, to his own
view of art. Milton was not offering the consolation of beautiful
fiction in a world without meaning; he was raising echoes of lost,
precious truths in our hearts. The essential insight is not that his
truths are true because, and to the degree that, our hearts respond to them; but that our hearts respond to them, given grace
and the proper occasion, because they are true.

The romantic tradition of criticism has witnessed to the fluidity
of Milton's archetypes, whether by antinomianism, as in Blake
and Shelley and modern critics such as Waldock and Empson,
or through Jungian interpretations of Zwi Werblowsky's kind.
But fluidity and ambivalence are not gods, demanding total
homage; it is not Christian or Platonic – not Miltonic – to call

all insights 'true'. We may believe that truth itself is relative, and conditioned by the needs and structures of believers; or we may believe that some insights correspond to reality and that others do not. The nature of Heaven and Hell, love and hate, salvation and damnation are clearly involved in this; and Milton's position cannot be in doubt. He did not believe that beauty, goodness and truth are relative and subjective; he believed that they are revealed in nature; in scripture; and supremely in Christ.

In *Paradise Lost*, the archetypal romantic is notoriously Satan, who ascribes power over reality itself wholly to the mind :

> The mind is its own place, and in itself
> Can make a heaven of hell, a hell of heaven. (1 254–5)

Like almost everything satanic, this is an important half-truth, perverted in its context into a lie. From the aspect of consciousness, Satan is entirely right, since it does lie within ourselves to celebrate God, or to reject. But God remains real and unchanged, whatever our attitude; we can alter our vision, our 'self', but not Him.

On this matter, we confront one of the great and unbridgeable divides in human thinking, between those who understand the great verities as truths beyond themselves, received by revelation, and those whose final appeal is always to the court of the self. 'What I feel', 'what I think', 'what it means to me' become final criteria, offered from inside the imprisoned, and usually the contracted, heart.

Milton's place on this issue is with Christians and Platonists; for him Heaven is the supreme reality, made by God and inhabited by Him; Hell is the reality of any consciousness alienated from God. Milton's readers may be on Milton's side here, or in the other camp; but they must recognise that if they take the satanic interpretation of events, as a whole, or even partly, they are shut with Satan, in Milton's understanding, away from the truth. Milton's method in his poem however is not to assert his great beliefs intellectually, in equal argument with Satan, but to demonstrate them by arousing echoes in ourselves of the divine.

Milton's view would be that art itself is a witness to the truths it celebrates, in that it incarnates the creative mind in union with the mind's chosen themes. Formally, *Paradise Lost* is among the symbols in time of timeless realities, the still point (to use T. S. Eliot's image) of the turning world. Throughout *Paradise Lost*, the timescale is as shifting and fluid as the images, but at every point – as in the passages we have been examining – there are timeless resonances of paradise, paradise lost, and paradise regained. The 'truth' is in the existence of these in art, and in their power over us; our denial of the poem, if we choose to deny it, must 'get round' them.

Since Milton is not staking his poem on anything quasi-historical or on anything merely literal, his scriptural fundamentalism is not, in this matter, to the point. We are no more forced to believe in the place and the occasion in Eden literally, than we are forced to believe literally in the fluctuating pictures and images of Heaven and Hell. We do not need to believe that Adam and Eve walked, in history, in a garden, as long as we are made to feel that they existed and still exist in us. The fallen Adam and Eve are doubtless easy to credit; it is the unfallen and the restored that we must also be persuaded to endorse. These images reach beyond their own powerful – and often inherently impressive – rational structures, to the place where great memories and promises haunt our lives. We have to feel again that these are not vain hopes; memories of the womb; desires for lost childhood; longings for escape, or bliss, or opium, or simple extinction; but that they are the spirit of God testifying within.

And in this, Milton's theme unites with his form to help him, since both exist to salute glory from the heart of loss. *Paradise Lost* is the epic of exile; of greatness in ruins; of restoration possible and promised in the end. Beyond the 'event perverse' of the last morning in Paradise, and of our daily experience, there is another image that readers will always have in their minds. In balance with the moment when creatures tried to be as gods, and moved into exile, there is that other moment when God, made man, went to His death. Eve's noontide repast is still lost to our human experience, but there are words spoken to a criminal now triumphant in history : 'Truly, I tell you, today you will be with Me in Paradise.'

So, just as the shadow of coming loss falls over scenes in Paradise, the coming triumph of God holds, even in scenes of the Fall. Omnipotence is really itself, though it seems defeated; Satan's nonsense is still nonsense though it seems to win.

'O felix culpa' : in this cry is the heart of the poem, the testimony to an event 'turned aside' but still to come. As in *Samson Agonistes* Milton insists that since man is free, he is also guilty; and human guilt is the centre of hope. To blame God or Satan is to lock ourselves in Hell and to cast the key away; in Hell we rejoice in our 'freedom' and 'growth' as we wither away. Milton fully understood that the nonsense of Hell is also daily experience, and that if his poem were to succeed it would have to dispel in us that particular enchantment of evil to which he had given marvellous expression in *Comus* :

> And they, so perfect is their misery,
> Not once perceive their foul disfigurement,
> But boast themselves more comely than before . . .

Like Wordsworth he knew that most men pass gladly into 'the light of common day' at adolescence, making 'growing up' a permanent excuse for growing down. Fewer and fewer glances are cast back at the lost land, guarded by angels with swords against our re-entry; the lost land is forgotten or denied. Milton's triumph is to bring it back to us, so clearly and unmistakably, that we can forget or deny it only by forgetting or denying ourselves. If Keats's words can be adapted, *Paradise Lost* is indeed like Adam's dream for its readers; they awake, and find it true.

The balance of tensions in language and structure which have been explored here in particular passages can be traced in almost any of the parts. *Paradise Lost* is a poem where the whole to an extraordinary degree inhabits individual episodes, and individual episodes radiate out to the whole. Book by book Milton builds his verbal cathedral, so skilfully, that his main image can be released, with the whole poem in it, as the final touch. We note the conjunctions of 'providence their guide' with 'wandering', of 'hand in hand' with 'solitary'; we do not miss the ironies in 'all before', 'where to choose', 'place of rest'. But as Adam and Eve move away, God is justified. Love has power, the lines also testify, to bring *this* to good :

> The world was all before them, where to choose
> Their place of rest, and providence their guide :
> They hand in hand with wandering steps and slow
> Through Eden took their solitary way. (XII 646–9)

SOURCE : From a work in progress; first published here.

SELECT BIBLIOGRAPHY

The definitive biography is now William Riley Parker's *Milton: A Biography*, 2 vols. (O.U.P., 1968).

In the sphere of critical biography, E. M. W. Tillyard's *Milton* (Chatto & Windus, 1930) is still useful.

MAJOR CRITICAL BOOKS

The books from which extracts have been reprinted here are all well worth reading in full. Publishing details will be found at the end of extracts and in Acknowledgements, p. 7.

In the Introduction, we mention C. S. Lewis's *Preface to Paradise Lost* (1942) as one of the best books on Milton. Two other short books of great value are Helen Gardner's *A Reading of 'Paradise Lost'* (O.U.P., 1965) and Northrop Frye's *Five Essays on Milton's Epics* (University of Toronto Press, 1965; Routledge & Kegan Paul, 1966).

There is also an excellent article by Helen Gardner 'Milton's Satan and the Theme of Damnation in Elizabethan Tragedy' which was first published in 1948, and can be found reprinted in Arthur E. Barker's anthology of criticism listed below.

On a shortlist we would put next the three books from which we should most have liked to include extracts if there had been more space : Arnold Stein's *Answerable Style: Essays on 'Paradise Lost'* (University of Minnesota Press, 1953; paperback, University of Washington Press, 1967); Joseph H. Summers's *The Muse's Method: An Introduction to 'Paradise Lost'* (Harvard, U.S.A., and Chatto & Windus, 1962); and Dennis H. Burden's *The Logical Epic: A Study of the Argument of 'Paradise Lost'* (Routledge & Kegan Paul, 1967).

Two other books which yield valuable insights are J. B. Broadbent's *Some Graver Subject: An Essay on 'Paradise Lost'* (Chatto & Windus, 1960), and B. A. Wright's *Milton's 'Paradise Lost'* (Methuen and Barnes & Noble, N.Y., 1962).

For readers wishing to pursue the 'satanist' argument, three other books have to be read. First, A. J. A. Waldock's *'Paradise Lost' and its Critics* (C.U.P., 1947). This is critically blunt, and not very helpful, but it was the first attempted 'answer' to C. S. Lewis. Then, John Peter's *A Critique of 'Paradise Lost'* (Columbia U.P. and Longman, 1960), which has moments of insight, and is more perceptive than Waldock, especially in incidental asides. Finally, William Empson's *Milton's God* (Chatto & Windus, 1961), which is brilliantly perverse, and indispensable to students of Empson.

BACKGROUND BOOKS

E. S. Le Comte's *A Milton Dictionary* (U.S.A., Columbia and Peter Owen, 1961) is a useful reference book.

For those interested in Milton's political background, two useful books are Don M. Wolfe's *Milton in the Puritan Revolution* (first published in a limited edition in 1941; reprinted by Cohen & West, 1963), and Michael Fixler's *Milton and the Kingdoms of God* (Faber & Faber, 1964).

On the philosophical and religious background, we would particularly mention Irene Samuel's *Plato and Milton* (Cornell U.P., 1947) and C. A. Patrides's *Milton and the Christian Tradition* (O.U.P., 1966).

COLLECTIONS OF ESSAYS

Three volumes of essays specially commissioned stand out. First *The Living Milton: Essays by Various Hands*, ed. Frank Kermode (Routledge & Kegan Paul, 1960). This includes the fine essay by Kermode from which an extract is reprinted here. Then *Approaches to 'Paradise Lost'*, ed. C. A. Patrides (Edward Arnold, 1968). Finally *'Paradise Lost': A Tercentenary Tribute*, ed. Balanchandra Rajan(University of Toronto Press and O.U.P., 1969).

Two other anthologies of Milton criticism also contain essays of interest to students of *Paradise Lost* : *Milton: Modern Essays in Criticism*, ed. Arthur E. Barker, A Galaxy Book (O.U.P., 1965) (this includes the essay by Helen Gardner mentioned above), and *Modern Judgements on Milton*, ed. Alan Rudrum (Macmillan, 1968).

Books on Milton are legion, and it will be appreciated that this is a personal selection. For a fuller select bibliography with comments, see the chapter on Milton by Douglas Bush in *English Poetry: Select Bibliographical Guides*, ed. A. E. Dyson (O.U.P., 1971).

For a fuller selection of background books, see also the section of the bibliography devoted to Milton in D. Bush's *English Literature In The Earlier Seventeenth Century 1600–1660* (O.U.P., 1945, revised version 1962 : and note that this covers *Paradise Lost,* despite its dates).

NOTES ON CONTRIBUTORS

A. E. DYSON is Honorary Fellow of the University of East Anglia, where he has taught for many years. His books include *The Crazy Fabric: Studies in Irony*, *The Inimitable Dickens*, *Between Two Worlds: Aspects of Literary Form* (and with Julian Lovelock) *Masterful Images: English Poetry from Metaphysicals to Romantics* (1976) and *Yeats, Eliot and R. S. Thomas: The Hidden Echo*. He has also edited volumes in the Casebook Series, of which he is General Editor.

T. S. ELIOT, who died in 1965, was one of the major modern poets and critics. His main criticism is available in three volumes: *Selected Essays*, *The Use of Poetry and the Use of Criticism* and *On Poetry and Poets*.

STANLEY E. FISH is Professor of English at the University of California at Berkeley. His books include *John Skelton's Poetry* and *Surprised by Sin: The Reader in Paradise Lost*.

FRANK KERMODE is a Fellow of King's College, Cambridge, where he was King Edward VII Professor of English Literature 1974-82. His books include *The Romantic Image*, *The Sense of an Ending*, *Continuities* and *Modern Essays*.

C. S. LEWIS, who died in 1963, was Professor of Medieval and Renaissance Studies at the University of Cambridge. His critical books included *The Allegory of Love*, *Preface to 'Paradise Lost'*, *English Literature in the Sixteenth Century*, *Studies in Words*, *An Experiment in Criticism* and *The Discarded Image*. He was also an outstanding Christian apologist.

JULIAN LOVELOCK studied English at the University of East Anglia and is currently the Headmaster of Akeley Wood School, Buckingham. He is co-author with A. E. Dyson of *Masterful Images: English Poetry from Metaphysicals to Romantics* and editor of the Casebooks on Donne's *'Songs and Sonets'* and Milton's *'Comus'* and *'Samson Agonistes'*.

B. RAJAN was Senior Professor of English at the University of Windsor, Ontario. His critical books include *'Paradise Lost' and the Seventeenth Century Reader* and *W. B. Yeats: A Critical Introduction*. He also edited books on T. S. Eliot and on Modern American poetry, and has written two novels.

CHRISTOPHER RICKS is Professor of English at the University of Cambridge. His books include *Milton's Grand Style*, *Tennyson* and the Longman complete edition of Tennyson, *The Poems of Tennyson*.

E. M. W. TILLYARD, who died in 1962, was Master of Jesus College, Cambridge, and a leading figure in the English School at Cambridge, of which he wrote the history (*The Muse in Chains*). His critical books include *The Elizabethan World Picture*, *Shakespeare's History Plays*, *Shakespeare's Problem Plays*, *Milton*, *The Miltonic Setting Past and Present*, *Studies in Milton* and *The English Epic and its Background*.

R. J. ZWI WERBLOWSKY was lecturer in Semitics at the University of Leeds when he wrote *Lucifer and Prometheus: A Study of Milton's Satan* (1952). His book had a preface by Jung, and brought Jungian insights to bear on literary criticism.

BASIL WILLEY (died 1978) was King Edward VII Professor of English Literature at the University of Cambridge. His books include *The Seventeenth Century Background*, *The Eighteenth Century Background*, *Nineteenth Century Studies* and *More Nineteenth Century Studies*.

INDEX